The Compact
Encyclopedia of
PSYCHOLOGICAL
PROBLEMS

BOOKS BY DR. NARRAMORE . . .

How to Tell Your Children About Sex
The Psychology of Counseling
Young Only Once
Encyclopedia of Psychological Problems
Counseling Youth
Life and Love

The Compact Encyclopedia of

PSYCHOLOGICAL PROBLEMS

Clyde M. Narramore, Ed. D.

Zondervan Publishing House
Grand Rapids, Michigan

Zondervan Publishing House, 1415 Lake Drive, S.E.,
Grand Rapids, Michigan 49506

ISBN 0-310-29900-4

Library of Congress Catalog Card Number 64-22835

Printed in the United States of America

84   85   86   87   88   89   90 / 10   9   8   7   6   5   4   3   2   1

ACKNOWLEDGMENTS

The author is indebted to many persons who have had a part in the development of this volume. Indeed, it would be impossible to adequately acknowledge all who have made a contribution to it.

Appreciation is extended to former teachers who have left indelible imprints. Included are faculty members at Columbia University, the University of Southern California and Arizona State University.

During the preparation of this manuscript the author often considered the thinking of his professional colleagues with whom he has worked for many years. Among them are the psychologists on the staff of the Los Angeles County Superintendent of Schools and the professional staff of the Christian Counseling Center at the Narramore Christian Foundation Headquarters.

Acknowledgment is made of the careful work of Robert D. Carpenter, M.D., full-time physician on the staff of the Narramore Christian Foundation. His meticulous review of the manuscript and his suggestions are deeply appreciated.

Special acknowledgment is extended to the author's nephew, Stanley Bruce Narramore, for his professional and scholarly contribution.

Many books have been researched to gain information and opinions on the subjects discussed. A basic bibliography from which the author has drawn is included under REFERENCES. It contains the books, periodicals and journals referred to throughout the volume.

Thanks is also expressed to Bernice R. Elford for the final typing of the manuscript. To all others not personally mentioned, the author expresses his deepest gratitude.

TABLE OF CONTENTS

The Compact
Encyclopedia of
PSYCHOLOGICAL
PROBLEMS

1. Human Problems

The past few years have ushered in an intriguing age of unprecedented change. One only needs to look around to see momentous progress taking place. The field of chemistry, for example, is ablaze with bright new wonders. Engineering, too, is making dramatic strides that seemed impossible only months ago. The medical profession is opening up brilliant new vistas of understanding. And so it goes—every sphere of human learning and achievement is exploding with progress, offering the promise of a thrilling new future for mankind.

But one great problem still exists—human behavior!

It seems that recent advances in knowledge have snatched up human beings and mercilessly ground them under the so-called wheels of progress. From every corner of the world come cries for help. The depressed mother in Europe, the bewildered boy in Africa, the tormented adolescent in the Orient, and the deviate father in America all plead for better adjustment.

As important as each profession may be, none offers a greater challenge than the field of human understanding, especially on an individual basis. The counselor who sits face to face with a disturbed person is challenged by an important question: "How can I help him to be a well-adjusted human being so that he can function adequately during his years on earth?"

To say that the human organism is complex would be an understatement. God's eternal Word eloquently describes man when it declares in Psalm 139:14: "I will praise thee; for I am fearfully and wonderfully made: marvelous are thy works; and that my soul knoweth right well."

Thus, the man who is called upon to counsel is in great need of wisdom. Nothing is more intricate than humankind. And to understand people, a counselor whether he is a minister, psychologist or psychiatrist, should devote much time to the study of human behavior. Equally important is the challenge for a counselor, himself, to be the kind of person who presents an example of excellent integration and adjustment.

How does human behavior develop? Especially unhealthy

behavior? What are the classical experiences that cause a person to turn to deviate paths? What are some of the basic approaches to help adults and children who are in trouble emotionally? These are some of the questions discussed in this volume.

When considering human problems and how they develop, one may picture three large circles which represent the basic causes of human behavior. Each of these impinges upon the other. Although they are somewhat discrete, they continually affect one another.

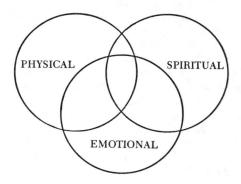

Physiological Aspects of Problems

Nearly everyone recognizes the relationship of bodily functions to human problems. In fact, many people undoubtedly think only of the medical bases of their difficulties. A homemaker, for example, may feel that her headaches are the result of insufficient sleep, excessive work, or some other physical ailment which she does not understand. She may not, on the other hand, give consideration to the fact that her headaches may stem from unresolved emotional conflicts. Similarly, a businessman who is experiencing extreme discouragement or depression may accept the possibility that he is having a medical problem which perhaps his physician has not been able to identify or correct.

And so, many people, like this businessman or homemaker, think readily in terms of physiological causes and solutions to problems. This is natural since the medical profession has made a remarkable contribution to the solution of problems of mankind by indicating their physical causes and medical treatment. Recent research in medicine points to even greater understanding of the human body. Every counselor, therefore, should seriously consider the possible physiological causes of problems and, when indicated, refer clients to medical doctors.

Emotional Aspects of Problems

During recent years psychologists, psychiatrists, ministers and others interested in human problems, have brought forth much evidence relating to the emotional bases of these difficulties.

Psychological facts which were little known even a few years ago are now gaining household acceptance. Mass media such as radio, television, and literature are continually bringing a wealth of understanding to the average person about the nature of emotional conflicts.

This trend in understanding and accepting the emotional aspects of problems is also evidenced by the number of people who are seeking psychological and psychiatric care. It is noted, also, in the emphasis which is being given in college and seminary curricula to understanding the emotional nature of man. Although many individuals prefer to think only in terms of the physiological causes of their problems, they are willing to consider the emotional causes once they learn that there is no physiological basis for their symptoms.

This volume presents a discussion of most of man's major psychological problems. It emphasizes the psychological nature of these difficulties. Indeed, all counselors, whether of a medical, religious or other background, should consider man's emotions and their effect upon his general well-being.

Spiritual Aspects of Problems

Because man is a spiritual being, it is important to consider the spiritual aspects of human adjustment. This volume expresses the fact that problems not only have physical and emotional bases, but spiritual as well. And since many problems do have spiritual causes, it follows that they have spiritual solutions. But unless a counselor has experienced spiritual conversion himself, he cannot understand spiritual causes or solutions of problems. "But the natural man receiveth not the things of the Spirit of God: for they are foolishness unto him: neither can he know them, because they are spiritually discerned" (1 Corinthians 2:14).

In fact, the man who is not born again is not only without spiritual insight; he often rejects consideration of spiritual matters. This is natural since their very consideration may be convicting to him. Yet, seeking to understand and help people who have psychological problems, without recognizing the spiritual causes and solutions, is to counsel ineffectively and unscientifically. Indeed, the professional counselor should seriously consider the spiritual aspects as he seeks to help individuals with their problems.

Life, therefore, is a process of developing and maintaining an adequate level of physical, emotional and spiritual adjustment. Each day a person has experiences which may threaten his well-being in each of these areas. Healthy adjustment is the degree to which one is successful in meeting these daily stresses. This volume deals with individuals who have not been able to cope successfully with the tensions and strains of everyday living. It discusses the reasons which have led to their inability to adapt to frustrations, and offers suggestions for resolving these difficulties.

Classification of Problems

In every area of scientific endeavor a system of nomenclature and classification is necessary to insure an orderly approach to the problems studied by that discipline. In the field of mental and emotional disturbances there are a number of factors which make such categorization necessary. Among the most important of these are:

- The need for a classification which will group similar maladjustments in like categories. This allows for more effective understanding of the interrelationship of various mental disturbances.
- The need for a shortened method of communicating infor-

mation about individuals with mental and emotional problems. Lengthy discussions of all of the personality dynamics involved in a person's emotional difficulty are often impractical because of the time factor.

- Without a systematic approach to mental illness, students of the field must wander through the maze of maladjustments lacking a clear understanding of the logical processes involved.
- Classifications are necessary for conducting research in mental illness. By grouping individuals into relatively discrete categories, a scientific researcher can study the similarities and contrasts between a number of mental disturbances.
- Through years of study a wealth of information is developed around the classification system and much meaningful material is transmitted through the use of psychiatric terminology.

Although a classification system for mental and emotional disturbances has many advantages, the professional person working in the field of human adjustment should be on guard for possible detrimental effects of such a system. Unless a psychologist, for example, has a genuine interest in the well-being of each of his clients, he may treat his patients as though they were diagnostic classifications rather than human beings suffering from emotional disturbances. Care must be taken to maintain an individual interest in each client and to think of each person as a human being with a problem rather than as a problem which happens to have a person attached.

Another pitfall to avoid is the indiscreet use of psychological and psychiatric jargon. Sometimes a counselor unwittingly uses a diagnostic label in talking with a client. When this occurs the client often becomes apprehensive and immediately goes home or to a library to read everything he can pertaining to the label the counselor has applied. Since the diagnostic label has reference to a number of people within a general category of adjustment, the client may read and apply things to himself which are inaccurate and inappropriate, as well as detrimental to his therapy. Naturally, such practice should be avoided.

Psychologists and psychiatrists must also exercise care in their use of technical terms when talking to lay people and those engaged in other professions. When a counselor has studied abnormal behavior for many years, he often forgets that the large majority of people have little or no comprehension of the meanings of his psychological terminology. In speaking to groups and in writing, the professional person must be sure to communicate on a level which is appropriate and easily understood.

Across America there is currently controversy over the use of psychiatric classifications. Some men stand vigorously for the use of these labels, saying that they furnish the best means for transmitting meaningful information about an individual. Others are just as adamant in their belief that all such diagnostic labeling should be avoided. The latter feel that it is much more meaningful to discuss a person in terms of the dynamics involved in his individual case rather than in terms of a diagnostic label.

Each of these viewpoints has its proponents, but most are agreed that if psychiatric classifications are properly used they can provide an orderly and systematic approach to the study of human maladjustments. The most widely accepted of these diagnostic systems is that prepared by the American Psychiatric Association in 1952. The following general outline of emotional and mental disturbances is taken from the *Diagnostic and Statistical Manual, Mental Disorders*, of the American Psychiatric Association.[1] This diagnostic system is used throughout America in most mental hospitals and outpatient psychological clinics.

The three major divisions of this classification system are: (1) Disorders caused by or associated with impairment of brain tissue function, (2) mental deficiency, and (3) disorders of psychogenic origin or without clearly defined physical cause or structural change in the brain.

Disorders Caused by or Associated with Impairment of Brain Tissue Function

Brain disorders are divided into two major types—acute and chronic. Cases of brain pathology which are temporary and may

[1]Committee on Nomenclature and Statistics: *Diagnostic and Statistical Manual, Mental Disorders*, American Psychiatric Association, Washington, D.C., 15th Edition, 1962.

be alleviated are called acute. Those which are irreversible are referred to as chronic. The mental disturbances in this section are either caused by or closely associated with actual organic dysfunction of the brain. Factors such as infection, trauma and intoxication are among the most common of these causes. This group of disturbances includes cases of mental deficiency which are associated with known organic diseases or prenatal causes for the intellectual deficit.

Disorders included in this classification which are discussed in this volume are:

Aphasia
Brain damage
Central nervous system disorders
Cerebral palsy
Epilepsy
Mongolism
Senility
Syphilis

Other conditions treated which may be related to this classification either as a primary or secondary diagnosis include:

Addiction
Alcoholism
Endocrine dysfunction
Mental deficiency
Thyroid dysfunction

Mental Deficiency

This diagnostic classification includes cases of limited intellectual functioning which are not due to a known organic or prenatal cause. It includes cases of low intelligence due to hereditary or familial diseases. One entire section of this volume is devoted to mental deficiency which includes disorders falling into this classification.

Disorders of Psychogenic Origin or Without Clearly Defined Physical Cause or Structural Change in the Brain

Mental and emotional disorders included in this third category are those which are believed to be due basically to emotional or psychogenic causes. This major classification is further divided into five basic classes of maladjustments resulting from emotional causes.

I. Psychotic Disorders.

Emotional disturbances classified as psychotic disorders are among the most severe of all personality maladjustments. Individuals suffering from these disturbances frequently show severe disorganization and inadequate contact with reality. They live partially in a world of fantasy and their maladjustments may require hospitalization. Their ability to relate to other people or to carry on a normal level of adjustment in daily living is usually inadequate. The psychotic disturbances discussed in this volume include:

Depressive reaction
Involutional psychotic reaction
Manic depressive reaction
Paranoid reactions
Postpartum psychoses
Psychotic disorders
Schizophrenic reaction

II. Psychoneurotic Disorders.

Mental and emotional disturbances in this category do not evidence the severe personality disorganization of the psychotic conditions. Anxiety is the basic characteristic of the psychoneurotic disorders. The neurotic individual is a tense and anxious person who is unable to gain the most from life because much of his energy is spent in defending himself against various frustrations, threats and conflicts. In treating mental disturbances it is important to distinguish between neurotic and psychotic disorders. Since the dynamics involved are different, therapeutic techniques must be altered to meet the individual problem.

The basic distinguishing factors between neurotic and psychotic disorders are outlined in the chart below:[2]

[2]Similar information is outlined in the following book: Thorpe, L., Katz, B., and Lewis, R.: *The Psychology of Abnormal Behavior*, Ronald Press Company, New York, 1961.

Differential Diagnosis Between Neurotic and Psychotic Disorders[3]

	Psychoneurotic	Psychotic
Daily functioning	The anxiety level affects only a portion of the individual's total personality functioning. Daily activities may be hindered but the individual is usually able to carry on basic duties.	The total personality is affected and the individual shows severe personality disturbances. His ability to function normally may be obviously impaired.
Symptomatology	There may be both physical and psychological symptoms but they are not obviously bizarre. Delusions and hallucinations are not present.	There are frequently very bizarre symptoms such as delusions and hallucinations and other forms of extremely inappropriate behavior.
Reality contact	The person is in contact with reality. He is aware of his environment and is oriented in time and space.	There is often much confusion of general orientation and inadequate contact with reality. This person may spend much time in a world of fantasy.
Insight	There is usually some insight into his feelings and behavior.	This person often has no insight into his behavior. In extreme instances he is unable to realize that he has severe problems.
Social relationships	Although social contacts may be hindered, the person is usually of no harm to his friends or community.	Because of the severity of the disturbance and lack of control, this person may be dangerous.
Therapy	Most of these disturbances can be handled on an outpatient basis. Institutionalization is not generally needed.	Hospitalization is often required. Therapy may include medical and psychiatric care, and prognosis is poor because of the severe personality disorganization.

---

[3]For a discussion of the treatment of psychoses see PSYCHOTIC DISORDERS in this volume.

The psychoneurotic disorders discussed in this volume include:

Anxiety reaction
Asthenic reaction
Conversion reaction
Depressive reaction
Dissociative reaction
Hypochondriacal reaction
Obsessive compulsive reaction
Phobic reaction

Other problems which are often related to these psychoneurotic disorders are:

Inferiority
Insecurity
Jealousy

III. Psychophysiologic Autonomic and Visceral Disorders:

This classification contains emotional disturbances often referred to as "psychosomatic disorders." These disturbances represent the somatization of emotional conflicts and chronic tension. Rather than allowing conflicts and anxieties to come into consciousness, the individual attempts to repress them. Being refused an emotional outlet, this tension is channeled into the body, resulting in physiological symptoms. The psychophysiologic disorders discussed in this volume are:

Anorexia nervosa (psychophysiologic gastrointestinal reaction)
Asthma (psychophysiologic respiratory reaction)
Headaches (psychophysiologic cardiovascular reaction)
Neurodermatitis (psychophysiologic skin reaction)
Obesity (psychophysiologic endocrine reaction)
Peptic ulcers (psychophysiologic gastrointestinal reaction)

IV. Personality Disorders.

The emotional maladjustments labeled "personality disorders" are characterized by developmental deficiencies. Whereas in other basic emotional maladjustments there is evidence of personality deterioration under undue stress, "personality disorders" are longstanding patterns of overt behavior. While other basic personality disturbances show many emotional and mental symptoms such as worry, tension, anxiety and depression, the individual with a "personality disorder" is usually without a significant high level of anxiety or distress because he often acts out his conflicts and thus avoids such feelings. During early years of life these persons have developed a personality structure with minimal anxiety and tension. This volume discusses the following maladjustments which are diagnosed as "personality disorders":

Addiction
Alcoholism
Delinquency
Exhibitionism
Homosexuality
Impotence and frigidity
Incest
Masturbation
Pyromania
Sexual deviation
Sociopathic personality

Other maladjustments discussed which are often associated with dynamics similar to those in "Personality Disorders" include:

Lying
Profanity
Stealing

V. Transient Situational Personality Disorders:

Maladjustments classified in this category include only those which are basically temporary in nature. They are patterns of behavior which may arise under extreme stress or a temporarily overwhelming environmental circumstance. When the behavior is indicative of rather serious underlying personality disturbances, the maladjustment is not classified in this category. The severity and duration of each individual case will determine whether these maladjustments can be genuinely termed "Transient Situational," or if they actually belong in another classification indicating a longstanding personality maladjustment. The continued presence of any of the disturbances listed below indicates they would more accurately be classified under another diagnostic category. The following such disturbances are discussed in this volume:

Anorexia nervosa
Enuresis
Pica
Speech disturbances
Tics

In dealing with human adjustment, psychologists and other counselors often counsel with individuals whose adjustment difficulties do not fit clearly into any one diagnostic classification.

There are three basic reasons why a number of problems cannot be put into a specific diagnostic category: (1) The problem is a mixture of several personality disturbances and does not fit discretely into any one category. (2) Some problems a counselor faces are not of a clinical nature and no place has been reserved for them in the diagnostic classification. An example of this is the adjustment necessary in working with adopted or gifted children. (3) Some problems are basically of a spiritual nature. Secular psychologists and psychiatrists have made no allowance for these disturbances in their psychiatric nomenclature. Problems discussed in this volume which cannot be discretely diagnosed because of one of the above reasons include:

Adoption
Assurance of salvation
Depression in childhood
Endocrine dysfunction
Giftedness
Guilt
Hostility
Lack of faith
Menopause
Obesity
Sleep disturbances
Suicide
Unfaithfulness in marriage
Unwed mothers
Withdrawal

2. Addiction

Description

Drug addiction may be defined as the continued use of drugs which produce psychological and physiological habit formation. Drug addicts can be classified into various categories according to the onset of their addiction. Only a small percentage have become accidentally addicted through the extended use of drugs for medical purposes. The use of narcotics for medical treatment presents no problem to those possessing a well-balanced personality. The great majority of addicts have turned to habit-forming drugs as a result of serious underlying personality maladjustments.

Addiction is no respector of class, sex or economic status. It is found among all races and economic levels. Young and old alike are affected by the tragic results of chronic usage. The chronic addict often engages in a variety of amoral and criminal activities. A combination of the personality maladjustment and the effect of the drugs leaves him vulnerable to participate in many antisocial activities. When a person has a strong dependency upon a drug, he will go to any extreme to obtain the needed drug. Men frequently turn to burglary to gain money needed to purchase drugs, while women often resort to prostitution.

Alcoholism and narcotism are related since chronic intoxication in either often leads to addiction. Younger addicts use the intoxication of alcohol or drugs primarily as a means of stimulation, while older individuals use it to blunt the pain, trials and stresses of competitive living and to relieve a sense of personal failure, disappointment and frustration.[1]

Specialists in the field of drug addiction often refer to "true addiction" or "false (pseudo) addiction." True addiction basically involves physical dependence, psychological dependence (habituation), and tolerance to the drug being used. False addiction, on the other hand, indicates that there is only a

---

[1]See: "Drug Addiction," *Collier's Encyclopedia*, vol. 8, p. 394.

psychological dependence upon a drug. The opiates, the barbiturates and alcohol may fulfill all the criteria of true addiction. On the other hand, the amphetamines, cocaine and marijuana have only the habituation factor.

The effects of drug addiction vary with the type of drug, the size of the dosage and the personality of the user. The drugs most commonly used are: opiates, related synthetics, barbiturates, the derivatives of Cannabis sativa (Indian hemp) such as marijuana, the amphetamines, cocaine and glue. The varied reactions to these classes of drugs necessitate separate consideration of their effects.

Opiates: Opium and its derivatives (morphine, heroin, paragoric and codeine) act as depressants of the central nervous system. (Ninety per cent of addicts use heroin.) They may be introduced into the body orally, by smoking or by injection. The physical effects of these drugs include lessening of physical energy, decrease in sexual desire, desensitization to pain, and pleasurable feelings ranging from a simple removal of depressive feelings to extreme euphoric conditions.

Within a few hours after administration of the drug, the pleasant effects begin to wear off. If another dosage is not supplied between six and fourteen hours, the addict will begin to experience withdrawal symptoms. The first withdrawal symptoms are yawning, secretion of tears, sneezing and perspiration. As the addict gains an increasing desire for the drug, these symptoms are increased. He loses his appetite, becomes depressed, develops muscle spasms and cramps, diarrhea and vomiting. As the symptoms reach their peak between forty-eight and ninety-six hours after the last dose of drug, the addict becomes extremely restless, his pulse and blood pressure rise, and he may experience hallucinations. Within five days of the last dosage, the withdrawal symptoms begin to lessen. It may take another four or five days before these symptoms completely disappear.

Synthetics: Synthetic drugs related to opium, such as Demerol, are used by drug addicts. The action and effect are similar to that of the opiates.

Barbiturates: These drugs are classed as hypnotic drugs.

They are basically depressants, commonly used as sleeping medications and widely used by those addicted to them. Most of these are taken orally but can be taken by injection. Long-standing use produces a serious type of addiction. Examples are Nembutal ("yellow jackets") and Seconal ("red devils").

Marijuana: This is the most common of the narcotic drugs. It is rather cheap and easy to obtain, and is often the first step in the chain leading to complete psychological and physiological dependence on other narcotics. Marijuana does not cause a physiological change in the user such as the severe withdrawal symptoms associated with opium and its derivatives.

Marijuana ("weed") is typically smoked as a cigarette. The user experiences a euphoric state accompanied by increased self-confidence and a breakdown of restraints. As the effects of this drug begin to wear off the individual may fall into a sleep which lasts several hours. Since marijuana does not produce physical dependence, its major threat lies in the fact that it is frequently a steppingstone to the more powerful opium derivatives. The marijuana user is often introduced to heroin or codeine while under the influence of marijuana.

Amphetamines: Amphetamines are used medically for such things as weight reduction and are taken orally. They are commonly called "pep pills" because of their stimulating action. Like most other drugs, when used properly amphetamines have a beneficial effect. Over-usage, however, can lead to addiction. Drivers who are traveling long distances and become sleepy sometimes use these, which are nicknamed "bennies." The National Safety Council, however, has warned against their use, stating that drivers taking them have more accidents than other people because these pills lower muscle control and interfere with coordination.

Cocaine: Unlike the opiates, cocaine is not, strictly speaking, a narcotic. Users of this drug do not experience severe physiological dependence. Cocaine is a stimulant which releases inhibitions. It differs from opium which acts as a depressant. Administration of cocaine is followed by a state of excitement, euphoria and self-confidence. When the drug begins to lose its effect a few hours after administration, the addict becomes depressed and irritable. He may also become weak and confused and experience digestive disturbances.

Glue: Some adolescents turn to other drugs which are harmful in themselves and which may lead to dependence upon the major drugs just discussed. Glue sniffing, for example, is used for temporary excitement. Users may take airplane glue, gasoline or solvents, and inhale the fumes from a cloth soaked in these solutions. Continued use of these products causes serious physical deterioration. Among the organs most susceptible to glue sniffing are the heart, liver, kidneys, brain and stomach, as well as the blood system.

Dependence is the most striking and devastating aspect of addiction. The body becomes so accustomed to functioning in the presence of the drug that it cannot function properly without it. A person dependent on a drug cannot take it or leave it as he chooses, for when the effect of the last dose subsides, he begins to suffer. Later, he may become so ill that he has to be hospitalized.

Etiology

The etiological factors in drug addiction are similar to those found in alcoholism.[2] The drug addict is typically an emotionally immature person who is unable to develop long-range goals. He may lack controls and be prone to seek immediate gratification of his desires.

The person who has serious personality conflicts and is leading an unhappy, frustrated life may turn to drugs in order to gain temporary relief. Often the dope addict is educationally and vocationally deprived and is not engaged in work for which he is suited. The addict seldom feels equal to situations. He, therefore, attempts to compensate for his inadequacies by taking narcotic drugs that will make him feel differently. He may also be ridden with guilt. The effect of drugs, however, only compounds his difficulties. The addict is defeated before he begins. He now has two problems: (1) his basic personality inadequacy, and (2) his addiction to drugs.

[2]See the discussion of ALCOHOLISM in this volume.

Unrealistically high goals, which have been set either by the person's parents or by himself, sometimes accompany these inadequate feelings. As he is unable to meet these goals he feels himself a failure. He then turns to drugs to gain a feeling of strength and importance which he is unable to achieve under normal conditions.

A teen-ager often takes his first drug as an experiment. He is seeking excitement, rebelling against authority, or seeking recognition. As he begins to have greater need for this crutch, he associates with more undesirable persons. His friends are other users and peddlers, usually engaged in many types of lawlessness and crime. The user's whole life is quickly in ruin by his associations and by his addiction to a drug.

There is usually a strong dependency between the addict and his (or her) *mother* or *spouse*. He needs to depend on her; she, in turn, because of her own emotional immaturity, often encourages this dependence.

Mothers of Addicts

An addict's mother is often overprotective and this role seems never to cease, regardless of her son's age. She often fosters her son's dependency on her. She frequently has a neurotic, masochistic need to keep him in a state of addiction, and is most happy when he is ill and dependent upon her. Then she seems to have a purpose in life. Where there are several children in a family, the addict usually becomes the favorite because he is the most dependent. The emotional illness of the addict's mother often feeds upon the sickness of her child. It prolongs his dependence on her and prevents him from becoming mature and resourceful.

It is common for a young addict to pawn his clothes when he is desperate for money to feed his habit. The mother frequently redeems his clothes when he is released from the narcotic hospital or correctional institution. Rarely does one hear of an addict who makes his own bed, helps around the home, or does other simple chores. Unconsciously the mother does not want him to develop a sense of responsibility because that would take him out of his dependent infancy stage.

The amount of abuse taken by the mother of an addict is almost unbelievable. There are many instances in which the son has ransacked her home, stolen her rent money, and even physically assaulted her. Yet, even in such circumstances, she may strongly oppose her husband if he makes an attempt to discipline the son.

Inconsistent behavior by the mother is a common phenomenon. She may lament to the parole officer about how terrible it is to have a son who is a drug addict. At the same time, by her deeds and attitudes, she fosters his drug usage. She frequently tells the officer she is willing to make every sacrifice to stop her son from using drugs, but she decries legislation which forbids the use of drugs. She may go to work, ostensibly for her son's psychotherapy, but somehow she manages, in addition, to support him in his narcotic daze at home.

To summarize, the mother must often maintain her child's emotional illness for her own emotional survival, thus contributing largely to the poor adjustment of the drug addict.

Fathers and Parents of Addicts

Studies by the New York University Institute of Human Relations reveal that, in the majority of cases of drug usage by adolescents, the father is either absent or, if present, weak. To some extent, separations and divorces of parents of drug addicts are caused by the emotional imbalance of the mother, who makes the home situation unbearable for the father. Wives are often known to leave their husbands because the latter insisted on taking a firm and positive approach to the son's derelictions. Invariably, in such broken home situations, the son remains with the mother and suffers from the lack of parental guidance.

Wives of Addicts

The woman who knowingly marries an addict may be emotionally disturbed herself. She often unconsciously feels that, in his addicted stage, the husband can remain the child that she yearns for. If the addict is basically passive—and he generally is—the wife can easily assume the dominant role. In personality, she frequently resembles the mother. The fact that the wife and her mother-in-law are the dominant personalities may account for the ill-feeling frequently existing between the two, with each blaming the other for the addict's state.

Many wives have an unconscious need for a drug-using, incompetent husband because only then can they be dominant. Sometimes, as the husband matures emotionally and stops using drugs, the wife's emotional disturbance becomes fully evident.

John, an addict for over five years and now eager for help, committed himself to a state facility for adults despite his wife's objections. His wife was so upset by his decision that on the day he left for the hospital she used the remains of a ten dollar "bag" of drugs and, within a short time, used drugs herself. She deserted her child, resorted to prostitution to maintain the habit and, when John was released from the hospital, she attempted to "turn him back on." Unsuccessful at this, she taunted him with accounts of her experiences with other men and even brought some of them into the home for John to meet. She persisted in her efforts to break down his morale and he finally succombed. In time, she withdrew from further drug usage and was thus able to retain her dominance.[3]

In another case, the wife so dominated her husband that she insisted on what she said was her right to attend the group therapy sessions with him. When permission was refused, she resorted to sitting outside the therapy room during the hour and a half session. Merely being there gave her a feeling of some control over his activities.

Studies of dope addicts reveal that spiritual conversion and dynamic Christian growth are seldom known among them. They have rarely experienced salvation and close communion with Christ. This lack of spiritual experience and Christian maturity leaves them vulnerable to many unwholesome experiences. It also prevents them from meeting their basic emotional needs.

Illustration

Identification: Mexican-American Male, age 20
Presenting Problem: The subject was apprehended by the law

[3]Wolk, Robert L., Psychologist, and Diskind, Meyer H., Parole Officer: *Special Narcotic Project*, New York.

when he was seized with drugs on his person. He was living with two other young men, one of whom had been apprehended previously for using addictive drugs. *Personal and Family History:* The subject was born in Mexico but moved to Southern California when he was ten years of age. In addition to his mother and father, there was an older sister and a younger brother.

As a child, the subject had very little formal education and when he came to the United States, he felt out of place with the other children. In addition to his language barrier, he was placed in school with boys and girls two years younger.

His confusion and turmoil were compounded with the lack of any spiritual training. In addition, he found himself in an unstable home where his older sister and father were engaged in sexual immorality with partners outside the home. The neighborhood was undesirable and the boy had few, if any, associates whose situation in life was better than his own.

The subject began smoking cigarettes at thirteen. Within a year he started drinking beer and liquor. He dropped out of school by fifteen and shortly afterward was introduced to marijuana. By the age of seventeen he was actively engaged in the dope traffic. He was apprehended twice for stealing before he was finally jailed as a dope addict.

Treatment

Treatment must include medical, psychological and spiritual aspects. In severe cases of drug addiction it is necessary to hospitalize the patient in order to insure complete removal of the drug. With users of opium derivatives, strict medical attention is imperative during the period of withdrawal.

The United States Public Health Service operates two hospitals for the treatment of drug addiction. These institutions are located at Ft. Worth, Texas, and Lexington, Kentucky.[4] Some individual states also maintain special facilities for narcotic addicts.[5]

---

[4]Information concerning these institutions, as well as literature regarding drug addiction, may be obtained from the Surgeon General of the U.S. Public Health Service, Washington, D.C.

[5]An example of an outstanding state facility is the California Rehabilitation Center for narcotic addicts, Corona, California.

Medical treatment may be beneficial in temporarily removing the necessity of drugs. However, if long term benefits are to be made, it is necessary that the addict receive concentrated psychotherapy. This therapy is aimed at resolving the basic conflicts which have led the patient to turn to narcotics. (For a discussion of counseling procedures with personality disturbances similar to the addict, see the discussion of SOCIOPATHIC PERSONALITY in this volume.) In addition to the therapeutic procedures outlined for sociopathic personalities, the drug addict needs special considerations.

Educational and vocational arrangements should be made so that the patient may find satisfaction learning and working. Since enjoyment comes from learning something which interests a person, education is important to one's good adjustment. In addition to suitable training and education, the former dope addict will benefit from job placement which takes into account his potential. The counselor should help the addict to understand his abilities, then seek employment where these talents can be utilized.

Those who have engaged in dope addiction also need a new circle of friends. Through better self-understanding, a person can perceive of himself differently and consider social contacts which he may have felt were closed to him previously. Practical aspects of counseling will take into account steps which a client may take to meet new, interesting people who are well-adjusted. These new friends may be found at work, at church and elsewhere.

Drug addiction is symptomatic of basic underlying personality disorganization due in large measure to faulty family relationships. Because of this, treatment of the addict alone is not enough; it should be accompanied by therapy with his family. In treating an adult addict it is important to have the mother or wife gain an understanding of her own emotional needs in relation to him. Her treatment should start before the drug user returns from the institution so that she will be prepared to receive him properly. She must be ready to deal with him in a constructive manner and at the same time experience a feeling of self-satisfaction herself.

Of special significance to the addict is spiritual conversion and subsequent Christian growth. Through the Word of God he can realize that God *does* care for him and can guide him into paths of righteousness. The facts of complete forgiveness and a bright future hold great promise for anyone, but especially for the individual who has been a slave to dope. As the Holy Spirit gradually takes over in a person's life, he becomes more mature. He finds both control and power which transcend all human effort.

3. Adoption

Description

One of the greatest joys that can come to any couple is to plan for a child. And it makes little difference whether the planning is for an adopted child or for one born to them.

The child without a home is usually headed for a life which will fail to meet either his emotional or spiritual needs. Individuals raised without stability of a home environment often enter adulthood with serious problems. By taking a homeless child into their family, a couple can make a wonderful contribution to his life. They can see that his basic physical, emotional and spiritual needs are met. Instead of growing up with many adjustment difficulties, the child may develop into a well-adjusted person with an abounding love for the Lord.

But adoption is not a one-way venture. To a childless couple a new family member brings great joy and satisfaction. The child gives the parents an opportunity to invest themselves in the life of another and to take interest in seeing the child develop into a mature adult. Indeed, the adoption of a child can result in a fuller and more complete life for the parents. Each year, in the United States alone, approximately 121,000 children are taken into homes for adoption.[1]

Pre-Adoptive Counseling

Many couples who are contemplating adopting a child wish to talk with a counselor about the different aspects of this decision. It is often wise to arrange for several sessions with this counselor to thoroughly consider the possibilities. There are a number of basic areas which should be discussed with each couple planning to adopt a child.

It is important to work through a reputable adoption agency. By dealing with an organization that has handled many adoption cases, the prospective parents will benefit from valuable ex-

[1]See: "Statistical Abstract of the United States," *U.S. Bureau of Census, 1964 (85th edition)*, Washington, D.C., 1964, p. 309.

perience. Difficulties may be encountered when dealing with an unstable agency with inadequate methods and personnel. Many legal factors are best dealt with through a well-known adoption agency.[2]

Careful planning is important. Sometimes a young couple loses a child in a tragic accident and immediately sets about to adopt another. Such impulsive decisions are often regretted later because the parents failed to carefully consider all the ramifications of adoption. When this occurs, neither the child nor the parents receive full benefit from the new arrangement. Adopting a new family member is an important step and should not be entered into without much forethought and planning.

Another responsibility of the counselor is to *help the prospective parents carefully evaluate their own attitudes.* In many instances those who anticipate adopting children are unable to bear their own; hence, it is important to help the parents consider their attitudes toward their inability to have their own children. Some people may be resentful of this inability or they may have serious feelings of guilt or inadequacy. Other parents may unwittingly be adopting a child largely to meet their own neurotic needs. A mother may feel lonely and insecure without a child and may attempt to fill this need by adopting a new baby. When this occurs, the mother may be so entangled with her own problems that her behavior adversely influences the child's emotional development. When a couple is adopting a child to replace their own which was lost through illness or accident, they need to carefully evaluate their "substitute" attitudes. While this can be an excellent arrangement, the parents must realize that they are adopting a new and different child and they should avoid trying to put the new family member in the mold of their former child. Some parents also adopt a child out of pity for his unfortunate circumstances. Although this may be a noble thought, a couple needs to be sure of their ability to meet the child's needs. The child is not in need of

[2]Evangelical Welfare Agencies are maintained in certain cities. These may be located through the Evangelical Child Welfare Agency, 127 N. Dearborn, Chicago 2, Illinois.

pity and sympathy; he needs a home characterized by stability, love, affection and security.

Another important consideration is a *knowledge of the background of the child to be adopted*. A child from an illicit affair between two highly intelligent people, for example, will likely have superior intellectual and physical characteristics. On the other hand, a child from a man and woman with meager educational and vocational backgrounds (possibly dropouts) may have limited intellectual ability as well as physical problems. Although it is not necessary to know the names of the parents, it is of value to know their general background. Some parents have been deeply disappointed by adopting an infant and later finding that he was mentally retarded or physically impaired. Much of this heartache can be avoided by knowing the child's background.

It is often wise to adopt a young child. Sometimes adoption arrangements can be made during the pregnancy of the mother so that immediately after birth the child can begin life with his new parents. This avoids the unnecessary instability associated with a number of foster home placements. Children who have been shifted from one home to another and are not finally adopted into one family until later, naturally build up more emotional disturbance than those who are adopted soon after birth.

Parents who already have children of their own should *evaluate their own children's attitudes toward a new brother or sister*. If these children are not properly prepared for the new child, they may react negatively. Talking with the children usually enables them to look with joy and anticipation to the day when their new brother or sister will arrive.

By thoroughly evaluating each of these areas with the prospective parents, the counselor will help build a strong foundation for an excellent relationship between the new parents and their child.

Counseling with Parents of Adopted Children

Some parents do not approach a counselor until they have completed adoption procedures and have received their new child.

In such cases there are several basic areas which need to be explored with the parents.

As in the case of preadoptive counseling, the parents of a new child need to consider their attitudes toward the new child. The reasons they decided to adopt the child and their current feelings toward him are important areas to explore if the parents are to develop wholesome attitudes toward the child.

One of the first questions parents ask a counselor is, "Should we tell our child he is adopted?" There are two points of view concerning this question. Those who think they should not, believe that it is dangerous to tell a child. "Keep it a secret," they say, "and he'll never know the difference. If you tell him, he may never really love you and he'll resent any discipline you must give him." Most people who have worked closely with many adopted children, however, feel that it is best to tell a child about his adoption. There are several reasons for this. One is that life is best when it is lived aboveboard. Yet some adoptive parents go through life hiding the truth of an adoption.

One such mother finally confided to her pastor that she and her husband had never told their daughter she was adopted. "But it isn't easy," she said. "Last week my husband and daughter and I were visiting in the home of some friends. While we were talking, the doorbell rang. Surprisingly, it was the natural mother and father of our adopted girl. They did not realize we were visiting in the home. They asked if this was 'Shirley.' I told them it was, and they remarked that she was getting to be a big girl. A few minutes later Shirley asked me privately, 'Mommy, who are those people? They acted so strange.' We go through life like this—just living a lie. We can't be ourselves, we can't be natural, we can't be truthful. And I know it is not honoring to the Lord."

Naturally, this is not a desirable way to live. We are much happier and God blesses us more when we are honest. God teaches this in His Word. "Providing for honest things, not only in the sight of the Lord, but also in the sight of men" (II Corinthians 8:21).

The child may discover his background in spite of his parents' attempt to conceal his adoption. Consequently, it is better if the parents tell him first. Friends or neighbors who know that the child is adopted may unwittingly say something. Finding it out in this "roundabout" manner is not good for the child. He would much rather have learned it from his parents.

If parents do not tell a child, they may always have guilt feelings about not telling him. One couple, for example, revealed their guilt feelings concerning their adopted boy. With deep concern the father told the counselor, "Nearly every night after tucking him in bed and praying with him, I think how deceitful I've been. It makes me feel awful. Jimmie has such confidence in me. He thinks that I am his father—but, of course, I have never told him. Sometimes I wake up at night thinking about it."

This situation is not good—neither for the boy nor for his parents. How simple it would have been if they had only lovingly told him that he was an adopted boy, assuring him how much they loved him and how important he was in their family.

A child's love for his parents does not depend upon blood relationship. Ronnie, for example, was a chubby little first-grader whom the psychologist was testing. At one point in the test, he started telling about his love for his mother. When asked why, he said with great delight, "Because she 'borned' me." Actually, Ronnie was adopted. He loved his parents because they loved him and cared for him. A child responds to those who love and care for him.

Parents often will ask, *"At what age should a child be told that he is adopted?"* A child should be told sufficiently early so that he will "always know it." Parents should not wait until a child is old enough to receive a "surprise" or a shock from the news. As one man said, "I am adopted and I have always known it. I guess my parents must have told me when I was very small because I never remember their breaking the news. I'm glad it was that way."

A third question parents will raise is, *"How do we tell our child he is adopted?"* To be sure, there are poorer as well as better ways. One woman told how her parents "informed" her that she was adopted:

"It happened when my husband was serving overseas. My

two babies and I were living with my parents. But during the last few weeks my folks and I had been getting on each other's nerves. Mom and I had locked horns in a few word battles. One day when we were arguing, Mom lost her temper. Her eyes flashed as she said, 'Well, no wonder you act this way. You're not my child anyway!' I knew Mother, and I could tell that she was in earnest. It was coming from down deep inside. So I asked her what she meant. She was still angry and she went on to say, 'Well, you're just an adopted child. We got you when you were three months old. We don't know who your parents were. If you had been anything like me or Daddy, you surely wouldn't be acting like this. You've always been hard to live with—such a nasty disposition!'

"My whole world fell from underneath me. I spent the rest of the day—in fact, several days and nights, crying bitter tears. But the heartbreak was this: I didn't have anyone to talk to— my husband was thousands of miles away. And the babies were too young to understand. Believe me, I was crushed. And I've never gotten over it."

Parents also frequently ask what they should tell an adopted child about his own mother and father. An attempt should be made to put the child's natural parents in as good a light as possible. Nothing is accomplished by running down the natural parents. A child can be told that if his parents were anything like their child, they must have had wonderful characteristics.

No child likes to feel that his parents were "no good." Some people feel that the worse they picture the natural parents, the more the child will love the adopted mother and father. But this is not true. Instead, the child resents it and develops unhealthy attitudes.

If parents know some unpleasant things about the natural parents, they shouldn't bother the child with the unsavory details. Not one of us can boast a perfect family tree. Furthermore, derogatory information doesn't edify; it usually casts dark, unhappy shadows.

Another question often raised by parents of a newly adopted child is, "*What should we tell our friends?*" The fact that a child is adopted does not need to be told to all of the parent's acquaintances. As a child becomes a part of the family, the thought of adoption should disappear. It is not an issue. Rather, it is a happy fact.

On the other hand, it need not be kept a secret. A psychologist visited an elementary school where he was requested by the principal to make a case study of "Dick." As the psychologist worked closely with the child and his parents, he sensed that these people were not the natural mother and father. When asked about it, they glanced around the room, then said in soft voices, "Yes, he's adopted, but no one here knows it. That's why we left Texas. But please, don't tell the school authorities or Dick's teachers, will you?"

The counselor kept their confidence, but suggested that they might benefit from discussing their true feelings about Dick's adoption.

On the other hand, some parents talk too much about adoption. One couple, for example, continually discussed their "adopted boy." The subject never seemed to rest. They appeared to need reassurance that they had done the right thing in adopting this child. They felt "adoption" was an excuse for his misbehavior. It must have been tiresome and unhealthy for the boy and, of course, unwise for all concerned.

In summary, adoptive parents might share such information with those who would benefit from it, but should not bring it up without cause.

Counseling Parents Whose Adopted Children Have Problems

Adopted children are vulnerable to the same emotional disturbances as all other young people. Some do poorly in school and evidence behavior which is very disturbing. Other adopted children suffer from emotional problems such as feelings of insecurity and withdrawal.

In addition to the common causes of emotional and behavioral problems, there are a number of other factors which may place an added burden upon an adopted child.

Serious adjustment difficulties may arise when parents fail to tell a child at an early age that he is adopted. When a child suddenly learns that he is adopted, he may immediately feel rejected and unloved. These feelings may then result either in depression and worry or in poor school adjustment or a behavioral disorder.

An important causal factor in some cases of emotional disturbances among adopted children is the fact that parents have too high standards of accomplishment. They expect the child to maintain a certain level of performance in order to receive parental approval and acceptance. Since an adopted child's physical and intellectual endowment is often much different from his parents', it is important for the mother and father to understand these differences and not attempt to conform the child to their preconceived notions.

Another factor which may be detrimental to an adopted child's adjustment is the fact that he likely has a different intellectual level than the parents. When parents have above-average intellectual gifts they may attempt to force the child into a mold for which he is not suited. They may expect high achievement in school, and become openly disappointed when the child fails to reach these standards. Such parents do not realize that this child does not have the intellectual gift of other members in the family. When they try to make him conform, the child may develop serious emotional disturbances.

Problems may also arise when an adopted child has different gifts than his parents. This may be the case, for example, with two musically gifted parents. Having such abilities, it is natural that they attempt to develop their adopted child's musical talents. In many cases, however, the child simply does not have ability in this area. His strengths may be entirely different from the parents. In such instances, it is important that the mother and father realize that God has given their new child abilities of his own. Parents should strive to determine their child's true abilities and to develop his innate potential. They can then deal realistically with his educational and vocational needs.

In seeking a better understanding of their child's abilities and his emotional makeup, many parents will want a thorough psychological evaluation. Through testing, a well-trained psychologist can determine the child's intelligence, the areas where he has special abilities, and his personality strengths and weaknesses. This type of psychological evaluation is helpful in preventing many problems. It furnishes information which enables parents to work with their child in a more understanding manner.

Unwarranted comparisons with other children is a pitfall to be avoided. In a subtle manner some parents make comparisons between children which put the adopted child in a poor light. This results in feelings of inadequacy and rejection and may lead to serious emotional disturbances.

Some parents try to impress others that they did the right thing in adopting a child. They put the child on display to prove to themselves and to others that adoption was a wise decision. This, of course, is no solution. Children soon sense these unwholesome attitudes and it causes them to develop feelings of rejection and worthlessness.

In other instances, emotional difficulties may arise from the fact that an adopted child is the couple's first and only child. Some parents have little understanding of child growth and development, and matters of discipline. When such is the case the counselor may offer helpful suggestions and recommend books on child training.[3]

When counseling parents of an adopted child who has problems, full discussion and ventilation of feelings are important. As parents begin to discuss their child's difficulties, they take the first step toward resolving the conflicts. The counselor can assist parents to develop insights into the causes of the child's behavior and into their own feelings and attitudes toward the child. They may have unresolved feelings toward the child which hinder an effective parent-child relationship. By getting their own feelings out in the open and gaining insight into their reactions, the parents will then be free to deal more effectively with the child and his disturbances. In dealing with specific problems, the counselor will want to consider each of the etiological factors discussed above, as well as related discussions under individual topics in this volume.

[3]See author's book, *Discipline in the Christian Home*, Zondervan Publishing House, Grand Rapids.

4. Alcoholism

Description

Alcoholism is a disorder associated with the excessive use of intoxicating beverages. It is estimated that there are over four million excessive drinkers in the United States alone.

Alcohol has deteriorating effects on the user's personal and social life. It often leaves the home of the alcoholic in a shambles. He is unable to maintain effective interpersonal relationships with family members and his mismanagement of finances causes serious difficulties. Separation and divorce are often left in the wake of excessive drinking. In short, the alcoholic is usually left financially, physically and spiritually bankrupt.

Occupational difficulties also arise. The alcoholic may perform inadequately at work, may miss complete days of labor, and may eventually lose his employment. Alcoholism is no respecter of persons, affecting all socioeconomic levels. Malnutrition often follows alcoholism, since the heavy drinker usually has a disrupted routine and does not receive proper nourishment.

In small quantities alcohol acts as a stimulant. However, in increasing amounts it is a depressant. It has an anesthetic or depressing effect on the central nervous system. By turning to intoxicating beverages the alcoholic can temporarily escape feelings of insecurity and inferiority and achieve false but gratifying feelings of adequacy. Studies reveal that most alcoholics are dependent individuals with inadequate self-concepts. They frequently have a poor sex role identification and are emotionally immature. These characteristics must be considered by the therapist who deals with an alcoholic. Factors which undermine feelings of adequacy and security are commonly found in studies of the childhood experiences of alcoholics.[1]

The development of alcoholism passes through several general phases. The alcoholic typically begins as a social drinker.

[1]Schilder, P.: "The Psychogenesis of Alcoholism," *Quarterly Journal of Studies on Alcohol*, vol. 2, pp. 244-292, 1941.

Finding that alcohol depresses his nervous system and temporarily relieves tension and anxiety, he gradually increases his consumption. In time, he finds that he is unable to control his drinking. Following this phase, the alcoholic turns to the most critical step in chronic alcoholism. He is taken over almost entirely by alcohol and is unable to control the amount he drinks.

If heavy drinking is continued over a period of years, permanent personality deterioration may occur. Mental disturbances often develop and memory and comprehension may be disrupted. The alcoholic may show a low threshold of tolerance as well as depressive reactions.[2] Physical symptoms may also appear. Cirrhosis of the liver as well as other internal disorders and an overall physical and muscular degeneration frequently result from chronic alcoholism.

Etiology

Physiological: Physiological disturbances are sometimes influential in the development of alcoholism. Although these disturbances are not sole etiological factors, people who suffer from certain brain disturbances are more likely to become alcoholics than physically healthy persons. Two of the more prominent physiological conditions associated with alcoholism are anoxia or hypoxia (insufficient oxygen at the time of birth) and neurological complications either during or after birth. In some cases people turn to alcohol as an attempt to escape physical pain. When this practice is continued, it may lead to chronic alcoholism.

Emotional: The chronic alcoholic is emotionally maladjusted and in most instances was maladjusted prior to becoming addicted to alcohol. He is often suffering from a neurotic disturbance which he is unable to resolve. In order to relieve the anxiety associated with his neurotic conflict he turns to alcohol.

Although no universal personality pattern has been found among alcoholics, certain characteristics are common to many.

[2]See: Seliger, Robert V., M. D., and Cranford, Victoria; edited by Goodwin, Harold S.: *Alcoholics Are Sick People*, Alcoholism Publications, Baltimore, 1945.

Alcoholics are usually emotionally immature and passive-dependent. They have not developed to the point where they can assume adequate responsibility in taking care of themselves and their families. They prefer to rely on others rather than accepting leadership themselves. In some cases, alcoholics are extremely disturbed, needing intensive psychotherapy.

The alcoholic is often a person with high aspirations. His inability to reach unrealistic goals leads him to turn away from these failures and attempt to find temporary feelings of adequacy and superiority by drinking.

Feelings of hostility are important in some instances of alcoholism. A hostile, rebellious person who is afraid to express these feelings under normal circumstances may turn to alcohol in order to lower his inhibitions and enable free expression of previously repressed feelings.

Basic to these emotional disturbances are childhood experiences. Rather than developing normally, the alcoholic has grown up with feelings of inadequacy and insecurity. Consequently, he feels unable to respond normally in most situations without the aid of a "crutch."

Many people take the first step toward eventual alcoholism during adolescence. When this happens there are usually four basic dynamics. First, the adolescent who begins to drink generally has an unsatisfactory home environment. There may be tension and misunderstanding between the child and his parents. Frequently the teenager has strong hostile feelings toward his parents.

A second factor often found in adolescents who begin to drink is a dissatisfaction with life in general and a search for thrills and excitement. It is normal for a teen-ager to want to try new activities to gain a sense of independence and joy, but when he turns to drinking it is generally indicative of emotional conflicts beyond the range of normal adolescent strivings. This person finds life dull and uninteresting without the "thrills" of drinking.

A third cause of teen-age drinking is the influence of group pressure. One of the adolescent's major goals in life is to find acceptance by the group. If it is necessary to begin drinking to gain this acceptance, the teen-ager frequently gives in to the encouragement of the "gang." In this way he is meeting his need for acceptance and finding a sense of identity by associating with the group.

A lack of spirituality is a fourth important consideration in teen-age drinking. The young person who has a love for the Lord sees the fallacy of drinking and has no desire to become engaged in such degrading activities. Instead, this person finds his sense of purpose and accomplishment through serving the Lord Jesus Christ. The unsaved adolescent, on the other hand, is seeking the thrill of the moment. He gives little thought to the future, especially to eternity.

This combination of emotional and spiritual factors is usually the root of alcoholism which began with teen-age drinking. In other instances alcoholism is only one segment of maladjustment of a broader sociopathic personality pattern.[3]

Illustration
Identification: White male, age 36
Presenting Problem: The patient's drinking had become increasingly worse. His wife had encouraged him to seek professional help but he refused, saying that he could stop if he wanted to do so. In time, he was unable to hold employment, so he went to see a physician who referred him to a local minister.
Personal and Family History: A review of the subject's family background showed an extremely overindulgent mother and a strict, perfectionistic father. The mother satisfied the child's every whim and did not allow him to develop independence. The father criticized the boy's efforts and supervised him closely to see that all of his work was done perfectly. As a result of these parental influences, the patient grew up as a dependent person who did not feel adequate to take adult responsibilities.

The patient went to college away from home and began having difficulties with his studies. Finding it impossible to live up to his father's high expectations and feeling insecure in social

[3]For a full discussion of this disorder see SOCIOPATHIC PERSONALITY in this volume.

relationships, he started drinking in order to forget his failures. Finally he left college before receiving his degree. The patient was married at twenty-four and became the father of two children.

Now that he has a wife and children he is finding it extremely difficult to provide leadership in his home and is also upset over the quality of his work at the office where he is employed. He has begun to turn more frequently to alcohol as a means of escape.

Treatment

One step in the treatment of an alcoholic is the removal of liquor. Medical treatment is available which is effective in conditioning the individual to stop drinking. Unless he is able to stop, at least for a time, he is unable to seek professional help and benefit from counseling.

Although medical treatment may be effective in discouraging excessive use of alcohol, it will not resolve the basic conflicts which have led to the disorder. Through counseling the individual needs to become aware of the factors in his life which led to his inability to tolerate stress and anxiety. He needs to realize that his drinking is an attempt to escape problems, but not a solution to them. He needs to discuss the fact that continued drinking will only exaggerate his present condition. Motives for his drinking need to be examined. When he learns "why" he is drinking he has a better basis for finding other approaches to his problems. The alcoholic needs help in facing his failures without the crutch of a drink. He also needs to take special precautions when he is discouraged and "down in the dumps." If he can verbalize, in advance, the danger of "low" times emotionally, physically and spiritually, he will be forearmed for such occurrences. The alcoholic must learn to take responsibility and to develop a more mature and realistic attitude toward his capacity for adjustment without resorting to the crutch of alcohol.[4]

[4]The following organizations provide recent information on alcoholism: National Committee on Alcoholism, Academy of Medicine Building, 2-103rd St., New York 29, N. Y.; Alcoholics Anonymous, Box 459, Grand Central Annex, New York 17, N. Y.; Yale Center of Alcohol Studies, Yale University, 52 Hillhouse Avenue, New Haven, Connecticut.

One who is addicted to alcohol also needs to understand the relationship between good physical health and nondrinking. Many alcoholics who have improved their general health have found that it is much easier to control their drinking.

One of the greatest hopes available to the excessive drinker is spiritual conversion. Jesus said, "Come unto me, all ye that labour and are heavy laden, and I will give you rest" (Matthew 11:28). There is practical hope for the alcoholic in receiving Christ as his personal Savior. This trust will bring about a new life for him. The Bible declares: "Therefore, if any man be in Christ, he is a new creature: old things are passed away; behold, all things are become new" (II Corinthians 5:17). This new nature, implanted by God, provides one with new desires as well as new power.

If the alcoholic has acknowledged Christ as his Redeemer but is not living in close fellowship with the Lord, his hope is also in Christ. He still has the assurance that God will not forsake him. "If we confess our sins, he is faithful and just to forgive us our sins, and to cleanse us from all unrighteousness" (I John 1:9). The Scriptures promise that ". . . God is faithful, who will not suffer you to be tempted above that ye are able; but will with the temptation also make a way to escape, that ye may be able to bear it" (I Corinthians 10:13). This spiritual help is thorough, affecting the personality in depth. It is also lasting, bringing permanent relief. Among other benefits of spiritual conversion and growth is the new circle of Christian friends which comes with new life in Christ.

For the person who has turned to drinking to escape feelings of failure associated with unrealistic goals, spiritual concepts are especially beneficial. These individuals feel they must reach a certain level of attainment in order to be loved and accepted. Because they feel they have not measured up to this level they have turned to drinking to escape feelings of unworthiness. The fact that the whole human race is unworthy in God's sight, and that every individual's acceptance of God is totally dependent upon Christ is a concept of utmost importance to the alcoholic. The alcoholic must learn that he does not need to strive to please God and gain acceptance. God's love is unconditional.

"Therefore we conclude that a man is justified by faith without the deeds of the law" (Romans 3:28). "But to him that worketh not, but believeth on him that justifieth the ungodly, his faith is counted for righteousness" (Romans 4:5). As the alcoholic comes to realize that he is justified by faith through Christ, rather than by his works, the need to escape will begin to disappear.

In summary, the alcoholic often needs medical therapy to help him stop drinking. Following this, psychological diagnosis is important in learning the causes of the problem. Psychotherapy which takes into consideration spiritual conversion and dynamic Christian growth is especially effective. Rehabilitation centers and farms have proved helpful in providing desirable environments and friendships during a crucial period of readjustment.

5. Anorexia Nervosa

Description
Anorexia Nervosa is a disorder which is characterized by loss of appetite. The person suffering from this ailment may say, "I'm just not hungry," "I don't feel like eating" and "I don't care for anything." If this condition continues the person will exhibit other symptoms, such as exhaustion due to lack of nutrition. He may have scaly skin, lowered pulse rate and low body temperature.

In children, loss of appetite is often accompanied by other symptoms such as thumb-sucking, bed-wetting and various nervous habits.

Etiology
Anorexia may be either physical or psychological in origin. Among the most prominent *physical causes* are disease with high fever, nervous excitement, tension, allergy and chronic wasting diseases. Diseases affecting glandular function (especially the pituitary) and digestive processes sometimes lie at the root of a poor appetite.[1] Lack of fresh air, inadequate exercise, and insufficient sleep may contribute to such a condition. Improper diet, whether it be attempted overfeeding, eating between meals, or vitamin imbalance may also be responsible for loss of appetite.

Emotional difficulties are the root of many cases of anorexia. A child may refuse to eat in order to gain attention or to get his way. He may be disturbed by lack of harmony in the home. If so, his unhappiness may very likely carry over into his eating habits.

Extreme discipline at the table may also be the cause of poor appetite. If mealtime becomes a period of discipline and unpleasantness, it is only natural that a person will develop negative feelings toward eating. *Forced feeding* or *inconsistency*

---

[1]For a discussion of the interrelationship between emotions and endocrine functions in Anorexia Nervosa see: Alexander, Franz: *Psychosomatic Medicine*, W. W. Norton and Company, Inc., New York, 1950.

in feeding habits are also disturbing to a child, sometimes causing him to dislike eating.

Some children refuse to eat in order to demonstrate *hostility toward their parents.* In this way they hope to make the parents worried and anxious over the possibility of physical illness. The child gains satisfaction when he sees the parents worry, as he has successfully discharged hostility toward them.

Parental rejection or *extreme problems at school* are also common causes of anorexia. The person who does not eat properly is often insecure. A home or school atmosphere characterized by criticism and punishment rather than by sympathy, love and understanding may be responsible for the insecurity.[2]

In adults a continued refusal to eat is often associated with a personality structure characterized by *extreme sensitivity, introversion and perfectionistic behavior.* In childhood these individuals have frequently had many unhappy experiences and are generally insecure and fearful. Many women suffering from chronic lack of appetite have had poor relationships with their mothers and still harbor strong feelings of *unresolved hostility.*

One factor which is frequently found among individuals suffering from anorexia nervosa is a *self-punitive dynamic.* In these cases the individual feels unworthy, guilty and in need of punishment. His refusal to eat is an unconscious effort to punish himself by denying basic bodily needs.

Secondary gains are influential in many cases of chronic lack of appetite. In addition to serving other unconscious emotional needs, the patient finds satisfaction in the attention, sympathy and affection he receives by being ill. Since he is in need of love and affection, the person's refusal to eat enables him to become the center of attention, thus meeting his emotional deprivation.

Illustration

Identification: White female, age 13

Presenting Problem: The patient was brought to the family phy-

[2]For a discussion of various feeding problems, see: Kanner, Leo: *Child Psychiatry*, Charles C. Thomas, Springfield, Illinois, Third Printing, 1960.

sician because her mother had become alarmed over the girl's refusal to eat. "I'm afraid she'll starve to death," remarked the mother to the doctor. "She just picks at her food and she doesn't eat enough to keep a bird alive."

The physician's examination found the patient to be much underweight and nervous, with a mild skin rash.[3]

Personal and Family History: The patient's parents were married at an early age. Although they became reasonably secure financially, they had moved several times and their marriage was marked by much turmoil and quarreling. For a year after their marriage the couple attended church, but in time both gave up regular attendance. During the last three years the husband had become interested in other women and had become sexually intimate with several.

The patient was referred to a psychologist who found that the girl was very insecure and deeply concerned about the unhappy conditions in her home.

After several months of counseling with the patient and with her parents, conditions in the home improved. This was reflected in the patient's improved appetite.

Treatment

The first step in treating anorexia should be a medical examination to rule out any possible physical conditions which might be causing the problem.

Therapy for a child or adolescent with a poor appetite is directed to the parents as well as to the child. The parents must come to realize that the child's difficulty is primarily a reaction to family surroundings and that, if the child is to overcome the problem, his environment as well as his attitudes must be improved.

Parents and teachers need to realize that inflexible rules or ultimatums, such as requiring a child to eat a certain amount at each meal, only complicate his problem. As the home and school atmosphere become more relaxed, the child will suffer

[3]See the discussion of NEURODERMATITIS in this volume.

less from emotional tension and his difficulty will usually resolve itself.

In dealing with adults, the basic underlying personality dynamic must be uncovered and resolved. If the person has an inadequate self-concept and is unconsciously attempting to punish himself by this behavior, the dynamics of this should be explored in detail. As this person comes to understand the reasons he feels in need of punishment and as he begins to appropriate the Lord's gracious forgiveness of sin, this self-punitive attitude will disappear. When anorexia is associated with a broader picture of neurotic behavior, the feelings of insecurity and inadequacy must be explored and resolved.[4]

---

[4]See the discussion of INSECURITY in this volume.

6. Anxiety Reaction

Description

Anxiety neuroses are characterized by marked degrees of unfounded dread, worry and apprehension. The person suffering from anxiety reaction may be continually concerned about his future. He is upset over little errors he has made. In addition, he worries about problems which he feels are sure to befall him in the future.

This disturbance differs from other neuroses because the individual is unable to pinpoint his uneasiness and apprehension. His total life is characterized by anxiety and dread which seemingly has no objective origin. This apprehension is known as "free floating" anxiety. Whereas the person with a phobic reaction has attached his anxiety to a specific object, the person with an anxiety neurosis is anxious in all situations.

Some people are subject to periods of intense worry and concern. These times are accompanied by a variety of physical symptoms such as breathing difficulties, excessive perspiration, headaches, dizziness, tremors, palpitations of the heart, restlessness and inability to sleep. Anxiety attacks may become extremely severe and medication is sometimes necessary to relieve physical symptoms. The person may come to fear some great catastrophe which he believes will occur. Such attacks may be quieted by administering a sedative or they can be allowed to run their course, which may last from a few minutes to more than an hour.

An anxious person is subject to feelings of apprehension and tension in situations where a well-adjusted person experiences little or no anxiety. The slightest stress is often sufficient to provoke serious feelings of impending danger in the neurotic individual.[1]

One who is suffering from anxiety may become unusually dependent upon someone such as a relative, spouse or close

---

[1] For a brief discussion of anxiety reactions, see Gregory, Ian: *Psychiatry: Biological and Social*, W. B. Saunders Company, Philadelphia, 1961.

friend. In the event of the death of this loved one, the person may suffer greatly and show marked symptoms of illness.

A child suffering from an anxiety reaction may be overactive. He is continually in action and unable to sit still for long periods of time. He may walk rapidly about the room, with his hands and legs in constant motion. Because of his hyperactivity this child often does poorly in school. He is unable to concentrate for prolonged periods of time and his restlessness hinders effective study. Other indications of nervousness such as inability to sleep and nail biting may also be present.

Etiology

Severe anxiety is a result of *basic feelings of inadequacy and inferiority*.[2] Throughout early life the person has usually been subject to criticism, failure and guilt. He has come to be fearful of new situations and insecure in social relationships. Even the slightest stress situations may cause great discomfort and anxiety. Any threat, personal criticism, direct suggestions, or forceful personality in his environment will immediately re-emphasize the individual's feelings of inadequacy and inferiority.

Another cause of this basic anxiety is to be found in *feelings of guilt*. One may fear the social consequences of certain immoral acts, yet have a very strong desire to engage in such behavior. The conflict between the individual's personal desire and his need for social approval may create a real source of apprehension.

A person may harbor *feelings of fear and guilt from a traumatic event in the past*. For example, an individual may blame himself for the accidental death of another in an automobile crash, a fire or because of some carelessness. This may cause him to go through life with vague feelings of guilt and condemnation.

The person with an insecure childhood, who constantly strove for commendation from his parents, may become extremely upset as an adult when his actions reap disapproval and correction rather than endorsement.

[2] See the discussions of INSECURITY and INFERIORITY in this volume.

The causes of childhood anxiety reactions can usually be traced to *the child's present home adjustment or to recent traumatic events*. When a child's parents are having marital difficulties, the turmoil associated with this can cause serious feelings of worry and anxiety. Any situations in the home which lead to stress, frustration and conflict may be influential in the etiology of anxiety reactions among children.

Illustration
Identification: White female, age 38
Presenting Problem: The patient has been experiencing severe anxiety when entering new and unfamiliar situations. If she attempts to go out for dinner, for example, she perspires, her heart beats rapidly, and she has shortness of breath.
Personal and Family History: The patient's mother was described as harsh and cruel. She continually nagged and criticized her children. The father was a passive man who worked long hours and spent little time with his family. As a child the patient was obedient, timid and fearful. She was afraid to express her anger for fear her mother would punish her.

In school, the subject had few friends and was very withdrawn. She studied hard and made good grades, but failed to take part in social activities. She married at eighteen, after a short courtship, and now has three children. She describes her marriage as unhappy. Through the years her feelings of anxiety and fear have increased, especially when approaching new situations.

Treatment
People who suffer from anxiety neuroses usually respond well to psychological treatment. Since the causes of an individual's anxiety lie in feelings of insecurity and inferiority, successful therapy usually requires many sessions.[3] During therapy the counselor helps the patient to evaluate his past experiences and

[3]For a more detailed discussion of self-confidence and personal assurance see the author's publication, *Self-Confidence*.

All of the author's books are published by Zondervan Publishing House, Grand Rapids, Michigan.

examine their binding influence upon him. The conflicts and frustrations which are at the base of the anxiety must be resolved. In this way the anxious person can strengthen his self-concept and face life as a more confident, secure and well-adjusted individual.

One important therapeutic technique with the person suffering from anxiety is to demonstrate the relationship of his anxiety to a particularly threatening situation. For example, a young woman whose counselor realizes that her anxiety is related to fearfulness of heterosexual relationships might be asked to keep a record during the week of the times when she feels most anxious and apprehensive. During the next session she can discuss these situations and come to see that in several instances her anxiety was increased when she was in close proximity to men. As she sees this relationship the subject is encouraged to delve more deeply into her relationships with men and to gain an understanding of the factors underlying this difficulty.

Spiritual growth is an important factor in overcoming anxiety. As a person walks in close fellowship with Christ, he becomes increasingly aware of the security and peace which he has in Him. The realization that God is interested in each one personally gives a child of God added confidence which helps him overcome his feelings of apprehension. Such spiritual concepts, however, are not gained automatically from a lecture. Instead, they are usually developed over a period of time as a client identifies himself closely with a dedicated believer (often a counselor) and as he discusses his problems and their origins. A gradual understanding of Biblical teachings will eventually take root in the heart and mind of the one suffering from anxiety and will help to permanently dispel his apprehensions.

The basic considerations in dealing with children and adolescents suffering from high levels of anxiety center upon improved family relationships. In these cases a major portion of the counseling time will actually be spent with the parents rather than with the child.

The parents must come to see the influence of an unstable home environment on the child. Parental patterns such as rejection or open discord associated with marital conflicts must be resolved if the child is to develop a more healthy emotional adjustment.

In working with the parents of children who have emotional problems, the counselor must be very alert. When a counselor merely discusses the effect of the home environment on the child's adjustment, little help is achieved. Even when the counselor offers specific suggestions for changes in the child's surroundings, little profit may be gained. People do not change their emotional reactions by hearing a lecture or even by taking time to discuss the basic home problem. Although parents may make overt changes in their behavior patterns as a result of the counselor's suggestions, too often these changes are of a superficial nature. What is usually needed is an actual time of therapy with the parents. In many cases of childhood problems, the counselor must turn from a discussion of the child's difficulty to a treatment of the parents' maladjustments. As the parents begin to consider their own emotional adjustment and as their behavior changes, the problems of the children will likely disappear. In some instances, anxieties of children can be alleviated even though little time is spent in therapy with the child. Instead, the counselor deals with the parents.

When a counselor first brings up the parents' responsibilities in the formation of their child's emotional disturbance, there may be considerable resistance. Parents may reply, "It's his problem, not mine. Why don't you spend your time with my son?" When this occurs the counselor should explain in a kindly way the influence of parent behavior on children's reactions.

The counselor may want to explain to the parents that many of their own feelings and actions are operating on an unconscious level. Because of this they are unable to clearly understand their own attitudes and behavior. They can be told that the counseling sessions will include consideration of these unconscious motivating elements (of both parents and children) in addition to factors of which they are currently aware. Usually, with this explanation and several initial sessions, the parents will come to the point of recognizing their own maladjustments and will be willing to continue therapy for their own personal problems.

When a counselor is able to spend time with both the parents and the child, most effective progress is made. In addition to individual counseling hours, some of the sessions may be devoted to family therapy. In such sessions, the counselor meets with all family members at once to work through various aspects of home adjustments. As the environment in the home improves, and as the child develops an improved sense of security and adequacy, his fearfulness and anxiety will disappear.

7. Aphasia

Description

Aphasia is a disorder which is characterized by an inability to articulate speech and to understand the meaning of written or spoken words. Three classifications of aphasia have been distinguished: (1) Motor aphasia or expressive aphasia, which is the inability to express ideas through speech, (2) Sensory aphasia or receptive aphasia, which is the inability to comprehend written or spoken words, and (3) Expressive-receptive aphasia, in which all language processes are limited. In addition to disturbances resulting from structural abnormalities, there are rare occurrences of loss of ability to communicate resulting from severe emotional conflicts. These cases occur most frequently as a result of some traumatic experience and are not genuine cases of aphasia.

Because of the individual's failure to understand speech and to communicate, serious emotional problems may arise. The person may become fearful of new and unfamiliar situations and may be overly dependent on parents or close loved ones. Continual failure and frustration can lead to depression and other serious emotional disturbances.

Etiology

Aphasia is basically the result of abnormalities of the brain. This condition may be due to injury at birth or to damage later in life. Among the major postnatal causes are meningitis, cerebral hemorrhage and injuries to the head.

Illustration

Identification: White male, age 8
Presenting Problem: This boy was brought to his family physician following a serious fall which resulted in a period of unconsciousness. A few days after the injury, the boy began experiencing difficulty speaking and also complained of headaches.

From medical examinations the presence of a blood clot on

the brain was suspected. Surgery confirmed this diagnosis. In removing the blood clot, brain tissue damage to the area which controls speech function was noted. After surgery, a program of speech therapy was initiated which resulted in gradual improvement. Because of the brain lesion, total recovery was not achieved.

Treatment

Therapy with the aphasic person is usually a specialized technique.[1] It consists of stimulating interest in speech by talking and reading to the person and by showing pictures and describing them. All means of association are used. Gesture language and the kinesthetic approach are valuable methods. The ear is trained by having the patient do something whenever he hears a sound. Next, he is helped to make a sound whenever he sees a movement. Vocalization is taught gradually by showing the patient how a certain sound is produced. The objective is toward gradual improvement.

In the case of children, especially those who have never spoken, training should be started early so that they will not become accustomed to a nonverbal existence. Various specialists, including medical doctors and speech therapists, may be utilized to help these individuals.

---

[1] For a thorough discussion of the treatment of this disorder, see: Longerich, M. C., and Bordeaux, J.: *Aphasia Therapeutics*, The Macmillan Company, New York, 1954.

8. Assurance of Salvation

Description

This is a condition in which a person is unsure of his personal relationship to God. Such an individual may know the Bible plan of salvation. He may give assent to the Gospel of Jesus Christ, and may have presented a public testimony to his faith. Yet he is plagued with gnawing doubts that his life in Christ is not genuine. He harbors fears that he may not have met all the requirements necessary to become a child of God, or he may feel that he has lost his salvation through some act of transgression.

Any believer in Christ may have temporary questions concerning the validity of his salvation. He may be tempted by Satan to doubt his position in Christ. But when such feelings become frequent and extend over long periods of time, they seriously cripple a person's day-to-day functioning. Many areas of an individual's life are affected negatively. He feels defeat and utter discouragement as he continually compares himself unfavorably with other Christians who seem to radiate happiness and security. Such a person may go forward to church altars again and again, seeking to assure himself of the reality of salvation. Yet he is never really sure.

Etiology

A person who lacks the assurance of his salvation may be suffering from a *spiritual* problem. Frequently, it *results from an insufficient knowledge of God's Word.* Although a person understands the Gospel generally, he may have heard undue emphasis placed on some aspects with a corresponding omission of others. Some individuals have only an incomplete picture of salvation—perhaps the need to repent and to turn from sin. Paramount as these truths are, they may have been unduly stressed, to the near exclusion of the security which is given by God.

Not only ignorance of Bible truth, but a *misunderstanding of Scripture* may be a spiritual cause for lack of assurance.

Scripture passages that refer to the importance of good works in the life of a Christian may become confused with basic truths of the plan of salvation. Warnings to those who merely profess a form of religion or portions dealing with judgment to come upon believers may be misinterpreted as applying to the person who has accepted Christ.

Sometimes the spiritual cause will be the feeling that one does not have sufficient faith or the right kind of faith. Lack of assurance is often bound up with looking within—feelings of introspection. *Confusing one's own feelings with Biblical facts* and the promises of God usually brings doubt and a greater lack of faith.

Lack of assurance of salvation can be expected as a natural consequence of a Christian's *disobedience to the Word of God,* being content to dabble with questionable practices, or following Christ from a distance. Neglect of Christian fellowship, little or no prayer life, failing to study the Word of God, bitterness and resentment toward other Christians, and indifference to the claims of God regarding the stewardship of time, talents and possessions—any or all of these will contribute to doubt about salvation.

Occasionally this problem is the result of *having trusted something or someone other than the Lord Jesus Christ Himself.* In other words, a person may consider himself a Christian and wonder why he has no assurance, when actually he has never been saved. It is an impossibility, of course, to expect assurance if one has never trusted Christ personally, apart from all else. Church membership, creeds, ceremonies, rituals, good works, and even mental assent—valuable as they may be in their proper place—are not substitutes for a heart experience. The Bible says, "The devils also believe, and tremble" (James 2:19).

Physical problems may also be factors in lack of assurance. Illness and fatigue affect one's whole outlook on life; and the spiritual life of man is often influenced by his physical health. Physical, emotional and spiritual aspects relate to each other in a very real sense, and are constantly interacting. It is impossible to categorize them into isolated compartments. The psalmist said ". . . I am fearfully and wonderfully made: . . . Thine eyes did see my substance, yet being unperfect; and in thy book all my members were written, which in continuance were fashioned, when as yet there was none of them" (Psalm 139:14, 16). Man is a complex being, a "whole" person. His physical, spiritual and emotional health are all influenced by each other. Whatever affects one part of man, affects the whole.

A series of *difficult circumstances, hardships or trials* may sometimes result in discouragement, which makes one susceptible to Satan's suggestion that he is not really saved. An immature Christian may blame God for extremely trying experiences. He may come to feel that since God has permitted these difficult circumstances, He must not really love or care for him. Therefore, he wonders whether he is saved. Periods of suffering, disappointment in other people, or false accusations from so-called friends may be the straw that finally upsets the normal balance of emotional well-being. After the initial glow has faded, a young Christian may be specially tested, and temptations may seem stronger than ever. He may come to what seems to him the logical (but erroneous) conclusion, "Surely I can't be saved or God wouldn't permit this to happen to me."

Emotional disturbances are high on the list of causes that make Christians feel uneasy and anxious about the security of their relationship to God. The life experiences of some people have left them feeling basically uncertain about themselves. Their own inadequate self-concepts have never permitted them to feel emotionally secure about anything. They have never found satisfactory answers to the vital questions of "Who am I?" and "Why did God make me?" or "For what purpose am I here?"

Feelings of insecurity and fearfulness present a special problem in certain cases of those who lack assurance of salvation. One of man's basic psychological needs is to feel reasonably secure. But this need may never have been met throughout childhood, adolescence and even adult life. When emotional deprivation has left deep scars in an individual's personality structure, they are not automatically erased by spiritual conversion. These experiences of repeated frustration and disappointment may condition a person to feelings of insecurity in *all* relationships. This may be carried over into his spiritual life, causing him to feel unsure about his relationship with God.

A *history of lifelong rejection and criticism in interpersonal relationships* may be another factor causing a person to be unsure of his salvation. The child or young person who seeks love and affection from those closest to him, yet finds constant rebuff or negligence, sooner or later comes to think of himself as basically unworthy. He then comes to feel that God must also reject him, since everyone else has. Having been deprived of love, the vacuum becomes filled by suspicion and fear. This kind of fear is not, of course, the Biblical fear of God which is clean and wholesome and implies a reverential trust in the Almighty and an abhorrence of that which is evil. Rather, it is the detrimental fear mentioned by the Apostle John when he said, "fear hath torment" (I John 4:18).

Treatment

The solution to the problem of lack of assurance of salvation is usually complex. It is not sufficient, for example, to merely tell a person that he should have assurance. In most cases a person needs a series of counseling sessions to understand the true causes of his feelings. In addition, he needs a vital spiritual program which will help him to develop adequate assurance. Such a program includes regular Bible study, prayer, fellowship with believers and witnessing.

Ministers and other Christian counselors who have been successful in helping people to develop assurance of salvation have found that it requires time for the counselee to express his feelings. For years he may have harbored strong feelings of insecurity and may have felt that he should not have had these attitudes. Consequently, he may think that he should not tell anyone. Full expiration of this feelings, then, is essential if he is to have confidence in the counselor and if he is to gain adequate understanding.

As the counseling sessions progress, the counselor will need insight into the client's knowledge of the Word of God. The client's understanding of the Bible may be meager or confused.

When this is so, the counselor should patiently point the counselee to the Word of God.

The counselor will also want to determine whether the client is projecting his own feelings into his interpretation of the Bible. A person's life experiences may have distorted his thinking to the point that he believes the Bible must surely teach certain things, when in fact the Bible may teach the opposite.

If the client's major problem is disobedience to God's Word, he should be led to a place of contrition and humility. He must want God's will in his life. Unresolved guilt and unconfessed sin in a Christian's life may cause him to feel that he has lost his salvation, or that he is uncertain of his position in Christ. The counselee must not only understand the teaching of God's Word; he should also see the importance of obedience to the Lord.

When an individual places his trust in another person—possibly a minister, a Christian leader, or a special friend—rather than in Christ, it usually results in confusion and unrest. A person who is insecure often has a tendency to idolize a Christian friend or a leader whom he greatly admires. When his "ideal" does not live up to his expectations, he loses confidence in him. To the client, the admired friend was a symbol of Christianity. Now that he is disappointed, his confidence in Christ has also been shaken, and he is not sure that he is saved.

It is important to lead the counselee into full discussion of his experiences, especially in childhood, which may have brought about serious emotional disturbances, and of their relationship to present feelings. He will then begin to separate his emotional insecurity from his feelings of spiritual insecurity.

The wise counselor should not overlook health factors since they vitally affect one's feelings of security. During times of illness, a person is more vulnerable to emotional stresses and strains. This same believer, upon regaining his health, may no longer doubt his position in Christ. Since physical problems may be hidden, the client should be encouraged to consult a physician.

The counselor's own stability and his acceptance of the counselee should not be minimized. Since the counselor is a strong factor of influence, it is important that he is stable and has a firm faith in God. As the counselee comes to feel that he is accepted by the counselor, he will generalize this feeling to other people and, in time, to Christ Himself. As one such client finally told the counselor, "When I first started counseling sessions with you, I was overwhelmed by the fact that you would accept me. In fact, I doubted your sincerity. But as time went on, I began to feel that you were genuine in your acceptance of me. This finally resulted in an acceptance of myself and, in time, acceptance of my position in Christ."

9. Asthenic Reaction

Description

Asthenic reactions are psychoneurotic conditions characterized by chronic fatigue and irritability. Other names for these disturbances include neurasthenic reactions and fatigue neuroses. The person suffering from neurasthenia often complains of tiredness, weakness, listlessness, headaches, indigestion, inability to sleep and lack of concentration. He may also exhibit a number of other ailments such as aches and pains in the back, abdomen and other body areas. Even though these symptoms are real, they stem from emotional rather than physical causes, and there is no actual tissue damage.[1]

Many housewives, office workers and others who complain of lack of energy and of poor health are suffering from neurasthenia. They are often self-centered persons who complain continually. They may attempt to overcome feelings of fatigue by excessive sleep and rest, but find themselves still arising each day with the usual amount of listlessness. Physical examinations may be conducted but organic causes for the fatigue are not discovered.

Etiology

The basic causal factors in neurasthenia are not well-defined, but appear to lie in frustrations and conflicts that are threatening to a person. By manifesting various physical ailments the individual is able to avoid or escape many unpleasant situations. If a person becomes tense and ill at ease, he may be able to avoid a frustrating condition by calling attention to various aches and pains.

The symptoms of neurasthenia may be employed unconsciously in order to get sympathy or special attention. When a child finds that he gets special notice during an illness, he may later turn to these methods of gaining attention and affec-

[1]For a discussion of asthenic reaction, see: Coleman, James: *Abnormal Psychology and Modern Life*, Scott, Foresman and Company, Chicago, 1964.

tion. This process is not always deliberate and is often on an unconscious level.

Parental overconcern for physical health may also be related to the development of neurasthenia. When parents become extremely concerned over the slightest sign of illness, a child may adopt attitudes of extreme worry that later develop into severe characteristics of chronic fatigue and ill health.

An asthenic reaction may also be related to a generally pessimistic and discouraging attitude toward life. The person who is unhappy and insecure may develop physical fatigue in order to avoid discouraging interactions with his environment.

Illustration

Identification: White female, age 35

Presenting Problem: The patient saw her regular physician several times, reporting that she was having various aches and pains. She also complained of constant fatigue. "I get up tired," she said, "I feel tired all day, and I go to bed tired. I am tired of being tired!" In time the physician indicated that the patient's problem might be psychological in nature. He then referred her to a clinic for counseling.

Personal and Family History: The patient is one of four children. Her father was a shy, quiet person who assumed a passive role in family affairs. Her mother was oversolicitous, seeing that the children had their every want supplied. She was overly concerned about their physical ailments, and became easily upset and very critical of her children's actions.

As a child, the patient was shy and withdrawn and had few friends. She found it difficult to mix with others, and became ill at ease in social situations. She recalled that during several childhood illnesses she greatly enjoyed freedom from her mother's constant nagging as well as the special sympathy and attention from the entire family. "I even remember the food they gave me," she told the counselor. "I'm ashamed to say it, but I think those times when I was sick were among the happiest times of my life. It was like being queen for a few days."

Treatment
Therapy for the neurasthenic individual centers upon the conflicts which give rise to constant fatigue and listlessness. The person who is unconsciously employing physical ailments to avoid stressful situations needs to gain an understanding of this defensive reaction and the reasons he is employing it. This may require a number of counseling sessions, since many of the factors may be hidden and little understood by the patient.

Finally, he needs to develop confidence and security in his own ability to handle new situations and to cope with stress more adequately. This may involve improved interpersonal skills. Such a person needs spiritual insight so that he can gain confidence and security through reliance on Christ and God's Word. Spiritual growth will help him to become emotionally more mature so that he can cope with stressful situations with increased poise and confidence.

10. Asthma

Description

Asthma is a disorder of the respiratory system characterized by breathing difficulties. Both children and adults are susceptible to this disturbance.[1] The person with this disorder usually makes a wheezing sound upon exhaling. Frequent coughing and chest constriction are also present. The severity of asthma may range from relatively minor attacks of coughing to a persistent pattern of wheezing, coughing and laborious breathing which greatly limits physical activity. Certain cases of asthma in childhood may be alleviated permanently, whereas others may become quite chronic, lasting a lifetime with possible complications.

Etiology

There is a complex interaction of physical and psychological forces in the etiology of asthma. In some instances the causes of this disturbance appear to be almost exclusively physical. Common physical causes include allergy and respiratory infections. In other cases the major etiological factors are emotional. Even when the basic causes are physical, an asthmatic attack is often precipitated by an unsatisfactory emotional reaction. Some children, for example, who are removed from an unhappy and tense home situation, show a relief of the symptoms of asthma.

Studies of the childhood experiences of individuals suffering from asthma frequently show similar patterns of parental behavior. The mothers of these people are often domineering and overprotective. They have tried to "protect" their children from physical harm by limiting and closely supervising their activities. The role of the father is often passive, or at least is second to the more domineering manner of the mother.

In addition to this pattern of parental behavior, there is frequently an absence of an overt demonstration of affection. Al-

[1] For a discussion of Asthma in children, see: Bakwin, H. and Bakwin, R.: *Clinical Management of Behavior Disorders in Children*, W. P. Saunders Company, Philadelphia and London, 1953.

though the mother may be domineering and overprotective, she does not show a genuine love for the child.

When a child grows up in this type of home environment he may become very insecure and dependent. He is accustomed to having his needs met by a domineering and overprotective mother; consequently, he has not developed a sense of individuality and the ability to meet new stresses and frustrations. When this person is placed in a difficult situation and is unable to turn to his mother for assistance, he may suffer an asthmatic attack. This physical complaint serves two functions. First, it removes the individual from a threatening and frustrating situation. By developing asthmatic symptoms, the person avoids unpleasant circumstances and has an excuse for his inability to meet daily pressures and conflicts. A second purpose served by this psychosomatic reaction is to provide the person with secondary gains. The sympathy, attention, and affection he receives from the illness are emotionally satisfying and are often important in the basic dynamics of asthma.

The person suffering from asthma is frequently a hypersensitive individual. When others are critical and rejecting, his sense of personal adequacy is threatened. This dynamic of extreme sensitivity is frequently found in asthmatics.

Another pattern associated with attacks of asthma is that of a general neurotic personality. In these instances the individual is an insecure person with a high level of anxiety who evidences much personality constriction. Being insecure, he is afraid to express impulses of sex and hostility. This inhibition of emotional reaction is common to many suffering from asthma.

Illustration
Identification: White male, age 42
Presenting Problem: This man had suffered from asthma since his early adolescent years. He had seen a number of medical doctors and had moved to a new area of the country to find a climate which was less aggravating to his respiratory disturbance. Medical care had succeeded in giving temporary relief from severe asthmatic attacks, but the patient still had consistent breathing difficulties. The last doctor this patient consulted

suggested that his difficulty might be partially related to an emotional problem, and referred him for psychological care.

Personal and Family History: This patient was the only child born to parents of upper-class socioeconomic status. The parents were devoted Christians and active in their local church. The patient's mother was very concerned over her son's development inasmuch as he was born six weeks premature. The mother was careful to protect him from any physical dangers and limited his participation in neighborhood activities. As he grew older, the parents watched him closely to see that he did not develop any unacceptable behavior. When he became angry, the parents scolded and punished him, saying that such temper outbursts were not acceptable for a Christian.

During school this patient did very well academically. Although he missed some school due to illness, he always made up the missed assignments. His social adjustment was hindered because he was insecure and afraid to take an active part in many school functions. During high school the first symptoms of a respiratory illness became noticeable. As an adult, these symptoms became more serious. The subject states that during the first two years of marriage he had little difficulty with the asthma. After his first child was born, however, the attacks became more serious.

Treatment

The first consideration with a person suffering from asthma is a thorough medical examination. The physical causes of this disorder and the basic symptoms need proper medical diagnosis and therapy. Medical care may continue over a period of time.

If medical examination indicates that emotional factors are influential in the disturbance, psychotherapy should be initiated. In determining the influence of emotional factors, a complete case history is of utmost importance. The history often brings to light the influence of emotional factors. For example, the times when attacks of asthma are most severe may be found to be associated with the presence of an emotionally disturbing situation. This understanding provides a foundation for exploring the personality dynamics underlying the onset of the asthmatic attacks.

Therapy with the person suffering from asthma will be directed toward the understanding and alleviation of the basic causes of his emotional disturbance. Factors such as a domineering mother or a fear of emotional expression must be evaluated. When the individual is unconsciously attempting to avoid responsibility and fulfilling his dependency needs through these physical symptoms, the underlying insecurity and dependency needs must be resolved.[2]

In dealing with children, the basic disturbances in the home which are causing the problem should be considered and alleviated. When the mother is overprotecting the child, he needs to be given new freedom from her domination and supervision. When the child is attempting to gain emotional gratification from attention associated with his problem, the parents must learn to better meet his basic emotional needs for love and affection. As the tensions and frustrations at home are resolved, the child will gain increased ability to meet life's daily activities in a secure manner without unconsciously resorting to physical ailments to avoid emotional conflicts.

[2]For a more complete discussion of this topic see INSECURITY in this volume.

11. Brain Damage

Description

Human behavior is the result of complex interaction between the individual and his environment. In recent years, specialists have become increasingly aware of the physical aspects of psychological problems. Many of the educational and adjustment difficulties which were previously attributed to emotional conflicts have been found to be closely related to physical functioning of the central nervous system. Psychologists have found that the reason some people do not respond to psychotherapy is the fact that they are suffering from previously undetected neurological impairments.[1] Such injuries to the brain and central nervous system vary widely in their severity. Some are minor and have no apparent ill effects while others are extremely severe and result in gross abnormalities of intellectual functioning.

Neurological impairments may be manifested in a number of ways. One of these is in mental retardation.[2] Although brain injury is found among many levels of intelligence, it is more commonly associated with lower intellectual functioning. An infant who had potentially superior intellectual gifts may be reduced to an average level of functioning while the already deficient individual may become even more severely retarded. The effects of such neurological impairments often go unobserved until the child reaches two or three years of age or later. At this time, parents may notice that the child in some way has been slow in developing.

In another child, the effects of injury to the brain may not become apparent until he enters school. At this time, even though the child is of average intelligence, he may have special difficulty learning to read and he may become confused in spelling and writing.[3]

[1] For a technical discussion of this disturbance, see: Birch, H. G.: *Brain Damage In Children*, Williams and Wilkins Company, 1964.
[2] See also MENTAL RETARDATION and CEREBRAL PALSY in this volume.
[3] For a discussion of reading disturbances, see: *Reading Disability: Progress and Research needs in Dyslexia*, Edited by John Money, The John Hopkins Press, Baltimore, 1962.

Neurological impairments may also result in behavioral problems. A hyperactive child who has frequent outbursts of temper and unpredictable behavior may be suffering from an undetected injury to the brain. Some types of neurological impairments have the effect of lowering the person's ability to control his actions, leaving him vulnerable to violent outbursts.

Another occasional consequence of neurological impairment is poor muscle coordination. The brain-injured person may have limited visual-motor coordination and be unable to perform a number of the physical tasks normally executed by those of his own age. Disturbed balance, inadequate coordination, and various perceptual difficulties are often indicative of organic impairments.

Etiology

Injury to the brain may be prenatal (before birth), perinatal (during birth), or postnatal (after birth). Among the most common factors resulting in brain injury before birth are infectious conditions in the mother during pregnancy. An example of this is German measles. When a mother suffers from this disease during the first three months of pregnancy, the child often suffers brain injury and mental retardation. Chemical imbalances of the mother during pregnancy and attempted abortions may also result in damage to brain tissue. Another factor suggested by many researchers is the transmission of a brain defect through heredity.

Among the most common birth injuries affecting intellectual functioning are intracranial birth lesions and asphyxia. Hemorrhage at birth due to difficult labor may lead to intracranial birth lesions. The most frequent causes of hemorrhage at birth are difficult labor, prematurity and improper handling of the infant. Asphyxia, or the inadequate supply of oxygen to the brain, is responsible for many cases of mental deficiency. An extended period without oxygen will result in permanent brain cell damage. Among the most common causes of asphyxia are early separation of the placenta and delayed breathing of the infant.

In some instances, neurological impairment may result from

conditions after birth. An abnormally high brain fever, known as encephalitis, is sometimes responsible for such injuries to the brain. Other factors include injuries or blows to the head and a prolonged inadequate supply of oxygen to the brain.

Illustration

Identification: Negro female, age 10

Presenting Problem: This girl was referred to a school psychologist because of poor academic achievement and related behavior disturbances.

Personal and Family History: The subject is the second of four children born to parents of middle-class socioeconomic status. The parents are born-again believers and the family adjustment is adequate. Since the girl first began school, however, she has had academic problems, especially difficulty in learning to read. Concentration on her work for prolonged periods of time has also been difficult. Because of poor motor coordination, she usually takes only limited part in physical activities.

After tests were administered by the school psychologist, it was recommended that the subject be examined by a neurologist. This examination revealed the presence of neurological impairment.

Treatment

After initial diagnosis of the presence of brain injury has been made, several basic steps need to be taken to assist the optimal development of the individual. The first of these is referral to a neurologist for a complete diagnosis. This specialist will determine the type and extent of the neurological impairment and prescribe medication if necessary.

In the case of a child, following the medical evaluation the parents need much help in understanding the causes of brain damage and how this will affect their child throughout life. In addition they must learn to accept the problem and to develop the most suitable methods of dealing with the child.[4] Psycho-

---

[4] A helpful book on this topic is: Lewis, Richard S.: *The Other Child: The Brain-Injured Child*, Grune and Stratton, Inc., New York, 1951. This book is particularly helpful in understanding the needs of the brain-injured child and contains suggestions for handling and educating him.

logical testing is helpful to determine the child's true assets and limitations. This objective evaluation will help the parents establish realistic goals for the child.

A major consideration for the parents is their attitude toward the brain-damaged child. Parents often take one of two extreme positions. They may be angry with the Lord for allowing such a thing to happen to their child, which may lead them to openly reject the child and give their affections and attentions to other siblings. Such an attitude only compounds the child's adjustment difficulties and may then result in severe emotional disturbances.

Other parents become overindulgent. They lavish love and attention on the brain-injured child and fail to let him develop a sense of individuality and accomplishment. Instead of encouraging him to try new activities, they pamper him and smother any of his attempts to achieve success on his own. In addition to denying the brain-injured child the opportunity to fully develop his capacities, this behavior also has a detrimental effect on other children in the family. They are aware of the fact that their brother has a problem and that the parents spend much of their time with him. This causes other siblings to develop feelings of rejection and insecurity.

Parents' reactions should be between these two extremes. They should be careful to avoid a rejecting attitude, but they should also be careful not to overindulge the brain-injured child at the expense of his own individuality and the emotional development of other siblings.

The classroom teacher, too, may receive help from the school psychologist and from curriculum specialists concerning ways of teaching the child and meeting his emotional needs. Specialized assistance for the child is helpful, such as remedial instruction in reading and speech, vocational and educational guidance, and counseling directed toward understanding and accepting his disturbances. It is important that the person learn to accept whatever limitations the injury places upon him and to realistically appraise his abilities.

In working with adults there are four major considerations. These include (1) complete medical attention, (2) an evaluation of the person's assets and limitations, including his vocational possibilities, (3) the person's attitudes toward his handicap, and (4) the importance of spiritual factors.

Medication for adults suffering from neurological impairments is usually less effective than with children. Some behavioral disturbances associated with brain injuries stabilize during late adolescence or early adulthood so that medication is no longer needed. With some adults, however, medication is of value in controlling the person's actions.

One of the important contributions a counselor can make to a person with a neurological impairment is to help him carefully consider his assets and limitations. This is best done by a competent psychologist who will utilize psychological tests to gain a scientific evaluation of the person's true abilities. This will enable the individual to better plan for his future and to consider various vocational possibilities.

A third consideration in counseling with the brain-injured adult is to help him evaluate his attitudes toward the handicap. Some people harbor strong resentments, feeling that the Lord has been unjust in giving them a physical disability. The counselor needs to encourage this person to express his feelings and to gradually gain insight into these attitudes. After this, the counselor can help the person see his assets, and realize that although the neurological impairment may have hindered academic performance, or some other functions, yet the Lord has given him gifts which he has many opportunities to utilize.

The final consideration with a brain-injured person is spiritual in nature. The individual needs to know Christ as his Savior and to walk in close fellowship with the Lord. By growing spiritually, he can receive continued guidance from the Lord and he will be able to lead a happy and fruitful life. Most neurological impairments do not result in severe limitations and need not serve as a serious handicap to an effective personal, social and spiritual adjustment.

12. Central Nervous System Disorders

Description

The central nervous system is that part of the body consisting of the brain and spinal cord. It is well-named in that it is the central portion of the nervous system and is essential to the proper function of the total organism. The central nervous system correlates and integrates the various body organs and parts by means of the peripheral nervous system. These main nerve trunks, which emanate from the brain and spinal cord, connect with every portion of the body through their millions of branches, so that it can function as an efficient unit.

Being the primary integrating structure of the human body, the central nervous system plays a major role in each individual's physical, mental, emotional and spiritual functioning. Injury or disease to this system may affect any one or more of these areas of functioning.

Other sections of this book deal with diseases and conditions which relate to the central nervous system directly or indirectly. Some central nervous system disorders are not mentioned in this volume since the emotional aspect is minimal. However, three of the more common ones are briefly described below.

Multiple Sclerosis

One of the most common chronic neurological diseases is multiple sclerosis. This disorder consists of several degenerative areas in various vital portions of the brain and spinal cord which hamper or prevent the proper functioning of the affected area. Consequently, the symptoms are quite varied. Relapses with long periods of remission characterize most cases. In others, the disease is intermittently progressive, ending in paralysis, loss of control and sensation disturbance. Some of the more common symptoms are transient or slowly progressive weakness or loss of control of limbs. Other symptoms include early loss of vision for a short duration and abnormal skin sensations.

There is an acute form of the disease which runs its course in a few weeks or months, ending fatally. Emotional symptoms such as dementia (impairment of mental functioning), euphoria (pathologic cheerfulness), or depression may also be present. Frustration and anxiety may occur due to the progressive on-and-off nature of the disease. Little is known about the cause of this disease. Many theories have been set forth but none have been proven. Treatment is basically symptomatic and supportive.

Huntington's Chorea

This disease of the nervous system is characterized by jerky, involuntary movements and mental deterioration. Individuals afflicted with this disorder manifest various twitching and jerking movements and an irregular gait. Speech is also affected, often becoming slow and indistinct. In addition to these physical symptoms, the person frequently experiences loss of memory, impaired judgment and inattentiveness. Feelings of severe depression may also accompany this disease.

Medical specialists have been unable to determine the causes of Huntington's Chorea. It does, however, run in families and is believed by many to be due to defective genetic inheritance.

At present there is no successful means of treating this disorder. It usually becomes progressively worse until ending in death. Since this disease appears to have a hereditary basis, some specialists advise afflicted parents against having children, fearing that it might be passed on to the offspring.

Paralysis Agitans

Commonly known as "shaking palsy" or "Parkinson's disease," paralysis agitans is a disorder of the central nervous system. It is characterized by tremors and contraction of the muscles. The contractions may cause peculiar positions of the limbs and a tendency to lean forward in walking. The face may also become rigid and speech is sometimes hindered.

This disease is usually found among persons over fifty years of age, but it is occasionally present in younger individuals. Since it is a progressive disease, the symptoms of tremors and stiffness become increasingly severe as time goes on.

Intelligence is not affected, but the disturbing symptoms may lead to emotional difficulties. Among the most common psychological symptoms are indifference, loss of concentration and lack of intellectual interest.

The causes of this disorder are still unknown and no effective treatment has been found.

13. Cerebral Palsy

Description

Cerebral palsy is a motor disability caused by a brain dysfunction. In many cases, this neuromuscular dysfunction is accompanied by other disturbances. The same brain injury which resulted in a motor disturbance may also be responsible for mental retardation, reading difficulties (dyslexia), language disorders (aphasia), and writing disabilities (agraphia).[1] Any one of these accompanying disorders may add to the palsied individual's motor impairment and cause other serious adjustment problems.[2]

Based upon the various forms of motor disturbances, cerebral palsy may be divided into these major types:

Spastic: Here there is a lack of smooth movement in one or more limbs. Movement of the affected limb is jerky and uncontrolled rather than smooth and well-performed.

Athetoid: Children with athetosis have uncontrollable, jerky, twisting movements of the extremities. Their movements are not rhythmical, their posture is uncontrollable, and they walk in a writhing, stumbling manner.

Ataxia: This person lacks balance and muscle coordination. His movements are unsteady, he walks with a high step, and he falls easily. He may also suffer from frequent dizziness and nausea.

Tremor and Rigidity: These types of cerebral palsy are less frequent than the above. The tremor or rigidity is usually less erratic than other motor defects manifested in the various types of cerebral palsy. The person suffering from either tremor or rigidity is usually better able to coordinate his actions toward a goal than is the athetoid or spastic type. In rigidity, the individual shows motion restriction and poor postural tone. In tremor, the whole body may be affected by involuntary vibrations.

[1] See the discussions of BRAIN INJURY and APHASIA in this volume.
[2] For an interesting account of how it feels to be cerebral palsied, read this book by a cerebral palsied medical doctor: Carlson, Earl R.: *Born That Way*, John Day Company, New York, 1942.

Etiology
Cerebral palsy may be caused by factors before birth (prenatal), during birth (perinatal), or after birth (postnatal).

Prenatal Causes: There are two major factors operating in the prenatal period which may result in cerebral palsy. The first of these is a genetic factor. Research findings show a higher than average incidence of cerebral palsy in siblings and relatives of cerebral palsied individuals. This evidences the possibility of an inheritance factor in this disorder.

Another prenatal condition responsible for cerebral palsy is inadequate oxygen supply due to premature separation of the placenta, undersized or diseased placenta, or impingement of the umbilical cord. This insufficient oxygen supply to the brain results in tissue destruction. Chemical imbalances in the mother during pregnancy are also thought to be causative factors in some cases of cerebral palsy.

Perinatal: Injuries at birth may also result in cerebral palsy. Especially important at birth is a good supply of oxygen to the brain. If this oxygen supply is diminished, damage to the brain tissue may result.

Postnatal Causes: Serious illnesses or accidents after birth are responsible for some cases of cerebral palsy. Among the most common causes are diseases such as meningitis, encephalitis, and other conditions in which the subject suffers from prolonged periods of high fever. Head injuries from falls or other accidents may also cause tissue damage resulting in cerebral palsy.

Illustration
Identification: White male, age 2 years
Presenting Problem: The patient was brought to a private physician at the age of two. The parents said that the child had been slow to walk and that they were concerned about his development. They also stated that he "jerked" when he walked and they wanted to know what caused it.
Personal and Family History: The patient is the son of parents who were in their late thirties when he was born. He has

two sisters, both older than he. Neither of the girls has any special physical or mental handicap.

The father is a postal employee and the mother a homemaker. Both enjoy average health.

The physician who examined the patient believed that the child sustained a damage at birth. The parents related the fact that the delivery was difficult and prolonged. In addition, the attending physician had requested that the child not be taken home until one week after the mother was released.

The child was slower than average in learning to walk. At present he shows spasticity in both arms and legs.

Treatment

The care of individuals who are cerebral palsied lies largely in the hands of medical and remedial specialists.[3] Throughout America there are numerous institutions which offer assistance to those afflicted with this malady. One type of service is a thorough program of diagnosis. Diagnostic centers give a complete evaluation of the patient's disabilities and assets. This evaluation is the basis for further therapeutic work. A thorough diagnosis usually includes an evaluation of the subject's hearing, intelligence and vision, in addition to his speech difficulties and the type and extent of his neurological impairment. Based upon this diagnosis, a well-integrated plan of therapy may be started. Depending upon the nature and severity of the disturbance, any one of a number of facilities may be utilized.[4]

Many who are cerebral palsied are also mentally retarded. These individuals are often cared for in state hospitals and schools.[5]

Some children have severe motor disturbances which restrict their attendance at a regular school, but they do have normal intelligence and can profit from home instruction. In these

[3]For a discussion of this topic, see: Cruickshank, W. M., and Raus, G. M., editors: *Cerebral Palsy*, Syracuse University Press, 1955. This book has excellent material on planning for the emotional, physical and vocational needs of cerebral palsied individuals.
[4]For recent information concerning cerebral palsy, write: The National Society for Crippled Children and Adults, Inc., 2028 West Ogden Avenue, Chicago 12, Illinois.
[5]See the discussion of MENTAL DEFICIENCY in this volume.

cases some school districts provide a special home teacher who works closely with the child and his parents in planning a program of development in both motor and mental tasks.

Many cities provide special classes or special schools for cerebral palsied children. They employ special educational aids as well as the equipment necesssary for working with these children.

In addition to the medical, educational and vocational planning, it is important that parents of the cerebral palsied child have an opportunity to thoroughly discuss their attitude toward the child's difficulties. It is not enough merely to provide the parents with information on the causes of cerebral palsy and the provisions that can be made for their child. The emotional reaction of the parents must be considered.

A handicapped child often brings to light the true feelings and character of the parents. If they are well-adjusted and love the Lord, they can gradually accept the problem, learn to live with it, and go on to live a happy, productive life. If, on the other hand, the parents are poorly adjusted and are not walking close to the Lord, these attitudes will reveal themselves.

Some parents become angry with the Lord for allowing such a tragedy to enter their home. They feel they have been dealt an unfair blow from life and are extremely upset over their child's disabilities. Sometimes this leads to serious spiritual problems since the parents are angry with God and consequently terminate all church activities. In other cases, they openly reject the cerebral palsied child, compounding his physical problems with rejection and consequent emotional disturbance.

Other parents feel that it is a disgrace to have a cerebral palsied son or daughter. They may be immature themselves and too filled with pride to accept the child's handicap. These parents may feel ashamed of their cerebral palsied child and attempt to keep him from the view of friends, making continual apologies about the child's disturbance. Such behavior only generates more problems. Parents of the cerebral palsied child need to realize that their friends and neighbors will soon accept the child in the same manner the parents do. If the parents are negative and apologetic, neighbors will likely develop similar feelings. If, on the other hand, the parents accept the child as a worthy and lovable member of the family, friends and neighbors will usually adopt this same attitude.

The opportunity to raise a handicapped child can be a real blessing. Many families have been brought into a close fellowship with the Lord through a seeming "tragedy." An excellent example of the effect a handicapped child may have on a Christian home is found in *Angel Unaware*,"[6] the story of the mongoloid daughter of Dale Evans and Roy Rogers. This well-written and encouraging book is often given to parents of handicapped children to show what an attitude of acceptance and spiritual dedication can do to enrich the lives of the parents of a handicapped child.

In other instances the parents of a cerebral palsied child may become extremely possessive and overindulgent. They meet the child's every need and do not allow him to attempt any new activities. While these parents feel they are being loving and helpful, they may actually be depriving the child of an opportunity to develop his own individuality and abilities.

Parents with a handicapped child sometimes bring undue pressure to bear upon him by continually attempting to help him improve. In their desire to see the child do his best, they may urge him beyond his limits. In such instances the child usually rebels and reacts negatively. For example, the parents of a cerebral palsied child brought him to a counseling center asking if there was anything more that could be done for him. "Also," the mother added, "we would like to know how much he has improved in the last two years. The people at the other clinic told us his intelligence was below average. So we have been working with him. We would just like to know whether we have gotten him up to average yet." The psychologist examined the boy and found that his intelligence was considerably below average and that he also showed signs of emotional tension. In this case the parents did not have a clear, basic understanding of human intelligence. They were doing everything

[6]Rogers, Dale. *Angel Unaware*, Fleming H. Revell, Westwood, New Jersey, 1953.

within their power to force the child to do things of which he was not capable.

In guiding parents of a handicapped child, a counselor should help them understand the nature and extent of the child's handicap. The counselor should also encourage them to strive for a balance between encouraging the child, on one hand and forcing him, on the other.

A cerebral palsied child may have sustained a handicap so severe that he needs care outside of the home. Although parents should be encouraged to understand and accept their child, they should not be led to feel that they are abandoning or depriving him if placement outside of the home is best. One family, for example, felt that their seriously retarded and physically handicapped child was a "cross" which they were to bear. Several friends, also, not understanding the nature of the child's disabilities, had told the parents that the worst thing they could ever do would be to "give the child away."

For several years the parents did their best to provide for the child in their own home. But the struggle was too great. He required almost constant attention, including continual lifting. Medical specialists and psychologists had advised placement in a state hospital but the parents felt that they would be shirking their duty if they did so. Finally, during a series of counseling sessions, the parents began to face their own true feelings and revealed the fact that they felt they could not continue keeping the child at home. "We have several other children," the mother said, "and I am not strong myself. We love the boy very much but we would almost have to have a small hospital staff to give him the care he needs." The counseling sessions afforded an opportunity to encourage the parents to tell just how they felt and also enabled them to look ahead and predict some of the problems which might arise and the type of care which their son would eventually need. Counselors can make a unique contribution to parents of a handicapped child by helping them to realistically appraise their responsibility to keep the child at home or to make other arrangements.

In order to thoroughly evaluate the attitudes of the parents toward a cerebral palsied child, a counselor should utilize several sessions. During this time he can encourage the parents to freely express their own feelings of fear, disappointment or hostility. After this they can consider the importance of their own emotional and spiritual attitudes. As this is done the counselor often has an opportunity to lead the parents into a closer walk with the Lord and to help them develop wholesome and realistic attitudes toward the child. Such counseling sessions can bring great changes in the lives of the entire family and, indeed, are very important in dealing with the cerebral palsied child.

14. Conversion Reaction[1]

Description

Conversion reactions are a group of neurotic disorders characterized by physical symptoms without the presence of identifiable organic pathology. These are also known as hysterical reactions. They are expressions of inner conflict and anxiety.[2] The various symptoms of hysteria are classified as follows:

Sensory: Hysteria may affect any of the bodily senses. Among the most common disturbances of sensory functions are those affecting hearing, vision and sensitivity to touch and pain.

Motor Symptoms: Impairment of mobility is a common symptom of hysteria. Its victims often suffer from paralysis of an arm or a leg, prohibiting the proper functioning of the limb. Another common symptom of this ailment is the impairment of a person's speech. The two most common speech disturbances are aphonia, in which the individual is able to speak only in a whisper, and mutism, in which the person is unable to speak at all. Tics, tremors, and other involuntary movements are also found in individuals suffering from hysteria. Tremors of the hands and fingers as well as various movements of the head are common in this disorder.

Visceral Symptoms: These symptoms include headaches, hiccuping, coughing, vomiting, belching, nausea, constipation and diarrhea.

Individuals suffering from conversion reactions often manifest symptoms remarkably similar to those resulting from actual organic illness. However, there are several means of distinguishing between organic and psychological causes.

1. One of the major ways to dintinguish between hysteria and actual physical disorders is by the presence of glove or stocking anesthesia. In this phenomenon the loss of sensitivity covers an area commonly believed to be affected as a unit rather

[1]This psychological term has no relationship to spiritual conversion, or regeneration, as presented in the Bible.

[2]For a definition and brief description of hysteria, see: *Dorland's Illustrated Medical Dictionary* (23rd Edition), W. B. Saunders Company, Philadelphia, 1957.

than following the true anatomical distribution of nerve fibers. In such an instance a person may claim that he has lost sensitivity in his entire hand, whereas if the complaint was actually of an organic origin, the anesthesia would follow a prescribed pattern and not cover the entire area.

2. A person suffering from hysteria typically shows less concern over his malady than one who is afflicted with organic pathology. He does not exhibit the anxiety and fear which characterizes an individual suffering from a true physical ailment.

3. Hysterical symptoms sometimes disappear during sleep or when the sufferer is extremely relaxed.

4. The physical handicap does not usually endanger the individual. When suffering from hysterical blindness, for instance, the person often avoids dangerous objects which a truly blind individual could not see.

5. The symptoms are transient. A loss of sensitivity may occur for a few minutes or hours, disappear temporarily, and return at a later time.

6. Under hypnosis patients may also be freed of hysterical symptoms.

The combination of a thorough medical and psychological examination can usually determine if the symptoms are the result of an actual organic disturbance or if they are due to emotional factors. The medical examination can generally rule out physical causes, while a psychodiagnostic study will often show the presence of personality dynamics sufficient to cause the apparent organic pathology.

Etiology

Hysterical symptoms are usually developed in an effort to avoid emotional conflicts and are an unconscious attempt to bypass threatening situations.[3]

A major etiological factor in many cases of conversion reaction is the repression of emotional conflicts. Some individuals, for example, harbor strong feelings of hostility. If they allowed these feelings to come to consciousness, however, they would be too threatening and anxiety provoking. Rather than

---

[3]For a psychiatric discussion of conversion reaction, see: Noyes and Kolb, *Modern Clinical Psychiatry*, W. B. Saunders Company, Philadelphia and London, 1963.

allowing this anxiety to come to consciousness, or rather than attaching it to a specific object as is done in phobic reations, the conflict is channeled into a physical symptom.[4] In this light, it can be seen that conversion reactions are the individual's attempts to resolve unconscious emotional conflicts. Because the hysterical personality is unable to face emotional conflicts and frustrations, his personality structure is often characterized by the defense mechanisms of denial, rationalization and repression. Rather than dealing with his problems on a conscious level, this person attempts to suppress the conflicts, thus avoiding the anxiety associated with it.

The person who develops hysterical symptoms is often one who has a deep need for attention and approval. He frequently has failed to develop emotional independence and is strongly influenced by his parents. He adopts hysterical symptoms as a means of obtaining security and status. A child, for instance, who has been the center of attention in his home may manifest hysterical symptoms because the attention and care previously bestowed upon him is now given to the new baby.

If a person becomes sick and through this experience is able to circumvent unpleasant experiences, he may continue in his illness even after the organic basis has been eliminated. The illness is real to the patient even though the organic disturbance is no longer the cause of his suffering. Hysterical reactions sometimes develop in the face of a frightening situation as a subconscious means of escape. For example, a newly-inducted soldier may become rapidly ill when he hears of some of the dangers he will have to face in his military career. His illness is a protective response which is triggered by his dilemma.

Conversion reactions may also arise from feelings of guilt. If a person believes that he is deserving of punishment for some immoral or illegal actions, he may punish himself by becoming ill. Of course, the hysterical victim is unaware of the relationship between his self-condemnation and his illness.

Precipitating conditions may also include such areas as threats

[4]For a discussion of emotional disturbances associated with consciously felt anxiety and phobic reactions, see the discussions of ANXIETY REACTION and PHOBIC REACTION in this volume.

to self-esteem or economic success. A person facing such a situation may attempt to solve his problems by becoming ill.

Illustration

Identification: White female, age 18

Presenting Problem: The patient is suffering from paralysis of the arm for which no organic basis has been found.

Personal and Family History: The subject is the only child of parents of high economic standing. The mother is very indulgent and has never allowed the daughter to develop her own independence. The mother has made all of the important decisions for the girl and directs her actions. Because of this the girl developed moderate feelings of insecurity. The subject had several close frinds and she always did well in high school. However, when she decided to attend college in another city where she would not be living at home, her mother registered strong disapproval. The subject went to college anyway but shortly after beginning college she developed paralysis of her right arm.

Treatment

Before initiating counseling with a person suffering from a conversion reaction, a complete medical examination should be undergone. This will rule out the possibility of a physical cause of the disturbance. If a physical disability which has an emotional basis is allowed to continue over a period of time, it can result in permanent fixation or stiffening through lack of use. Thus, a contracted joint, for example, may require specific medical care to prevent lasting damage, even though the cause is not physical in nature.

Those suffering from hysteria are prone to reject the psychological causes of their illness because this brings them face to face with the basic problem they are attempting to avoid. They are not willing to admit the emotional origin of their disturbance.

Since the hysteric is usually a person who is highly suggestible, it is sometimes possible for a physician to recommend medication which appears to help. Because the individual accepts his problem as being physical in nature, he is willing to follow a medical doctor's recommendation. Occasionally mere faith in the doctor and the treatment he prescribes is sufficient to ease the symptoms of the patient. This process may alleviate his present condition but does not correct the basic personality problem.

Since the person suffering from a conversion reaction is frequently unwilling to admit an emotional basis of his disturbance, psychotherapy is often very difficult. Because of this, some counselors feel they should scold the person and accuse him of not wanting to get well. This confrontation is usually ineffective and may cause the person to repress his emotions even further. Instead, the patient needs a long and gradual process of therapy in which he can understand his total personality adjustment. In this way the specific causes of his physical symptoms may gradually be brought into the forefront of therapy.

When the conversion symptom is due to feelings of guilt the counselor must help the person to come to an understanding of his attitudes and to determine if the guilt is real or pseudo-guilt.[5] If the guilt is a genuine concern for the transgression of God's laws it must be dealt with by repentance and the acceptance of God's forgiveness. If the person is unconsciously attempting to punish himself for his felt sins, he must understand this dynamic and come to a realistic understanding of his acceptance by God.

If the person is turning to a physical handicap in order to seek affection and attention and avoid responsibilities, this dynamic should be explored. In these instances the person needs to gain an understanding of the childhood factors which caused him to feel insecure and unwanted and to replace these attitudes with a sense of security and adequacy found through an understanding of his position before the Lord. In this way the person can develop an adequate self-concept which will enable him to meet daily frustration without retreating to a physical symptom to avoid emotional conflicts.

[5]For a discussion of this topic see GUILT in this volume.

15. Delinquency

Description

A delinquent is a minor (usually defined as under the age of 18) who engages in antisocial or illegal behavior.[1] These individuals, often called psychopaths or sociopaths, are not classified as either neurotic or psychotic, but exhibit antisocial behavior such as theft, prostitution and even murder.[2]

Some of the common symptoms of delinquency are:

- Disregard for rules and regulations
- Lack of restraint
- Deviant sexual patterns
- Inability to profit from mistakes
- Inability to postpone immediate pleasures
- Ability to impress and exploit others
- Superficial social relationships
- Little respect for the church
- Ability to rationalize and blame others for his conduct
- Incorrigible behavior
- Tendency to lie
- Frequent use of profane language
- The desire to be "important"
- Disregard for property rights of others
- Discrepancy between intelligence and conscience development

Etiology

Two major categories may be used to classify the origin of delinquency. The first includes social factors related to the person's environment. When continued into adulthood, this type of behavior is classified as a dyssocial reaction. These delinquents (or criminals) grow up in an environment which accepts

[1] For recent information concerning delinquency, write: United States Department of Health, Education and Welfare, Social Security Administration, Children's Bureau, Washington, D.C.
[2] For a discussion of related adult behavior, see SOCIOPATHIC PERSONALITY in this volume.

undesirable attitudes and behavior. Since the child's parents exhibited such behavior, it is only natural that the child adopts these antisocial attitudes. Individuals with this background are disturbed largely in relationship to society. If it were not for their antisocial actions, they would probably not show other evidence of personality maladjustment. They are not excessively hostile, they can form close emotional relationships, and they follow the standards of their own environment.

The second major classification of delinquent behavior is known as an antisocial reaction. Individuals in this category have not necessarily developed their unacceptable behavior because of living in an abnormal moral environment. Instead, their behavior is a symptom of a broader picture of personality maladjustment. These people may come from homes of above-average socioeconomic status and their parents may be community leaders. These delinquents have turned to antisocial acts as a result of their feelings of hostility, their inability to relate to other people, their irresponsibility, and their impulsive characteristics. Rather than being disturbed largely in relation to society (as in the case of dyssocial reaction) these individuals have more serious personality maladjustments.

Following are some of the significant factors underlying the development of delinquent behavior:

Neurological Impairment. In some cases of delinquency, cerebral dysfunction is a significant factor. Silverman found that 80% of a group of 75 criminal psychopaths had abnormal or borderline brain waves as recorded by electroencephalograms.[3] Although brain abnormalities are found in many cases of delinquency, it appears that this is rarely the single causative factor. Rather, brain injury is one of many contributing factors in the development of sociopathic personalities.

Broken Home. The emotional climate of the child's homelife is probably the most important factor in the development of delinquent behavior. Glueck and Glueck,[4] in a comparison of

[3]Silverman, Daniel: "The Electroencephalograph and Therapy of Criminal Psychopaths," *Journal of Criminal Psychopathology*, Chapter 5, pp. 439-466, 1944.
[4]Glueck, Sheldon, and Glueck, Eleanor: *Unraveling Juvenile Delinquency*, Harvard, New York, 1950.

500 pairs of juvenile delinquents and nondelinquents, found a very high per cent of the delinquents came from homes broken by separation, divorce, death or prolonged absence of a parent.

Parental Conflict. Some homes are characterized by a high degree of parental conflict. Children from such an environment are often caught in the cross fire of their parents' quarreling, and suffer emotional disturbances as a result. They not only lose confidence in their parents but they frequently develop poor attitudes toward themselves and all adults. Such boys and girls may then turn to almost any type of activity outside of the home in an effort to find satisfying experiences, or at least ones which will help to compensate for the conflicts at home.

Lack of Proper Discipline. Discipline in various homes differs markedly. But families that produce delinquents often have very poor discipline. In some cases, it may be too severe. In other homes punishment is inconsistent so that a child is bewildered by it. In still others, there is an utter lack of discipline. Studies of divergent youth indicate that in many instances there was no one at home who cared enough for the child to see that he did what was expected of him.

Parental Rejection. Many children engage in unwholesome activities and later turn to acts of violence because they have been rejected at home. In some cases the parents have had such serious problems themselves that they could not realistically consider the emotional needs of their children. Such boys and girls grow up feeling that they are not wanted. Consequently, they turn to "the street" for their security.

Rejection of a child may be passive or active. Some parents with adequate financial means do not show personal interest in their children and reject them by leaving them with others and by continually participating in social activities. This lack of parental-child companionship is interpreted by a child as rejection and he will often go to extremes to find individuals and gangs which will accept him.

Instability of the Home. Extreme instability characterizes some homes. The children may not feel a part of any community, having moved from place to place through the years. For them, life becomes a continual shifting about without an opportunity to put down emotional roots with any person or group. Children raised in such an environment often fail to develop a sense of responsibility. Since they have not really been an integral part of anything, they always feel like "outsiders," not personally accountable. Without strong home or community ties, they attach themselves to whatever is convenient. From this background, irresponsible delinquent behavior often becomes their way of life.

Overprotection by Parents. To develop normally a child needs a balance between parental support and self-development. When parents overprotect a child, they prevent him from making his own decisions and feeling accountable for them. Nor is he able to develop an adequate self-concept. Delinquent behavior is sometimes a reflection of a child's attempt to be on his own and to "grow up." Feeling that he has no opportunity to become mature at home, he is willing to engage in unacceptable behavior, if necessary, in order to develop a feeling of individuality. As he goes with a gang and gains their approval, he often becomes more hostile to his parents who "never let him grow up."

Poor Living Conditions. In nearly every city and in many rural areas there are families whose circumstances prevent them from having adequate food, shelter and clothing. Numerous families live in slum areas where children do not have proper places in which to play and develop in a healthy manner. They may receive little or no encouragement. In fact, they may have known virtually nothing except an abnormal environment. Growing up in this situation, a child may become resentful. He feels deprived of many gratifications and thinks that he has received a "raw deal" from life. Because of this he may leave home and turn to antisocial behavior.

Severe Emotional Disturbances. Studies of divergent youth point up the fact that many boys and girls who have entered crime are actually severely disturbed and in need of longterm professional care. The home and school may have interpreted the child's behavior as "being ornery" or "noncooperative." But, in fact, he may have been so disturbed that he could not act otherwise. His antisocial acts were a symptom of his underlying emotional disturbance. Since his behavior was unacceptable to the adults in his life, he had to turn to delinquents who would offer him a degree of acceptance.

Cultural and Language Barriers. Improved and extensive transportation facilities, coupled with relaxed immigration regulations, have enabled many families to move from their homeland to a strange, new country. Upon arriving in such a land a family may be forced to live in a neighborhood which is not conducive to good citizenship. Added to this are cultural and language barriers. Members of the family may not be able to communicate effectively because they do not know the new language. This lack of language skills seriously affects the adolescent, not only in his immediate neighborhood but also in his school. Since he is of a different nationality and background, he may not be understood by others. In some cases he faces continuous ridicule. In his effort to be accepted he may become discouraged and hostile toward authority figures. He may even feel that he has to make a break from his parents who tend to hold to their family customs. Such boys and girls can easily drift into patterns of delinquent behavior in an attempt to be recognized and accepted.

Inadequate Education. Most junior and senior high schools best meet the needs of "good students" who are above-average in intelligence and who are well-adjusted. Many schools have not seriously considered their responsibility for meeting the needs of boys and girls who have below-average ability or who need extensive remedial instruction. Such schools may not provide adequate guidance services to detect and assist those students who are making insufficient progress.

In one high school, for example, a study was made of entering freshmen who were failing algebra. The researchers found that in nearly every case pre-entrance tests indicated that these students had little mathematical ability and would probably not be successful in algebra. Yet the school made no other provision for them. Not only did they have to take algebra; they had to remain in the class for an entire year. No one was permitted to drop the course, even though he was failing. Consequently, these students were forced to take instruction in a subject in which they were almost predestined to fail. Inappropriate school procedures such as this often cause boys and girls to drop out of school and to begin a life of delinquency and crime.

Lack of Vocational Preparation. Adolescence is characterized by a desire to understand one's abilities and to put them to use. Many young people, however, do not have the benefit of vocational guidance. Neither the parents nor teachers may understand the student's specific abilities. Consequently, he is not encouraged in activities that will bring him increased skill and personal satisfaction. Naturally, one who is not challenged in some kind of productive work becomes discouraged and often turns to unwholesome pursuits.

Inappropriate Leisure Time Activities. Teen-agers need to budget their time wisely if they are to develop good habits and make the best use of their time. But many young people lack supervision and consequently spend much of their time in activities that are destructive. Still others are engaged in leisure activities that are inappropriate for their age levels. In some neighborhoods little or nothing is planned for young people. They are left to themselves to find something to do. Lacking constructive activities, they may engage in pursuits which lead to delinquent acts.

Wrong Companions. One of the most challenging influences in a young person's life is the companionship of others his own age. Since adolescents are anxious to conform to a group and to feel accepted, they often go to extremes in seeking those who will become their friends. In many instances, boys and girls who have not been accepted by their parents or other adults will choose each other. Such companionships often compound the problems of adolescents, bringing out the worst type of behavior. Once a young person is involved with others in delinquency, he achieves a certain success and he also finds it difficult to withdraw from his undesirable friends. As time goes on he may be introduced to even worse companions who lead him into a variety of criminal actions.

Poor Sex Education. During the adolescent years boys and girls develop physically and sexually at a very rapid rate. They suddenly experience new feelings and attitudes and find themselves capable of adult sexual behavior. In many cases, boys and girls have been given virtually no sex education. In other instances, their information regarding sex matters has all been negative and unwholesome. They may have gained immoral attitudes from their own parents or from close associates in the community. At any rate, they are launched into young adult life without proper attitudes and concepts of restraint. Ventures into delinquency are often attempts to gain information about sex. This may lead to fornication, pregnancies, venereal diseases and a host of demoralizing experiences.

Influence of Unwholesome Mass Media. The effects of current mass media upon the minds and emotions of young people should not be minimized. Printed materials, motion pictures, television and radio all leave their impact upon the lives of boys and girls. In many instances, there is little supervision or discretion concerning the type of information which reaches adolescents. In their eagerness to learn and gain information, many young people encounter books, entertainment and other elements of mass media which bring harmful influences into their lives and which eventually lead to immoral behavior and delinquency.

Lack of Spiritual Conversion and Christian Growth. Since all persons are spiritual beings with the capacity to know God, they are in need of spiritual conversion and Christian growth. One of the greatest impacts upon the life of any individual is to face the fact of his sinfulness, then to surrender his life to Christ. Without spiritual conversion a young person continually lives with his old nature and he does not possess the new nature which is implanted by God. Consequently, he is unable to discern what is best for him and he has little restraint to combat evil. Life without Christ leaves one adrift like a cork on the ocean. Such a person has no eternal moorings, no compass and no guide.

Illustration

Identification: White male, age 17

Presenting Problem: The subject was apprehended with two other boys, ages 17 and 18, for stealing a car. Records showed that he had been reported by school authorities for truancy when he was 15 years of age. One year later he was arrested for drinking and disturbing the peace. Since then he has been apprehended on two other occasions.

Personal and Family History: The subject was born and raised in a large city. The father was a mechanic and the mother worked outside the home part time during the early years of her married life. The family seemed to be quite happy and no problems were reported concerning the subject's two sisters and one brother.

The parents stated that the subject had always had trouble in school. Reading had been especially difficult. At the time he dropped out of school at 16 he was unable to read beyond the third grade level. The parents had been called to the school nearly every year to confer with teachers who felt the boy "could do better, but just wasn't trying." He was retained an additional year in the third grade, but the adjustment did not seem to help him. At 14 he became a member of a local gang of boys. After that the family had little control over him.

After his apprehension at the age of 17, the subject was given psychological tests which indicated that he might be neurologically impaired. He was then referred to a neurologist who administered an electroencephalogram and found that the boy had sustained a brain injury, probably at the age of two when he fell out of a car and suffered a brain concussion. Both the psychologist and the neurologist felt that much of the boy's behavior could be attributed to the results of this injury. Medication was then administered which helped to alleviate the subject's symptoms of extreme hyperactivity, temper outbursts and general irritability.

Treatment

A child who exhibits prolonged disobedience and rebelliousness needs immediate attention. If measures can be taken to relieve his disturbances before they become too serious, much future hardship will be avoided. Early referrals of students by classroom teachers to school guidance personnel are especially important. If parents see that their child is experiencing serious difficulty over a period of time, they should seek professional help.

Many of the present methods of dealing with delinquent behavior do not alleviate the individual's basic conflicts. Detention and punishment may actually make the person more hostile and rebellious, so that when he is released from confinement he will again turn to antisocial behavior.

Psychotherapy with delinquents is often difficult because they frequently have no desire to change. Skilled therapy, however, which includes a consideration of the person's total life adjustment, can bring significant and lasting changes in one's personality patterns.

The initial step in counseling is a thorough diagnosis of the underlying causes. Since many delinquents are suffering from undetected brain injuries, the counselor will need to consider referral to a neurologist for a complete neurological examination.[5] Without a clear understanding of the etiological factors, therapy will likely make little progress. When the counselor begins to understand the basic personality dynamics and how the person's current attitudes and actions have developed, he is in a position to help the client overcome these patterns of behavior.

In counseling with a young person in trouble it is important to work with the entire family. Improvement is generally limited unless the counselor deals with the parents as well as the child. One of the major goals of the therapist in family counseling is to help each family member gain insight into the feelings and motivations of others in the family. The rebellious teen-ager can come to see why his parents feel they must impose certain restrictions and why they react as they do. The parents can learn to see their teen-ager's world through his own perspective and can begin to picture the adolescent as a person striving for acceptance and individuality. As parents understand their child's motivations and the needs he is attempting to fill by his behavior, they can learn to help him meet those needs in a more wholesome and acceptable manner.

[5]See the discussion of BRAIN DAMAGE in this volume.

Another important aspect of therapy with the delinquent is the opportunity for him to express his feelings of resentment, anger and hostility. As the teen-ager begins to get these feelings out in the open, the counselor can gradually lead him to an understanding of the causes for his hostile attitudes. The feelings of insecurity underlying the hostile reactions need to be discussed and resolved.[6]

The most dramatic changes in the attitudes and behavior of a delinquent appear when the person comes to know Christ as his personal Savior. Many divergent youths have made an abrupt about-face in life as a result of having come face to face with spiritual realities. When a person accepts Christ as his Savior, however, the counselor should not feel that his work is done. The person still harbors the ill experiences of the past fifteen or twenty years which must be discussed and resolved. As the counselor gradually works with the person and leads him to increased spiritual understanding and growth, the teen-ager will begin to replace his old attitudes and actions with a new pattern of behavior which is honoring to Christ.

In addition to the actual time spent in therapy, the delinquent needs help in all of the basic areas of living. The counselor should evaluate the young person's school adjustment. If he is doing poorly in school and experiencing feelings of failure, the possibility of remedial study in reading or other areas should be considered. If he is enrolled in courses which are above his intellectual abilities, the school may be able to place him in other classes which are more appropriate. In this way the person has an opportunity to experience success and accomplishment which have been lacking in his life.

The counselor will also want to evaluate the individual's vocational opportunities and his leisure time activities. A very practical consideration is the use of free time. If the counselor can assist the boy to become actively engaged in wholesome recreation, church youth activities, and part-time work, he will find new meaning and purpose in life. Idle time which was previously occupied with antisocial acts can become precious

[6]See the discussion of INSECURITY in this volume.

minutes which are used to grow and mature into a well-adjusted adult.

When a counselor can develop a program of therapy including these spiritual, emotional and situational factors, dramatic changes may be seen in the attitudes and behavior of the delinquent.

16. Depression in Childhood

Description

In recent years much attention has been given to the emotional disturbances of children. School psychologists, child psychiatrists, and other specialists have devoted their time to the study of children and youth with various personality maladjustments. This focus on childhood problems has brought about a recognition of depressive reactions among boys and girls.[1] Today it is believed that many children as well as adults are suffering from the initial stages of depression. Naturally, such disturbances in children often go unnoticed since the symptoms are not so pronounced as in adults.[2] Parents, for example, may think of their child as merely being uncomfortable or unhappy. The fact that a child does not gain satisfaction from his social relationships may be attributed by his parents or teachers to individual differences, to certain developmental stages or to a child's preference to play alone.

Actually, the depressed child may appear to be active and interested in some activities, yet he may give other evidences of disturbing depression. He may be unable to concentrate on his school work and may make low grades in spite of above-average intellectual ability. He frequently prefers to play alone and refuses to mix in social activities. The depressed child has feelings of self-reproach and unworthiness. He often feels that life is not worth living, and in some instances he may attempt to take his life.

Etiology

The chief cause of depression in childhood is the feeling of being unloved. There are many reasons why a child may feel that he is not wanted, that he does not fit into the family picture, or that he does not measure up to the expectations of his

[1] For a discussion of this problem, see: Finch, Stuart M.: *Fundamentals of Child Psychiatry*, W. W. Norton and Company, Inc., New York, 1960.
[2] For a discussion of depressive reactions in adults, see DEPRESSIVE REACTION and MANIC DEPRESSIVE REACTIONS in this volume.

parents or teachers. It is not uncommon for a son or daughter who feels rejected by his parents to generalize these feelings to others. Basically, he feels unloved, uncared for and not appreciated.

A child may sense that he is not loved even though his parents provide him a comfortable home and offer him many gifts. For example, in the case of a boy who was under psychiatric care, the parents provided a beautifully-appointed home, expensive toys and many other advantages. Yet the child felt unloved and unworthy. A study of the family revealed that the parents spent much time away from home without the boy. They preferred going out with adults and leaving him with babysitters. The child longed for companionship with his father and mother, but since they failed to meet this need, he developed feelings of loneliness and rejection. These feelings carried over into school where he felt that other adults did not love him. In time he gave up and settled back into a world of his own. Little by little, feelings of depression overcame him until his parents had to seek professional help.

Some children develop serious feelings of depression because of the loss of a parent. When a home is disrupted by divorce or by the unexpected death of a parent, this loss may be seriously disturbing to the child.

Another cause underlying many cases of childhood depression is a *parental pattern of unduly strict discipline and overly high expectations.* When parents continually attempt to force a child to accomplish a high level of achievement, and punish him if he fails to reach this level, serious feelings of unworthiness and dejection often result. These feelings of unworthiness and inadequacy are basic to many children's feelings of depression.

Related to unrealistic goals imposed by parents are instances when parents continually hold before the child a pattern of perfection. When a child misbehaves he may be told that "God does not love you" or "that makes Jesus leave your heart." When this continues, even young children may develop severe feelings of guilt and worthlessness. Unless these misconceptions are corrected, the patterns of guilt and depression may develop even more seriously at a later age.

Physical factors sometimes play an important role in the development of depression in childhood. Although physical illnesses or handicaps are seldom the major causes of depression, they often serve to compound the child's feelings of insecurity and rejection. A weakened physical condition may lower the tolerance threshold to the point that he is more susceptible to emotional difficulties.

Illustration
Identification: Negro female, age 9
Presenting Problem: This girl was brought to an outpatient psychological clinic because she had threatened to take her own life. She had run away from home a number of times and was doing poorly in school.
Personal and Family History: This girl was the last of three children. She had two brothers who were six and nine years her senior. During counseling with this girl and her parents, her strong feelings of unworthiness and sinfulness became apparent. For a child of nine she showed an unusual sensitivity to sin and misbehavior. Every little misdeed was interpreted by the girl as a sin against God. It gradually became apparent that the parents were extremely critical of the girl's behavior. Every time she did not follow their wishes she was punished with the reminder that her behavior would make God unhappy. In addition to this punishment and criticism, neither parent was able to spend adequate time in play with the child. The father worked long hours and the mother was often busy with her teen-age boys and her own social activities. The girl was frequently left with a babysitter while the parents went out to visit friends.

Treatment
Since the major factor in depression is rejection and lack of love, treatment of the depressed child lies largely with the parents, as well as with teachers. If the child is to overcome depression, his home atmosphere and emotional environment

must be improved. Parents should come to understand the urgency of providing a loving and accepting home life if the child is to make adequate adjustments and reduce feelings of depression. As parents and teachers gain understanding of their own feelings and can discuss them freely, they will, in turn, be able to meet the needs of children with whom they associate. Treatment of the depressed child, therefore, is aimed not only toward him, but also to the adults in his life. As they are enabled to improve their own attitudes and actions, the child will respond favorably.

When parents are being overly critical of their children and setting unrealistic goals, this pattern of behavior should be corrected. When such an unhealthy parental pattern is replaced by one of acceptance, encouragement and praise, the symptoms of depression frequently disappear.

A thorough physical examination should also be given to a child who is exhibiting symptoms of depression. Proper medication or an improved diet will often enable the child to better cope with his feelings of unhappiness.

17. Depressive Reaction

Description

Depression is a condition marked by feelings of worthlessness, dejection and worry. The depressed person is an unhappy individual with a pessimistic outlook on life. He is vulnerable to threats, and even minor frustrations may cause increased feelings of depression. This individual thinks that all he does results in failure. He feels inadequate and unworthy of the love and respect of others. In short, he has an inadequate self-concept. In its more severe forms, depression may result in suicidal attempts.[1]

The person suffering from depression often has feelings of strong guilt. He feels sinful and unworthy and thinks that he is in need of punishment because of his failures, sins and inadequacies. He may worry constantly over some deed committed many years before but is unable to remove the feelings of guilt and concern. Because he feels unworthy and sinful, he misinterprets the Word of God by giving attention only to those verses which judge and condemn. He seems unable to accept the gracious Plan of God's love and forgiveness as outlined in the Scriptures because he feels he is unworthy of love and forgiveness.

A clinical distinction must be made between a person suffering from a psychotic depressive reaction and a neurotic depressive reaction. Neurotic depression is usually more situational then psychotic depression, and can often be traced to a precipitating event. The person with psychotic depression usually has a long history of continued mood swings and depressive episodes. In neurotic depressive reactions there is an absence of delusions and hallucinations which are frequently found in individuals suffering from psychotic depression.[2]

Because the symptoms and etiology of both psychotic and

[1]See also CHILDHOOD DEPRESSION, MANIC DEPRESSIVE REACTION, POSTPARTUM PSYCHOSES, and SUICIDE in this volume.
[2]For a contrast of neurotic and psychotic disturbances see the chart in Chapter One of this volume.

neurotic depression are often very similar, they are treated as a unit in this volume.[3]

Etiology

The depressed person is essentially an insecure individual who has developed feelings of unworthiness through a period of many years.

Parental rejection is a factor frequently found in the childhood experiences of the depressed person. Throughout childhood the parents have done many things to make the child feel inadequate. They may have failed to spend sufficient time with the child and refused to give him needed attention and affection. This lack of love is a basic factor in many cases of depression.

Overly-critical parents may also cause a person to develop serious feelings of inadequacy which result in depression. Instead of giving a child encouragement and praise when he attempts a task, parents may criticize him because he failed to do better. Parents may show their displeasure if the child does not obtain excellent grades in school. Instead of encouraging the child and complementing him for his efforts, they scold and criticize. These actions cause the child to minimize his own worth and feel that all he can do is fail. Similar experiences, multiplied through the years, are at the heart of many cases of severe depression. Parent criticism can also be of a passive nature. By neglecting a child, not spending time with him and overlooking him, parents can show their displeasure of a child.

Cruel parent behavior is another factor in many cases of depression. Sometimes parental rejection goes far beyond normal limits and the parents may be extremely punitive and physically abusive. Some children go through almost unbearable physical punishment at the hands of parents who are themselves seriously maladjusted.

Unconscious feelings of hostility are frequently associated with feelings of depression. An interesting dynamic often occurs with a depressed person. Reared in a home with inadequate

[3]For more specific therapeutic considerations of psychotic individuals see the section on SCHIZOPHRENIC REACTIONS and PSYCHOTIC DISORDERS in this volume.

affection and security, this person may have developed strong feelings of worthlessness and sinfulness. He strongly resents the way his parents have mistreated him, but fears to express this hostility toward them. If he expresses the hostility toward parents or others, he will be rejected and lose what little love and support he possesses. As an adult, when placed in a frustrating situation he is afraid to place the blame on another person. Feeling unworthy and no good, the depressed person will then blame himself for the problem, even though it was entirely the fault of another. In this way he avoids losing a friend, which may have happened if he reacted angrily, and he meets his felt need for punishment. This intropunitive manner of handling hostility is a frequent dynamic of depression.

A *past traumatic experience* may lie at the root of feelings of depression. The tragic loss of a loved one or a significant childhood sexual experience are often found to be factors in severe cases of depression.

Psychoanalytic theorists stress the importance of *conflicts between "instinctutal drives" and the demands of society.* The drives of sex and hostility are especially prominent in this orientation. These theorists point out that individuals have a need to satisfy the physiological sex urge and to vent feelings of hostility. Since this behavior is unacceptable to society, these impulses must be repressed. This repression results in anxiety and is seen as a major etiologic factor in many neuroses. The universality of repressed instincts in the formation of neurotic behavior cannot be accepted, but these dynamics are often found to play an important role in neurotic disturbances.

In addition to the many childhood experiences which can lead to depression, there are a number of *factors in later life which may create much anxiety and neurotic depression.* Many times a person has normal experiences as a child, but upon reaching adulthood is faced with circumstances which can lead to adjustment difficulties. Probably the most common experiences of adulthood center upon marital difficulties. Many times a young woman marries a man whose serious maladjustment is not apparent before marriage. Later on, sometimes after a number of years, his personality disturbances begin to reveal themselves in many ways. The husband may become abusive toward his wife, he may turn to drinking, or he may have illicit affairs with other women. Even though the wife has had an adequate adjustment level, these new crises and frustrations begin to raise her anxiety level and create much worry and depression.

In some instances of depression the subject is particularly *upset by some past sin.* There are instances where a sin is particularly threatening and upsetting to a person because of early childhood teachings. If the person then falls to this sin, he is unable to remove the plaguing feelings of guilt and depression. In individuals with adequate adjustment, such a sinful experience will not continually bother. The better adjusted person is able to ask the Lord's forgiveness and realize that the sin is forgiven. The insecure person with feelings of unworthiness, however, is unable to accept the forgiveness of God and will constantly dwell on his misdeeds.

Secondary gains (side effects of an illness) play an important role in depression. The dynamic here is that the person who feels unworthy and depressed may gain sympathy and attention through his illness. Feeling unloved and unwanted, this mechanism enables the person to gain some attention from a loved one. This behavior needs to be interpreted as the person's longing for unmet emotional needs.

Illustration

Identification: Spanish female, age 31

Presenting Problem: This woman came to an outpatient psychological clinic suffering from serious feelings of depression. She stated that she had no interest in life and that recently she had considered taking her life to "end it all."

Personal and Family History: This subject is the fourth of five children. It was necessary for both parents to be employed full time in order to meet the family's financial obligations. As the girl grew up she spent little time with her mother and never really felt a close bond of affection. The father was a hard-working man who had little time to spend with the children.

He was often harsh in discipline because he did not like to put up with "childish behavior."

In school the subject did average work. She was married soon after graduating from high school in order to get away from home and to find someone who would show interest in her and give her needed love and affection. The subject stated that she had always been a nervous person who worried a great deal, but in the last few years she has become more seriously depressed.

Treatment
Therapy with the depressed is typically a long-term process. Since his feelings of inadequacy and unworthiness have been years in formation, it usually requires a number of months to make lasting progress.

The foundation of successful therapy with the depressed person is the counselor's reaction of love and acceptance. In many instances the depressed person feels that the minister, psychologist or psychiatrist is the first one who truly understands him and is interested in him. A kind, sympathetic, noncritical counselor is the first step on the road back to happiness. The depressed person has often been told to "Snap out of it," "Quit feeling sorry for yourself," "It's all in your head," or "Pull yourself together." If the depressed person had been able to overcome his feelings, he would have done so long ago. What he needs now is not advice, but rather, understanding.

As the depressed person begins to place his trust in the counselor, he can feel free to discuss childhood experiences which have led to the feelings of worry and depression. The counselor can help the client understand the effect of his parent's rejection upon his current behavior. In the case of a person whose parents set unrealistic goals, for example, the client can be helped to recognize the fact that the parents' overly high standards and critical attitudes caused him to develop a sense of inadequacy and failure. As the person gains insight into the cause of his current feelings, they gradually begin to lose their hold.

Another important consideration in dealing with depression

is the problem of guilt. As indicated earlier, the depressed person is laden with guilt. The reason for this is usually not because he is any greater sinner than his neighbor, but rather because his childhood experiences have made him overly sensitive to failure. Such an overly strict conscience, or superego, causes the person to continually feel guilty and sinful. In dealing with this type of person, the counselor must help the client see the distinction between real guilt and "pseudo guilt." Real guilt is the conficting power of the Holy Spirit for the transgression of God's laws. Pseudo guilt is the feeling of unworthiness and sinfulness which arises out of inadequate childhood experiences. In this case, the individual often feels guilty even though he has not transgressed God's laws.[4]

If the counselor is to be effective in working with a depressed individual, he must make this distinction between real and pseudo guilt. Real guilt is the result of sin and can only be dealt with by true repentance and the forgiveness of God. Scriptures such as Psalm 103:12 and I John 1:9 are especially helpful in dealing with the forgiveness of sin. Character studies of Biblical personalities such as David or the woman taken in adultery may be used to show God's complete forgiveness to the person suffering from feelings of guilt and sin.

When a person continually feels guilty and sinful, yet has done no deeds to merit these feelings, the counselor must help the person to see the childhood factors resulting in his overly sensitive superego. He needs to carefully see that his thoughts of evil are not induced by the Holy Spirit, but are, instead, a psychological mechanism resulting from past experiences.

Related to feelings of guilt and sinfulness is the dynamic of intropunitive hostility. In therapy the counselor must explore this dynamic with the client to help him understand the fact that he is turning his feelings of hostility toward himself rather than giving them outward emotional expression.

Another important consideration with the depressed person is his fear of rejection. His need for love and affection have not been met. Hence, he is afraid that others are not interested in

---

[4] For a further discussion, see GUILT in this volume.

him and that he is unworthy of their love. Since the person has been rejected by his parents, he usually perceives of the Lord in like manner. If a person's father was strict, rejecting and unloving, it is likely that this person will think of God as strict, rejecting and unloving. Therapy with the depressed person must include patient, Biblical correction of these false concepts of God.

The depressed person feels that love is conditional. As a child he was loved and accepted only when he did certain things. As an adult he now feels that he must live up to a certain standard to be worthy of the Lord's love and forgiveness. In overcoming this attitude, the person needs a combination of factors. He needs to understand the experiences which have caused him to feel unloveable; he needs to experience the love and concern of his counselor; then he needs to recognize Scriptural teachings on the nature of God's love. When the person begins to accept the fact that God sees him as an important person and an object of His love, the depressed individual has made a significant step toward recovery.

In working with a depressed individual, the above concepts usually need to be dealt with a number of times. Merely quoting Scripture and telling the person how he should be may only compound the problem by making the patient feel depressed because he doesn't get better. Instead, with many counseling sessions the person can go over each insight a number of times until it has been internalized and is no longer strictly an intellectual fact. Each therapeutic concept must be throughly ingrained in the subject's personality structure.

18. Dissociative Reactions

Description

Dissociation consists of isolating certain mental processes from normal consciousness in order to ignore, refuse or blot them out. These "refused" experiences or factors are unpleasant or threatening to the personality and must be removed from consciousness to avoid negative emotional reactions.[1] The most common dissociative reactions are:

Amnesia: This is a disorder characterized by the inability to recall or identify past experiences. It may result from either organic pathology or emotional conflict. When amnesia is the result of an organic pathology such as a nervous system disorder or brain injury, the experience may be completely lost. However, in psychogenic amnesia the material is not lost, but is subject to recall if the individual returns to normal mental functioning. The amnesic person may be unable to remember his name and residence and to identify well-known friends and relatives. He is, however, capable of performing other functions normally.

Fugue State: A fugue state is an episode of nonremembered activity which may last over an extended period of time. In this condition the person may leave his home and family and wander to a distant city. He may carry on an apparently normal life until he suddenly comes to the realization that he is in a strange place and has no understanding of the weeks, months or even years which have passed since he entered into the fugue state.

Multiple Personality: Multiple personality is a rare disorder in which a person exhibits two or more distinct systems of personality. Each personality has its own characteristic patterns of behavior and the two personalities are usually vastly different. One personality, for instance, may be quiet and serious-minded, while the other is light-hearted and carefree.

[1] For a description of this problem see Gregory, I.: *Psychiatry: Biological and Social*, W. B. Saunders Company, Philadelphia and London, 1961.

Ordinarily, while the individual exercises one personality he does not realize what is going on in the other. Occasionally, however, one personality will be aware of the other. A person may switch from one personality to another within the space of a few hours. On the other hand, he may maintain one personality for as long as several months.

Somnambulism: In somnambulism a sleeping individual walks and engages in various activities that he cannot recall upon awakening. The activities of the somnambulist are usually directed toward some definite goal. The acts which he carries out are evidently desires which are repressed during waking hours.

Narcolepsy: Narcolepsy is an excessive, uncontrollable desire for sleep. The person is aware of his abnormal need, but is unable to control it. Even when the individual sleeps well during the night and has frequent naps during the day, he feels drowsy and in need of still more sleep.

Etiology

The basic causes for dissociative reactions are much the same. In each case the individual is attempting to gain relief from a stressful situation. He is unable to accept his own personality and his own ways of reacting to life's experiences. Consequently, he evades disturbing experiences by repressing them from his memory. If the emotionally painful situations were allowed entrance into consciousness, they would prove to be threatening and anxiety producing. By depriving certain experiences and feelings admission into consciousness, the individual can also protect himself from the unacceptable aspects of his Personality. A person with strong hostile feelings, for example, may completely repress these ideas through one of the dissociative reactions. In doing this he protects himself from admitting that he actually has such hostile and unacceptable impulses.

Many times the reason a person cannot accept some of his inner drives or past actions is because of an overly strict superego development. When parents continually stress the unacceptability of certain actions or thoughts, the child may accept these prohibitions. In later life, when the person experiences a desire to engage in the unacceptable activity, he may then attempt to cut this thought or experience from awareness.

Such mental mechanisms are usually on an unconscious level. The patient, himself, does not understand either the early causative experiences or the present conflicts that are resulting in bizarre behavior.

Illustration

Identification: White male, age 20

Presenting Problem: The subject was apprehended in a strange city, a victim of amnesia.

Personal and Family History: The subject had been attending college and working part time in a printing establishment. About six months before he became a victim of amnesia, he met a woman who was employed at the same company. After several dates at her apartment, they became sexually intimate—his first such experience. This relationship continued for several weeks, then he changed jobs and refused to see her again. Two months later she found that she was pregnant and returned to her home in another state. Three months passed before she was able to locate him by phone. She then told him that she had become pregnant and that he would soon become a father. She phoned him several additional times and begged him to marry her, but he avoided any arrangements to meet her.

Finally the girl's father called the boy and demanded that he meet her at the airport the following Monday and arrange for an immediate marriage. Two days later the boy disappeared. Some weeks afterward he was discovered in another city. He did not know who he was, where he was from or where he was going. There was no response either to his name or the girl's name. His amnesia kept him from facing the situation which he dreaded so greatly.

An early childhood history revealed that he often used the defense mechanism of repression whenever unpleasant situations developed. However, he had not developed amnesia until a major conflict presented itself.

Treatment
Treatment for various dissociative reactions is essentially the same. It consists of extended psychotherapy in which the patient is methodically questioned and encouraged to bring to consciousness all repressed experiences.

Psychiatrists have found that shock therapy is effective in some cases, but because of the severity of this treatment it is not widely used. Narcosis, which makes use of sleep-producing drugs to keep patients asleep for prolonged periods of time, is also used with some success.

Certain drugs are likewise being used to free patients from many of their repressed feelings. When these drugs are administered, the patient is enabled to more freely express his feelings to the therapist.

In counseling with the person suffering from a dissociative reaction, the therapist must center his attention on the aspects of the subject's personality which are too threatening and anxiety-provoking to be admitted to consciousness.

The childhood experiences and patterns of parental behavior which have caused the subject to feel that certain actions and thoughts are too evil to be expressed need to be evaluated. As the counselor gives the client the freedom to express even the most disturbing thoughts, the guilt and fear of these feelings gradually diminish. Spiritual understanding is also important in this therapy since it concerns such unacceptable attitudes. The fact that all men have sinful natures and that God freely forgives even the vilest sinner helps the person to thoughtfully consider and gain relief from condemnation. As a person grows toward spiritual maturity he realizes that he will do many things which are not desirable, but that God readily forgives these sins. He also may begin to replace evil thoughts and actions with behavior which is pleasing to the Lord. This spiritual understanding and growth is a vital factor in learning to accept oneself and overcome the tendency to repress and dissociate certain aspects of one's personality.

19. Endocrine Dysfunction

Description

The endocrine glands produce hormones which affect both the physiological and psychological development and functioning of a person. Adverse effects come from over- or undersecretion of the hormones.

The various glands and their functions are as follows:

Pituitary: This gland controls growth during the growing years. Oversecretion causes gigantism, and undersecretion produces midgetism. In the adult, oversecretion produces acromegaly.

Pineal: The function of this gland is not clearly defined.

Thyroid: This gland is discussed in this volume under THYROID DYSFUNCTION.

Parathyroid: Calcium and phosphate metabolism are regulated by this gland. Undersecretion produces tetany.

Thymus: This gland has to do with immune functions of the body.

Pancreas: This gland is partly hormonal; namely, the Islets of Langerhans, which are scattered throughout this gland. Oversecretion produces hyperinsulinism and undersecretion causes diabetes mellitus.

Adrenal: There are two adrenal glands, each composed of two layers. The outer layer, the cortex, acts on secondary sex characteristics and plays a role in metabolism regulation. The medulla, or inner layer, secretes hormones which help supply extra energy in emergencies. Addison's disease comes from a deficiency of secretion from the cortex. Puberty praecox (early development of secondary sex characteristics) can come from oversecretion of adrenal androgens in childhood. Cushing's syndrome is produced by excessive secretion of cortisone. The adrenals may fail to function due to long-standing emotional stress.

Gonad: The gonads consist of the female ovaries and the male testicles. Like the pancreas, they are only partially hormonal. They affect sex drive and the secondary sexual characteristics. Castration before puberty causes eunuchism, and male sex characteristics do not develop. Instead, the person may take on effeminate features and lack sexual drive and interest.

Etiology
There is still much to be learned about what causes the normal as well as the abnormal function of these endocrine glands. There is definite interaction between the glands so that malfunction of one may cause malfunction of another.

Specific causes of malfunction are injury, infection (both bacterial and viral), degeneration, tumor formation (both benign and malignant), heredity and psychogenic causes.

Prolonged emotional stresses have also been demonstrated to cause the malfunctioning of various glands. Although psychological factors apparently are not sole etiological considerations, emotional stress can precipitate a malfunction in an individual who already has a predisposition toward this physical problem.

Illustration
Identification: White female, age 35
Presenting Problem: The subject came to an outpatient counseling clinic with the complaint of depression and difficulty in remembering many ideas and facts.
Personal and Family History: The subject is the second of four children. Her parents are dedicated Christians and there has been no mental illness in the family. As a child the subject did well in school. She has always been a rather quiet person and slightly overweight.

At the age of 21 the subject was married. Her husband is professionally employed and they have three children. In recent years the subject has experienced greater feelings of fatigue and has become very sensitive to worry and depression. She has seen her minister about her discouragement but these feelings have persisted.

During the subject's first counseling session her therapist recommended a complete physical examination. This medical evaluation revealed a decreased functioning of the thyroid gland.

The subject responded well to medical treatment and in time her emotional symptoms disappeared.

Treatment

Although treatment of endocrine dysfunctions are basically medical in nature, often requiring the services of a specialist, psychological factors should not be overlooked. Even when a disturbance is basically physical, the person may need several sessions with her doctor or another trained counselor to evaluate her attitudes toward the physical disturbance. The limitations which glandular malfunctions place on an individual have emotional influences and these must be resolved if the person is to be effectively treated.

All counselors should be especially alert to medical referrals. Since many seemingly emotional problems have a physical basis, the counselor can waste much time in therapy if the real problem is physical rather than psychological. It is always wise to rule out the possibility of physical disturbances before initiating psychotherapy.

20. Enuresis

Description

Enuresis, commonly referred to as bed-wetting, is the repeated involuntary discharge of urine. Nighttime bed-wetting is known as nocturnal enuresis and daytime wetting is called diurnal enuresis. Research specialist, F. N. Anderson, places the average age of nocturnal bladder control among children of intelligent and educated parents at 23 months.[1] Other research substantiates his findings and points out that the majority of children at three years of age are consistently dry in the morning. There is, however, a wide range of normality at which bladder control is achieved. Some normal children continue wetting until three or four years of age. Occasional wetting beyond this age is common when a child becomes temporarily excited or upset. Moving to a new neighborhood or entering school sometimes precipitates a temporary relapse of bladder control.

A child is considered enuretic when he continues to regularly wet himself beyond the age of approximately four. When this happens the parents should begin to search for the causes of this persistent behavior and seek professional help if necessary.

Etiology

Enuresis may develop due to a lack of training, as a result of a physical disturbance or because of an emotional difficulty. Some studies also point to the importance of heredity as a cause of enuresis. Children who continue to wet themselves after the age of four or five usually evidence other symptoms of emotional maladjustment. Among the most common psychological causes of enuresis are:

Undue emphasis on early bladder control. When parents try to force a child to control his urinations at an early age, they may create anxiety associated with bladder movements. Since the child is not yet physiologically developed to the point of

---

[1]Anderson, F. N.: "Psychiatric Aspects of Enuresis," *American Journal of Diseases of Children*, vol. 40, pp. 591, 818, 1930.

exercising voluntary control, the parents are often encouraging their child to accomplish a task he is not developmentally ready to achieve.

Parental oversolicitude. Some parents are unwilling for the child to develop his independence. They continue to treat him as a baby and attempt to meet his every need. When this pattern of oversolicitude and overprotection is continued, the child may not attempt to gain control over his bladder functions.

Need for attention. Bed-wetting may also arise because of a child's need for attention. When a child feels rejected and unloved, he seeks many ways of gaining needed emotional gratifications. Since bed-wetting is a sure way of turning the parents' attention to him, the child may develop a pattern of enuresis. Even when the parents punish the child, he would rather receive this attention than be completely ignored.

Unfavorable home environment. A child with emotionally unstable parents may develop emotional difficulties which are manifested in bed-wetting. Extreme tension and anxiety are frequent causes of enuresis. When an insecure child is placed in a threatening situation such as changing schools or moving to a new community, he may react by wetting his bed frequently. The new environment has served as a precipitating factor of his underlying feelings of insecurity.

Birth of a new sibling. When a child is generally insecure, the presence of a new baby in the family may cause him to turn to attention-getting behavior. The child feels that the new baby is getting the affection which he deserves, so he turns to bed-wetting to direct the parents' attention to himself.

Illustration

Identification: White male, age 7

Presenting Problem: This boy was brought to the family physician by his mother because he continually wet his bed. He sometimes suffered from enuresis during the day.

Personal and Family History: The subject was an only child from a family described as upper middle class. The father was an administrator in the public schools and the mother was a homemaker who worked outside the home in an office two days a week. She had been married previously but had no other children.

During his conference with the mother, the physician observed her nervous symptoms. The mother said that her husband was a perfectionist and that they were both very concerned about the boy's bed-wetting.

The family had lived in three different homes during the past seven years, each move representing an improvement in neighborhoods. The father had been taking night and Saturday courses at the local university to meet the course requirements for his doctor's degree.

The physician referred the mother and her husband to a counselor who met with them for several sessions. He was able to help them see that their own problems were undoubtedly reflected in the child, resulting in his enuresis.

Treatment

Treatment for the enuretic child is directed toward uncovering the conditions which are creating tensions and interfering with his personal happiness. The first step in treating the enuretic child is a thorough physical examination.[2] In addition to disturbances of the urinary tract and the bladder, the child's total health should be considered. When the child is in good physical health he is better able to cope with possible frustrations.

Wise parents refrain from embarrassing the child who wets the bed. They do not criticize him or make remarks before his friends. The child must be enabled to build up his self-confidence by gaining increased independence and responsibility.

If the child's bed-wetting appears to have come about or is worsened after the birth of a new baby, it is important to give the child more individual attention. Parents can occasionally single out the child for special play activities and other times together. This added attention can help to meet the child's emotional needs and serve to resolve the enuresis.

Stresses and strains in home relationships should be elimi-

[2]For a discussion including physical aspects of enuresis, see: Bakwin, H. and Bakwin, B.: *Clinical Management of Behavior Disorders in Children*, W. B. Saunders Company, Philadelphia, 1953.

nated if the child is to be relieved of the emotional tensions which cause his difficulty.

In order to accomplish a more stable and emotionally gratifying home environment, it may be necessary to have a number of counseling sessions with the parents. During these periods the parents can evaluate their own emotional and marital adjustment and its effect on their child's behavior.

The parents can begin to replace the tensions of the home with an atmosphere of understanding and affection. As the parents gradually develop a better adjustment in the home, the child's symptoms of emotional disturbance will begin to disappear.

21. Epilepsy

Description

Epilepsy is a chronic disorder of the nervous system, characterized by attacks of convulsions and unconsciousness.[1] Epileptic seizures may be classified into four major types: Grand Mal, Petit Mal, Jacksonian and Psychomotor.

Grand Mal: This type of seizure is the most common form of epilepsy and also the most severe. It is characterized by gross convulsive seizures and a loss of consciousnesss. Four phases of symptoms may be identified in most cases of *grand mal* seizure.

a. Aura. An aura is a warning which precedes an epileptic attack. This aura may take the form of dizziness, headache, localized pain or some other sensory or motor discomfort. In some cases, the aura precedes the seizure long enough for the individual to prepare himself for the seizure by removing dangerous objects and lying in the middle of an open space where he will not injure himself.

b. Loss of consciousness. Shortly after the aura, the individual may cry out sharply, fall to the ground and lose consciousness.

c. Convulsions. As the individual loses consciousness, muscle spasms begin. The person's body may first become severely rigid, followed by jerking of the arms and legs and rolling of the head from side to side. The jaws may open and close tightly, causing the individual to bite his tongue. The person is unable to swallow and he may foam at the mouth.

d. Stupor. As the convulsions begin to lessen, the individual may regain consciousness, but he usually appears very confused. He may then fall into a deep sleep lasting anywhere from a few minutes to several hours. After the

[1]For a discussion of the medical aspects of this disorder see: *The American Handbook of Psychiatry*, edited by S. Areti, Basic Books, Inc., New York, 1959, vol. II.

individual awakens from his sleep, he is unable to recall the entire seizure. He is aware of the attack, however, as he is extremely tired and may have injured himself physically during the seizure.

Petit Mal: This form of epileptic seizure is marked by a partial loss of consciousness. In the lesser forms of this type, the only sign of an attack may be a glassy stare in the eyes. More severe cases show a twitching of the eyelids, loss of color in the skin and slight jerking of the head. The individual may pause in the middle of a sentence for a few seconds and, as the attack passes, resume exactly where he left off. These attacks are usually of only a few seconds' duration (up to thirty). A person suffering from *petit mal* attacks may have a number each day. On occasion, this type of seizure develops into the more severe *grand mal* attack.

Jacksonian: This type of seizure is similar to the *grand mal* attack, but less extensive. The loss of consciousness may not be as rapid as in the *grand mal* attack and the convulsions are usually limited to one area of the body. The convulsions may begin in one area, such as the face or an arm, and spread throughout one side of the body. Occasionally, the convulsions spread to the entire body.

Psychomotor: In this form of epileptic attack the individual experiences an impairment of consciousness, confusion and psychic disturbance rather than convulsions. These attacks are known as epileptic states or epileptic fugues. They may last from a common length of a few seconds or minutes to an occasional rare instance of several days. While in this condition, the individual may perform seemingly purposeful acts, but later he has no memory of these activities. Occasionally a person may perform injurious acts or antisocial behavior while in this state.

Due to the physical disturbances, many epileptics develop feelings of inferiority and inadequacy. They may begin to feel sorry for themselves and to withdraw from social contacts, fearing they are thought to be odd or queer. This withdrawal may lead to severe emotional disturbances if the individual does not take a more realistic attitude and learn to accept his condition.[2]

Another common emotional reaction to this handicap is the development of feelings of resentment and hostility. This person may become angry with society because of his disturbance and may act out this hostility in antisocial behavior.

Etiology

Some form of *brain pathology* is involved in every case of epilepsy. Numerous studies of electroencephalograms (brain wave tests) given to epileptics reveal consistent patterns of pathological brain waves. Any type of cerebral disorder can cause epileptic disturbances.

Studies of the families of epileptic individuals lead some investigators to conclude that epilepsy is *inherited*[3] Although there is a much higher frequency of epilepsy among children of epileptics, it seems that the children inherit a predisposition to epilepsy rather than a completely fixed condition.

Thorpe states that, "A number of factors may precipitate an epileptic attack in an individual who is predisposed. The most common *physiological precipitating agents* are hydration, alkalosis, low blood sugar, oxygen deficiency and alcohol."[4]

Psychological stresses sometimes serve as precipitating factors causing epilepsy in organically predisposed individuals. When a person is confronted with a frustrating situation, the resulting tension may precipitate an attack. Emotional factors may also add to the severity of epileptic seizures.

Intelligence does not appear to be a significant factor in epilepsy. Although some studies show epileptics to have slightly lower than average intelligence, this appears to be a result of the brain pathology associated with the disorder. Disruption of

---

[2]For information and recent bibliography regarding epilepsy, write: Federal Association for Epilepsy, The Epilepsy Foundation, 1729 F Street, N.W., Washington D.C.
[3]Lennix, W. G.: "Sixty-six Twin Pairs Affected by Seizures," *A. Res. Nerv. and Ment. Dis., Proc.*, vol. 26, p. 11, 1947.
[4]Thorpe, Louis P.; Katz, Barney; and Lewis, Robert: *The Psychology of Abnormal Behavior*, The Ronald Press Company, New York, 1961, p. 475.

school activities by consistent attacks and emotional factors may also influence these findings to some extent.

Treatment

Treatment of epilepsy is primarily medical. Beginning with the use of phenobarbital in the early 1900's, medical science has found a number of drugs which have effectively controlled epileptic seizures. It is now possible to obtain complete relief in a majority of epileptic seizures and to decrease the severity of seizures in most of the remaining cases. Some of the most widely used drugs for this purpose at present are Dilantin, Mesantoin and Tridione.[5]

Psychotherapy is an important adjunct to medical treatment of epileptics. One of the major areas of concern for the epileptic is social relationships. Because he believes that he is looked upon as being odd, or different, the counselor should help such a person overcome his fear of social contacts with others. He needs to understand his capacities for adjustment and success in life rather than continually dwelling on his limitations and handicaps.

Parents of an epileptic child should provide a balance of protection and care along with reasonable individual freedom. As any other child, he needs to develop independence and self-reliance. Each year he sould be given more liberty to make decisions and to assume additional responsibility which will serve him well in adulthood.

As parents encourage him to talk about his true feelings, he will come to accept his handicaps and will be more able to discuss and interpret his condition to schoolmates and friends.

Education of an epileptic child depends upon the severity and frequency of seizures, whether control can be maintained through medication, his intelligence and other factors. Some school districts provide special training for such children. Parents of an epileptic child should work closely with the school in order to realize the best education available for him. Parent

[5]Putnam, Tracy J.: *Epilepsy*, J. B. Lippincott Company, New York and Philadelphia, 1958.

conferences with teachers, counselors, principals and school psychologists usually result in improved educational arrangements.

Parents should seek periodic physical examinations for a child who is epileptic. With continued research in the field, newer drugs are becoming available which will better control epileptic seizures.

As a child approaches adulthood, parents must consider work opportunities and the possibility of marriage. Careful guidance during these years will result in realistic goals and appropriate skills affecting lifetime happiness.

Spiritual growth is an important factor in the epileptic's total adjustment. As this person lives close to the Lord, he is able to accept his handicap and to develop an emotionally stable and optimistic outlook on life.

22. Exhibitionism

Description

Exhibitionism is a sexual deviation in which an individual feels a compulsion to display the sex organs in order to gain sexual excitement. This type of deviation occurs most frequently among young adult males. The exhibitionist may display his genitals in a public place such as a park, school or theater, and usually to children of the opposite sex. Another term for the public display of the genitals is indecent exposure.[1]

The exhibitionist gains sexual pleasure from the tension accompanying the public display of his genitals. He usually gains special excitement when the person to whom he exposes himself shows unusual shock or horror.

Exhibitionism may be noted in varying degrees. Some individuals would not exhibit their genitals in public; however, they would do so privately to one or more persons, perhaps of their own sex. Still others would not make a complete public spectacle of themselves, but they would go nude in their own homes or even join others in private homes or in camps or colonies. Other individuals would dress as scantily as possible, especially at beaches, private or public swimming areas, or at other recreational centers in order to gain attention and attempt to prove their adequacy.

Etiology

The basic personality pattern underlying exhibitionism is usually that of *inadequacy, inferiority and insecurity.* One who has inferiority feelings or immature attitudes toward the opposite sex may turn to exhibitionism to gain sexual excitement and attention. Feeling inadequate in the male role, a man may have a compulsion to demonstrate his masculinity by publicly displaying his genitals. By shocking someone with this action, he gains feelings of power and sexual virility.

Hostility toward the opposite sex is another possible cause

[1]For a discussion of related disturbances see SEXUAL DEVIATION in this volume.

of exhibitionism. Just as some hostile individuals turn their anger onto society by crimes such as stealing, others may demonstrate their hostilities and frustrations by publicly exhibiting their genitals.

Inadequate sexual education is another factor often associated with exhibitionism. When parents fail to impart a realistic and wholesome concept of sex, the child often grows up with distorted sexual attitudes and actions.

Severe psychological maladjustments may also be the cause of exhibitionism. A study by Henninger,[2] for example, revealed that out of fifty-one cases of indecent exposure, ten were mentally deficient, eight were psychotic, four were chronic alcoholics, and three were classified as psychopathic personalities.

A lack of spirituality is another factor in exhibitionism. Without Christ as his Savior, a person is dominated by his old nature. He does not have the desire to live a moral life and to combat strong drives such as those in exhibitionism. This lack of control leaves a person more susceptible to sexual impulses associated with personality maladjustments.

Latent homosexuality is often found among individuals who have been arrested for indecent exposure. This dynamic is closely associated with feelings of inadequacy in the male role and with an improper identification with parent figures of the same sex.[3]

Illustration

Identification: White male, age 26
Presenting Problem: The subject sought psychiatric help as a result of a court referral. He was apprehended by the police after he had been reported by the parents of two 14-year-old girls. These girls were leaving the school grounds when the subject called them over to his car under the pretense of asking them directions. As they approached the car he stepped outside and exposed himself and when the girls turned and ran, he laughed, got into his car and drove away. When apprehended

[2]Henninger, James M.: "Exhibitionism," *Journal of Criminal Psychopathology*, vol. 2, pp. 357–366, 1941.
[3]For a discussion of this disturbance see HOMOSEXUALITY in this volume.

later that afternoon, he denied the charge, but later admitted it after he had been identified by the girls. Police learned that he had been apprehended several months earlier on a similar charge.

Personal and Family History: The subject is single, having been married for two years, then divorced. He lives at a YMCA and on week-ends usually visits his divorced mother who resides in a nearby community. He is employed regularly at a publishing company and attends a night class for adults at a community college.

During psychotherapy, it was learned that the subject was an only child, raised by his overindulgent mother who was divorced from her husband. During childhood the subject suffered from chronic ill health and was protected by his mother from normal, healthy contacts with other children. He grew up thinking of himself as inferior and inadequate. The mother arranged to have him excused from athletics in high school and discouraged any dating activities. His only extra-curricular activities were limited participation in drama and music.

The subject revealed that he had always envied other boys who seemed more masculine and competent. Several times during high school he exhibited himself to small children in the neighborhood but he was never apprehended. He admitted his inadequacy in his marriage and said that he received sexual excitement from exposing himself, especially to young girls. When asked why he enjoyed indecent exposure, he repled, "I don't know; I wish I did."

Treatment

Success in treatment of exhibitionism is largely dependent on the realization that this disorder is the outgrowth of a basic personality disturbance. Although exhibitionism is a problem, it is not the *causative* problem. After the counselor has established rapport with the client, the next step in counseling with an exhibitionist is to understand the dynamics underlying his behavior. If the person is one with inferiority feelings, or one who is attempting to prove his masculinity by indecent exposure, it is necessary to examine the ways in which he has developed these attitudes.

Since exhibitionists frequently have serious misunderstandings about sex, it is often necessary to devote time to sexual re-education. This should include an examination of the formation of their misconceptions about sex as well as the development of a new, wholesome attitude toward sexual functioning.[4]

Closely tied in with an overall personality improvement is the development of a positive, secure attitude toward social interaction. The exhibitionist frequently is a shy person who takes a minimal role in social settings. He needs to develop an improved self-concept so that he feels free to associate and interact with others.[5]

Spiritual growth is an essential part of therapy. Spiritual conversion and a close, honest walk with Christ will give the person added strength to withstand temptations. It will also assist him to develop an improved attitude both toward himself and society. As he studies and appropriates the Word of God, he will accept the fact that his adequacy is in Christ and he will no longer be overly concerned about his own adequacy. He will not feel that he has to call attention to himself in an effort to build up and fortify his own self-image. "And ye are complete in him, which is the head of all principality and power . . ." (Colossians 2:10).

[4]For a thorough discussion of the formation of wholesome sexual attitudes, see the author's book, *Life and Love (A Christian View of Sex)*.
[5]See the discussion of INSECURITY in this volume.

23. Giftedness

Description

Giftedness is a term applied to a wide variety of individuals who have superior ability to deal with facts, ideas and relationships.

Unusually high intelligence in a child may lead to various problems and challenges. Unutilized gift is a waste of talent and a concern to society. Furthermore, undeveloped talent often leads to much personal unhappiness. Misdirection of gifts, too, may bring unhappiness and problems, both for the individual and his environment. Since a gifted child may not be understood by his parents, his questions, interests, creativity and other actions may cause them much apprehension. The school room is also a setting of much concern about a gifted child. Teachers may find it difficult to challenge him. The gifted student, in return, may become bored and unhappy. The question of playmates and leisure time activities is also a concern for parents of a highly intelligent child. He may prefer to associate with older children because of similar intellectual interests. In some instances he will prefer to devote most of his free time to reading rather than learning to play with others and to develop socially and emotionally.

Some psychologists and educators define giftedness primarily on the basis of high intelligence. When this criteria is used, an intelligence quotient score between 130 and 140 is usually considered the minimum limit of giftedness.

The modern trend in identifying gifted children is a broader approach than the past tendency to rely solely on scores on intelligence tests. Specialists in the field now recognize the value of other factors. They realize that intelligence as revealed by tests is only one phase of giftedness. Consideration is also given to a person's social ability and to various talents that he may possess in areas such as music, art, mechanics or linguistics.

Studies of talents and abilities show strong tendencies for a person who is gifted in one area to have superior general ability.

De Haan and Havighurst[1] for example, in identifying the top high school students in several areas of talent, found that the school's upper fifteen per cent in intelligence included all of these talented students.

Some of the more common characteristics of the gifted child are:

Learns easily: The child with superior intellectual ability is able to learn new material much faster than a child of average ability. He often begins to walk and talk at an early age and frequently learns to read (often with minimal instruction) before entering school.

Has wide interests: The gifted child often shows an interest in many activities and fields of knowledge. Rather than limiting his interests to narrow fields, he shows a desire for broad understanding.

Remembers what he has learned: This ability to remember information is another characteristic of the person with superior intellectual gifts. This person is usually able to recall information long after it is forgotten by a person with average intelligence.

Evidences inquisitiveness: Even at a very early age the gifted boy or girl displays marked curiosity in many things. He asks numerous questions and may become upset if they are not answered to his satisfaction. He is alert and observant and often discovers many of the answers to his own questions.

Thinks in abstract terms: Slow-learning children learn best by dealing with concrete data. For example, in studying fractions, they like to see a picture of one-half a pie or one-third of some other object. The bright child, on the other hand, can discuss things on a highly verbal level without the use of illustrations or graphic material. He is able to grasp more complex ideas and concepts.

Has large vocabulary: Since the gifted child has superior learning ability, he usually develops a large vocabulary at an

[1]De Haan, Robert F., and Havighurst, Robert J.: *Educating Gifted Children.* University of Chicago Press, Chicago, 1957.

early age. He frequently surprises adults by his understanding and usage of complex words.

Has difficulty conforming: Because the person with superior intellectual gifts often has new ideas and wide interests, he may find it difficult to conform to activities planned for those of normal intelligence. He is not satisfied with programs planned for those with lesser ability.

Enjoys reading: The gifted child learns easily and has wide interests. Because of this, reading is both interesting and easy. He sometimes finds reading more stimulating than many of the normal playtime activities of other children.

Does well in school: Due to his superior intellectual ability the gifted child usually performs near the top of his class in school. He handles new material with ease and has little difficulty in completing his assignments.

Is physically advanced for his age: Research studies show a tendency for the gifted child to be above average in height and weight. The stereotype of the gifted person as frail and physically inadequate has been proven fallacious.

Prefers older playmates: Because he has superior intellectual ability the gifted child often finds that activities which are pleasing to others his age do not interest him. Instead, he generally turns to older children to find discussions and activities to his liking.

Chooses friends who are intellectual: The gifted child frequently prefers to spend time with other bright children in order to stimulate his intellectual curiosity.

Generalizes easily: The person with limited intellectual ability has difficulty generalizing the significance of one event to similar situations. The gifted child, however, has excellent ability to apply concepts and data learned in one setting to a new circumstance.

Likes school: Although there is no perfect relationship between intellectual ability and satisfaction in school, the gifted child is generally happy in his academic work. Since he has abundant intellectual gifts, he is not faced with the failure and frustration which sometimes accompany lower intellectual ability.

Organizes materials and ideas easily: A bright youngster usually organizes materials and ideas easily. He not only sees things in order, but he sees them as a whole, then in component parts.

Has an excellent sense of humor: Many individuals with superior intelligence have a keen sense of humor. They can see relationships, understand meanings, and know what others are interested in. The bright child frequently makes up jokes, and laughs at the humor of adults, often on an abstract or imaginary level.

Is highly creative: The gifted child tends to be original in many areas. He may show unusual skill in art or music and have a good sense of rhythm or of color. He often states ideas in a picturesque or novel way.

Understands elements of time: Concepts of time may be very complex for a small child. He cannot distinguish between a week, a month or a year. He may not know the difference between a century and a fortnight. When a child is gifted, however, he is able to grasp these concepts at an earlier age. He usually learns to tell time quite young and also comprehends larger units of time.

Is versatile: A final characteristic of giftedness is versatility. Most of the world's outstanding leaders could have been successful in many vocations. Gifted ministers could have been equally successful in business, industry or many of the professions. As children, these men have usually evidenced the ability to adapt easily to many new settings.

People with superior abilities may possess a number of the above characteristics. Further evaluation is possible through intelligence tests and actual achievement.

Etiology

Most investigators agree that heredity plays a dominant role in giftedness. Intelligent parents are much more likely to have intelligent children than are average or below-average parents. In his long-term study of over 1,500 gifted individuals, Terman found that his subjects also had children who were much above average.[2] However, this is no exact hereditary relationship. Some average parents have been known to have a child with superior intellect, while some gifted parents have children with only mediocre abilities.

Early life experiences may influence a child's performance on an intelligence test. A stimulating environment, for example, may enable a person to reveal his talents. The person who has had opportunity to develop his abilities is likely to score somewhat higher on intelligence tests than is another who has equal native ability but who has little education.

Illustration

Identification: White male, age 6

Presenting Problem: This gifted child was noticed soon after he enrolled in the first grade. His reading was at the fourth grade level and he demonstrated unusual knowledge in most subjects. He enjoyed talking to various school faculty members about science and mathematics.

He was referred to the school psychologist who found that the child's intelligence quotient was approximately 150.

Personal and Family History: The child's father was a successful minister and his mother a homemaker. There was one sibling, a younger brother two years of age. Both parents were college graduates and the mother had taught school for two years before marriage.

The boy evidenced unusual ability at a very young age. He preferred toys of a scientific nature when he was very young and he engaged adults in conversation at the age of three. He learned to read without special help when he was four. He has enjoyed good health and has been larger than most children his age.

Treatment

Gifted children and adults have the same basic emotional needs as others. They need a home characterized by love and security

---

[2]For the most thorough research study to date on giftedness see: Terman, Lewis M., and others: *Genetic Studies of Genius*, Stanford University Press, Stanford, 5 vol., 1925-1959.

and the opportunity to develop their independence. Their lives should be filled with the presence of God. At a young age they need to come to a saving knowledge of Christ and to begin growing spiritually.

Children with special abilities may also have some special requirements.[3] Parents should understand the type of child they have in order to best meet his individual needs. Gifted children need a stimulating environment if they are to develop their full potential. Parents should supply interesting games and experiences which will challenge them. They also need good literature and adequate educational opportunities.

In schools the three most common methods of meeting the educational needs of intellectually superior children are (1) acceleration, (2) enrichment, and (3) special classes.[4]

Acceleration involves moving the child ahead in school. Class placement is then based more upon mental age than chronological age. Since the gifted child has the mental ability equal to children older than himself, he may be placed in a more advanced grade.

Some schools make special provision for *enriching the curriculum* of the gifted student. They provide the child with opportunity to do special projects in literature, mathematics, science and other subjects. While being left with children of his own chronological age, he is enabled to work in academic material more suitable to his mental capacities.

In some schools *special classes* are also provided. This enables a student to spend most of the day in regular classes, yet take some time with other gifted students working on projects such as mathematics or science.

In planning for gifted students it is important that individual differences be taken into account. An academic program which is suitable to some may not be appropriate for others. Arrangements which may prove beneficial to some may cause others

---

[3]For a more complete discussion of the gifted child's academic, spiritual and psychological needs, see the author's publication *Is Your Child Gifted?*, Zondervan Publishing House, Grand Rapids, Michigan.

[4]For an excellent discussion of these educational arrangements see: Kirk, Samuel A.: *Educating Exceptional Children*, Houghton Mifflin Company, Boston, 1962.

to be nervous and unhappy. A counselor can help parents to see that simply because a child is gifted does not mean that he should have a "gifted program" outlined for him. A child with unusually high intelligence likes to play and create and spend his hours like any other child. He should not be pushed academically beyond reasonable limits. One young lady, for example, commented on her experience in junior and senior high school. "Because I was gifted they shoved me from one class to another and always put me in groups with superior children. I often found myself working with boys and girls who were older than I and whose interests I did not share at all. School became a grind for me. I faced nearly every day with the attitude that I was having to compete with someone. In senior high school I began to be concerned about my grades inasmuch as I knew that I had to make a certain grade average in order to be accepted into some universities. And yet I was competing with other gifted children and we all found it difficult to make the grades which were required for college entrance. In short, I suppose you would say that I felt pressured—and used."

Counselors can make an unusual contribution to gifted children by talking to their parents about the basic emotional needs of all children and encouraging parents to see that their gifted children develop emotionally as well as academically.

Spiritual factors, too, need to be emphasized in parent counseling. All gifts are from God and should be used for His honor and glory. "Every good gift and every perfect gift is from above, and cometh down from the Father of lights, with whom is no variableness, neither shadow of turning" (James 1:17). Gifted young people should grow up with a desire to honor Christ in all that they do. Counselors have a unique opportunity to help parents of gifted children understand this responsibility.

24. Guilt

Description

Guilt may be defined as feelings of sinfulness, evil, wrong-doing and failure to measure up. The realization of guilt comes at the time a person understands right from wrong. In dealing with individuals in a counseling setting, it is important to distinguish between two types of guilt.

Real Guilt: Because every human being has an inherent bent toward sinning, he transgresses the law of God and is guilty of sin. Feelings of evilness and wrongdoing as the result of transgressing God's laws are known as real guilt. "Wherefore, as by one man sin entered into the world, and death by sin; and so death passed upon all men, for that all have sinned . . ." (Romans 5:12). When the guilt of sin weighs heavily upon the unregenerate soul, it is only natural that he feels the pressure of it. When guilt feelings of this type lead to repentance and surrender to Christ, God forgives the sin and the pressure of guilt is removed.

The born-again believer is the recipient of a new nature. He has new appetites and desires; a new righteous position in Christ. "Therefore if any man be in Christ, he is a new creature: old things are passed away; behold, all things are become new" (II Corinthians 5:17). But he is not divorced from the old nature, which wars against the new. However, the believer *does* have immediate access to God through Christ who will forgive the erring son as he asks daily forgiveness. "If we say that we have no sin, we deceive ourselves, and the truth is not in us. If we confess our sins, he is faithful and just to forgive us our sins, and to cleanse us from all unrighteousness" (I John 1:8, 9).

Pseudo Guilt: Sometimes, however, the feelings of guilt that plague a person are not of a spiritual nature. Instead, they result from emotional causes. A person may have already committed his life to Christ but still cannot shake the feeling of guilt. He may continually ask the Lord's forgiveness for some past sin, yet be unable to remove the feelings of guilt and evil. This is an abnormal reaction which is brought on by certain environmental situations, usually from childhood, and may be referred to as pseudo guilt feelings.[1]

Both real and pseudo guilt feelings may show themselves in numerous ways. Since a person is a complex organism, capable of a great variety of integrated responses, it is only natural that he reveals his feelings of guilt in diverse and complex forms. Following are some of the more common symptoms of guilt feelings. They may be brought about by actual transgression of God's laws or by a person's emotional and maladjustment.

Exemplary behavior. The individual acts rather docile and well-behaved in order to cover his true inner feelings of guilt.

Somatic (bodily) complaints. These are of an emotional nature which show themselves in physiological reactions such as fatigue and headaches.

Feelings of depression. The person who feels guilty continually blames himself. This pattern of reacting can cause serious feelings of depression.

Further indulgence. This involves further indulgence in wrong practices which are the result of an attitude of defeat or are calculated to bring additional feelings of guilt, thereby inflicting a form of self-punishment.

Self-condemnation. The person continually condemns or blames himself for having done something wrong, shameful or wicked. This is related to feelings of depression.

Self-punishment. The individual punishes himself by denying himself food, clothing or other material necessities. Many primitive tribes inflict bodily harm upon themselves in an effort to atone for feelings of sinfulness.

Expectation of disapproval. The individual anticipates disapproval and condemnation from those about him and feels that the world considers him worthless.

Projection and undue criticism. The person continually finds fault with others and ascribes to them the faults and shortcomings he finds in himself.

---

[1]For a discussion of environmental factors which may result in severe feelings of pseudo guilt, see the discussion of DEPRESSION in this volume.

Hostility. The individual is generally hostile to others because of his own guilt feelings.

Compensation. This is an attempt to ease the individual's conscience by doing good deeds, joining respected organizations and giving to charity.

Etiology

Real Guilt. Actual feelings of sinfulness and guilt are the result of the transgression of God's laws and a refusal to confess these sins. The unsaved person who continues in sin is constantly faced with the fact of his own sinful condition. He suffers tensions, anxiety and feelings of guilt because of the convicting power of the Holy Spirit. "But the wicked are like the troubled sea, when it cannot rest, whose waters cast up mire and dirt. There is no peace, saith my God, to the wicked" (Isaiah 57:20, 21). Although men may strive for years to soothe their consciences and avoid facing the reality of sin; even though they may occupy their time with every conceivable activity, they still have occasion to realize their sinful condition. Even hardened criminals and sociopathic personalities are frequently touched with their sinful state and need of salvation.[2]

The born-again believer also experiences feelings of sinfulness and guilt which are very realistic. As the Holy Spirit works in the lives of believers to bring them more in conformity with His will, the Christian is frequently aware of attitudes and actions which are not pleasing to God. Until these sins are confessed to the Lord, the believer will suffer much anxiety and tension. "From whom the Lord loveth he chasteneth, and scourgeth every son whom he receiveth" (Hebrews 12:6). "As many as I love, I rebuke and chasten: be zealous therefore, and repent" (Revelation 3:19).

Pseudo Guilt. Severe guilt feelings often have their basis in childhood experiences. One of the most frequent causes of pseudo guilt is parental behavior characterized by condemnation, blame and accusation. Many children are made to feel

[2]For a discussion of this disturbance see SOCIOPATHIC PERSONALITY in this volume.

guilty for actions that have nothing to do with the transgression of God's laws. Parents, teachers and other significant adults often treat children in such a way that they are made to feel guilty and unworthy. When children grow up in an environment that causes serious feelings of insecurity and inadequacy, they begin to react to frustrations and conflicts in an intropunitive manner.[3] They blame themselves for all difficulties and create serious feelings of guilt and depression.

The person who is susceptible to pseudo guilt may also find it difficult to accept the forgiveness of the Lord for even confessed sins. Some insecure individuals go repeatedly to the Lord and beg for forgiveness of their transgressions. In spite of the fact that the Lord has promised to remove the stain of sin, this believer is unable to free himself from disturbing thoughts of his sinfulness and guilt. The basic dynamic of this problem is the fact that the individual feels unworthy and is attempting to inflict upon himself the punishment he feels he deserves.

Illustration: Pseudo Guilt

Identification: Spanish woman, age 43

Presenting Problem: This woman came to a counseling center suffering from feelings of guilt and depression.

Personal and Family History: This subject was the oldest of three siblings. Both parents were college graduates and were active in their local church. They set very high standards of accomplishment for the subject and often criticized her behavior. The father frequently punished the girl for misbehavior by serious scoldings and by withdrawing her privileges.

In school the subject received excellent grades and participated in many activities. In spite of these accomplishments, however, she did not feel worthy of praise and acceptance. She was very sensitive to what others thought of her and was easily discouraged by criticism.

The subject is married and has two children. Both she and her husband are active in their church. They also sponsor a Bible study in their home each week. Throughout her life the

---

[3]See the discussion of INSECURITY in this volume.

subject has been easily discouraged and has suffered from feelings of guilt. During counseling she related a number of sins from years past which were plaguing her. Although she had prayed often for forgiveness of these actions, she stated, "I know God has forgiven me, but I just can't quit worrying about them."

As a result of counseling this woman came to see that much of the cause of her guilt was the criticism and punishment she had received as a child. Since her parents had often punished her for misdeeds, this woman felt that she was unworthy and in need of punishment. Because of this she was unable to accept God's forgiveness for her sins. Her guilt feelings were an attempt to punish herself for feelings of sinfulness.

Illustration: Real Guilt
Identification: White male, age 25
Presenting Problem: This man came to a local pastor complaining of constant anxiety and feelings of guilt. He told the minister that he had done many deeds which continually bothered him.
Personal and Family History: This subject was the second of three children. His parents were unsaved and he had attended church and Sunday school only occasionally. During teenage years he had become involved in a number of delinquent acts but had not been apprehended by the police.

The minister encouraged him to express his feelings of sinfulness and conviction. Then the minister explained to the young man God's plan of redemption and forgiveness of sins. The man recognized his sinful condition and his need of forgiveness and asked Christ into his life. As the minister followed up with the subject, he found that new joy and peace had replaced the past feelings of guilt and worry.

Treatment
Pseudo Guilt: Feelings of self-depreciation and guilt which have been environmentally induced (by parents, teachers and others) must be dealt with by examining the experiences which have led to these attitudes. The therapist must help the counselee distinguish his pseudo guilt feelings from those which are the result of the transgression of God's laws. As a person begins

to see that he is suffering from guilt which is not resulting from the conviction of the Holy Spirit, he gains new freedom and relief from these attitudes. He can then be led to an understanding of the causes of his unfounded guilt.

The influence of parental criticism and unrealistic expectations upon the person's conscience development need to be examined. He needs to see that such criticism has resulted in an attitude of self-depreciation and unworthiness. When he sees the influence of these experiences and develops a more wholesome self-concept, the feelings of guilt begin to disappear.[4]

Real Guilt: If a person is suffering from guilt feelings which are a result of the convicting power of the Holy Spirit, the only solution lies in the forgiveness of Christ. "Come now, and let us reason together, saith the Lord: though your sins be as scarlet, they shall be as white as snow; though they be red like crimson, they shall be as wool" (Isaiah 1:18). As a person faces his need of forgiveness and accepts Christ as his Savior, he will be relieved of these feelings of guilt. This is God's miracle.

The Bible declares that "All we like sheep have gone astray; we have turned everyone to his own way; and the Lord hath laid on him the iniquity of us all" (Isaiah 53:6). Since man is a spiritual being, he must face the fact that sin is a reality and it must be dealt with in a real way. Genuine guilt feelings cannot be rationalized and dispelled by the efforts of a counselor. They have been implanted by God and can only be removed by Him. This guilt must be dealt with by the loving forgiveness of God's Son, Jesus Christ. "In whom we have redemption through his books, the forgiveness of sins, according to the riches of his grace" (Ephesians 1:7). Only through genuine repentance and a life lived in close fellowship with the Lord can true feelings of guilt be overcome.

---

[4]For a more complete discussion of therapeutic techniques with individuals suffering from feelings of guilt, see DEPRESSIVE REACTION in this volume.

25. Headaches

Description

Aches and pains are never welcome in any part of the body—but especially in the head. Many people, however, frequently suffer from seriously disturbing aches of the head. Rather than being a distinct disease entity, the headache is often a symptom of other physical or emotional disturbances.[1] About one-half of the patients seeing physicians name headache as one of their complaints. Two of the basic types of headache are migraine and tension.

Migraine headache: These disturbances can be most painful and severe. Some of the major characteristics of migraine headaches include:

Severe, persistent throbbing

Aches (often on only one side of the head)

Periodic pain, preceded by warning signs such as mood changes or eye spots

Nausea, with vomiting and sensory disturbances

A family history of migrane

Tension headache: These headaches are usually less severe than migraine although they may also accompany migraine disturbances. Among the most common identifying characteristics are:

Diffuse aching of the head (as compared with the one-sided pain of migraine)

Accompanying pains of the neck and shoulders

Minimal throbbing

Lack of warning symptoms

Etiology

Because the head is the control center of the entire body, it can be affected by a large number of physical and emotional disturbances. Among the most common *physical causes* of

---

[1]For a discussion of headaches, see Noyes, A. ., and Kolb, L. C.: *Modern Clinical Psychiatry*, W. B. Saunder Company, Philadelphia, 5th Edition, 1963.

headaches are blows to the head, poisoning, anemia, high altitudes, fever and intoxication.

Emotional disturbances appear to play a major role in the formation of headaches. In cases of individuals who have definite physical conditions which make them susceptible to headaches, emotional factors often serve to precipitate these conditions. Such physical disturbances frequently do not become apparent until undue emotional strains lower resistance to the disturbance. Emotional factors can also produce headaches in a direct manner. In many cases no apparent physical dysfunction is found. Instead, it is believed that emotional tension and stress have served as the basic causal factors.

The personality characteristics of the individual suffering from headaches of a psychological origin are similar to those of other psychophysiologic disorders.[2]

This person is generally an insecure individual who has a *high level of anxiety and tension,* frequently with an overly strong superego (conscience) development and exhibiting some personality restriction.[3]

During childhood this individual is often characterized by a *high level of striving,* achieving well in school and being very competitive. This pattern of striving arises from a home situation where parents set high standards of achievement and constantly encourage the child to high performance, causing feelings of insecurity which he tries to overcome by superior performance. An early pattern such as this initiates a basic personality characteristic which continues into adulthood. *This person is continually under stress.* He feels he must excel in order to gain recognition and acceptance. When he is unable to satisfy these strivings, he is under constant pressure and tension. If this continues for a long period of time, the person may begin to channel this anxiety into bodily disturbances.

Another characteristic of the individual suffering from headaches of an emotional origin is the *excessive use of denial and*

[2] See the discussion of ANOREXIA NERVOSA, ASTHMA, NEURODERMATITIS, and PEPTIC ULCERS in this volume.
[3] See the discussions of GUILT and INSECURITY in this volume.

repression. This person is generally fearful and insecure, afraid to express his true emotions, particularly those of a sexual or hostile nature. Fearing to exhibit such emotions, he develops a pattern of reacting in which he attempts to deny the presence of these feelings. In spite of attempted repression, however, these conflicts generate much anxiety. When this anxiety is not allowed conscious expression, it may then be channeled into a physical symptom such as headache.

Illustration

Identification: White male, age 36

Presenting Problem: This man went to his medical doctor complaining of frequent headaches. He reported that they were often accompanied by aching of his neck and shoulders. They had become increasingly frequent during the past two years. After finding no organic basis for the headaches, the doctor referred the patient to a psychologist.

Personal and Family History: The subject was the second of two children. His parents were of middle socioeconomic status and were active in a number of church and community activities. During childhood the subject's parents always set very high academic standards. Although they had not been able to go beyond high school, they wanted to be sure that their children had the advantages of a college education. Because of this they stressed academic achievement at a very early age.

The subject, above average intellectually, pleased his parents by studying hard and making good grades. During high school he was a member of the honor society in addition to participating in a number of extracurricular activities. He received a scholarship for college and took his bachelor's degree in business. After graduating from college, the subject married. He now holds an executive position in a growing firm. Over the past years he has worked hard and has put in much overtime to gain advancements. In addition to his business activities, the subject is very active in church. He serves as an usher as well as teaching a young adult Bible class.

In therapy the psychologist found that much of the cause of this man's difficulty was the constant tension associated with his drive to be a success. In essence, he was attempting to prove to his parents and to others that he was a capable person and could be highly successful at an early age. When he began to gain insight into these dynamics, the subject learned to relax his schedule and take more time with his family. With his increased self-acceptance, he was freed from the persistent need to prove his adequacy to himself and to others.

Treatment

In treating headaches the first important step is a thorough medical examination. If the disturbance is basically organic in origin, these causes can often be eliminated; even if emotional, proper medication will usually give relief of the distressing symptoms. After proper medical diagnosis and treatment, a program of psychotherapy can be initiated. This counseling process should be directed toward the factors underlying the person's high level of anxiety and tension.

Dynamics such as overstriving in order to meet parental expectations need to be explored and resolved. When this dynamic is found to be at the root of emotional disturbances, the person should be helped to adopt a more realistic and accepting attitude toward himself. This individual usually feels that in order to be accepted he has to meet the standards which others set. Since the parent's love and acceptance was conditional, he feels he must reach a high standard of achievement to satisfy others. This attitude, which leads to continual overstriving and tension, must be replaced with an improved self-concept and increased self-acceptance.

In overcoming the inability to accept one's self, spiritual concepts are especially important. As a person gains a better understanding of the nature of God's love and forgiveness, he comes to see that the Lord's acceptance is unconditional. No longer must the person strive for acceptance from others or from the Lord. Instead, he realizes that his source of security and adequacy comes from the finished work of Christ. Two portions of Scripture which are especially beneficial in this regard are the books of Romans and I John. In the eighth chapter of Romans, we read: "Therefore [there is] now no condemnation—no adjudging guilty of wrong—for those who are in Christ Jesus, *who live not after the dictates of the flesh, but after the dictates of the Spirit.* For the law of the Spirit of life [which is] in Christ Jesus [the law of our new being], has freed me from the law of sin and of death. For God had done what the Law could not do, [its power] being weakened by the flesh [that is, the entire nature of man without the Holy Spirit]. Sending His own Son in the guise of sinful flesh and as an offering for sin, God condemned sin in the flesh—subdued, overcame, deprived it of its power [over all who accept that sacrifice]. So that the righteous *and* just requirement of the Law might be fully met in us, who live *and* move not in the ways of the flesh but in the ways of the Spirit—our lives governed not by the standards *and* according to the dictates of the flesh, but controlled by the (Holy) Spirit" (Romans 8:1-4, Amplified Bible).

26. Homosexuality

Description

The development of adult heterosexuality is a long and complex process. Because of the numerous factors which influence this development, many people fail to achieve normal sexual adjustment. Homosexuality is characterized by an unnatural sex attraction for members of one's own sex. Although the term "homosexuality" may apply to either sex, the term "lesbianism" applies to women only. Three levels of homosexuality may be distinguished.

Latent: Some persons who appear normal sexually, who date, marry and have children, have homosexual tendencies of which even they are unaware. This sometimes shows itself as weakened or absent heterosexual interests or (through compensation) as abnormally increased heterosexuality. Impotence, frigidity, and compulsive masturbation are often associated with an underlying dynamic of latent homosexuality.

Passive: Persons at this level usually engage in homosexual acts only when invited by an active homosexual and may play a passive role. They are often capable of normal heterosexual relations and may be married and have a family.

Active: Those at this level actively solicit others to engage in homosexual acts and may commit homsexual rape. Active homosexuals are often repulsed by the thought of relations with the opposite sex. They may wear the clothes of the opposite sex (transvestism) and even change their names.

All individuals vary on a continuum from normal heterosexuality to the active level of homosexuality. Although certain body builds and personality characteristics are commonly associated with homosexuality, such is not necessarily the case. Some very masculine appearing men and some women with very feminine appearances are engaged in homosexual activities. The homosexual is a person who is afraid of normal involvement with the opposite sex. Fearing this contact, he turns to members of his own sex in order to receive needed gratification.

Etiology

Various theories have been given concerning the origin of homosexuality, but it is now widely agreed that this disorder is largely the result of abnormal personality development. A number of conditions may contribute to this deivation.

Glandular Disturbances: Some researchers give important consideration to hormonal causes of homosexuality. In a study of male homosexuals, Myerson and Neustadt found a relationship between homosexual behavior and the amount of sex hormones (androgen and estrogen) in the blood.[1] However, several factors minimize the importance of such an endocrine imbalance: (1) All homosexuals do not exhibit these imbalances, (2) many people who are not homosexuals exhibit similar disturbances, and (3) individuals have made changes from homosexual behavior to normal heterosexual adjustments without altering this glandular imbalance.

Genetic Causes: Some investigators have suggested hereditary influence in the development of homosexuality, but conclusive evidence for this viewpoint is lacking. It is natural that homosexuals attribute their disturbance to genetic factors, in this way removing any personal responsibility for their condition. The personality factors which lead to homosexuality occur subtly in childhood. In fact, many homosexuals cannot recall a time when they felt differently about their sex role than they now do. This, of course, leads to the erroneous conclusion that they were born this way.

Dominant Mother: Some mothers stifle and belittle their son's masculinity. When this happens the child loses confidence in his own sex. A dominant mother may have a strong, masculine component in her personality and may rival her son for the father's affection. This development is often on an unconscious level. As the son loses confidence in his masculinity, he may dread the thought of marriage or any intimacy with women.

Weak Father: When a dominant mother is paired with a weak father, and unhealthy situation is intensified. The son cannot

[1]Myerson, A., and Neustadt, R.: "The Bisexuality of Man," *Journal of the Mount Sinai Hospital*, New York, vol. 9, pp. 668-678, 1942.

look to his father for moral support in his fight to become a man. He may then lose respect for his father and his own sex. A daughter may lose respect for men in general because of her father's weakness.

Overindulgent Mother: The overindulgent mother is also a common cause of homosexuality. Her indulgence leads the boy to develop a strong attachment to his mother which he is unable to break as he grows older. He feels that no girl can measure up to his mother and he does not develop normal heterosexual friendships.

Cruel Parents: A mother or father who is continually cruel and arbitrary may cause the child of the opposite sex to develop ill feelings toward others of the same sex as the cruel parent. These hostile feelings result in the inability to establish adequate heterosexual relationships and lead the person to find gratification and acceptance from those of his own sex.

Poor Parental Marriage Relationships: In the case of many homosexuals, a portion of the underlying cause can be traced to the faulty marital relationships of the parents. The child in this home environment grows up with the attitude that marriage is an unhappy and frustrating institution. Reaching adulthood, he harbors these same feelings and thus avoids marriage. Since he still has strong sexual drives he may then turn to homosexual contacts to obtain needed sexual gratification.

Overly Close Relationship With a Parent of the Same Sex: When a young child has an extremely intimate relationship with one parent, to the exclusion of normal identification with the other, the child is unable to develop healthy heterosexual attitudes. Since the child's early experiences have been almost totally with the parent of the same sex, he is unable to relate to those of the opposite sex.

Lack of Appropriate Sex Education: Although not a singular cause of homosexuality, the lack of wholesome sexual education contributes to the misunderstanding and unwholesome sex attitudes of the homosexual. When parents treat the subject of sex as taboo, the child often develops poor sexual attitudes. Combined with some of the above etiological factors, this compounds the individual's struggle toward heterosexual adjustment.

The Society of Medical Psychoanalysts recently completed a nine-year study of the problem of male homosexuality.[2] They compared a group of 106 male homosexuals with a similar number of non-homosexual men. Among their findings is the following data on the relationships between male homosexuals and their parents.

Mothers of Male Homosexuals: The following factors were found significantly more frequently among the mothers of homosexuals than in the normal control group.

- The male homosexual was more frequently the mother's favorite child.
- The mother demanded to be the center of the homosexual's attention.
- The mother was dominating.
- The mother spent a greater than average amount of time with the patient.
- Mothers did not encourage masculine activities and attitudes.
- Mothers discouraged masculine activities and attitudes.
- Mothers encouraged feminine activities and attitudes.
- Mothers often tried to ally with the son against the husband.
- Mothers often openly preferred the patient to the husband.
- Mother was unduly concerned about protecting the patient from physical injury.
- Mother's concern about health or injury caused her to interfere with the subject's activities.
- In childhood the patient was excessively dependent on his mother for advice and direction.

Fathers of Male Homosexuals: The following findings were statistically significant in the father-son relationships of the group of studied homosexuals compared with the control group of non-homosexuals.

- Another sibling was favored over the subject.
- The patient was the least favored child.
- The patient did not feel accepted by the father.
- The father spent very little time with the patient.

[2]Bieber, Irving, and others (Society of Medical Psychoanalysts): *Homsexuality, A Psychoanalytic Study*, Basic Books, Inc., New York, 1962.

- The father failed to encourage masculine attitudes.
- The patient often knowingly hated his father.
- The patient often both hated and feared his father.
- The patient had little respect for his father.
- The patient did not accept his father.
- The father did not express affection for the patient.
- The father had less respect for the patient than for other male siblings.
- The patient did not side with his father in parental arguments.
- The patient found it more difficult to cope with the father than the mother.
- The patient feared his assertiveness would hurt or anger the father.
- The patient felt the father did not consider his needs.
- The patient did not currently feel respected by his father.
- The patient did not regard the father as admirable.
- The patient was not excessively dependent on the father.

Spiritual Causes: In a godless, secular society it is not surprising that men and women have turned to all types of sexual behavior. In Romans 1:24-27, we read of the sinful behavior resulting from the rejection of God: "Therefore God gave them up in the lusts of their [own] hearts to sexual impurity, to the dishonoring of their bodies among themselves, abandoning them to the degrading power of sin. Because they exchanged the truth of God for a lie and worshipped and served the creature rather than the Creator, Who is blessed forever! Amen—so be it. For this reason God gave them over *and* abandoned them to vile affections *and* degrading passions. For their women exchanged their natural function for an unnatural *and* abnormal one; And the men also turned from natural relations with women and were set ablaze (burned out, consumed) with lust for one another, men committing shameful acts with men and suffering in their own bodies *and* personalities the inevitable consequences *and* penalty of their wrong doing *and* going astray, which was [their] fitting retribution." (Amplified Bible). Homosexuality is one result of the apostasy of the world and sinful man's refusal to worship God.

Illustration

Identification: White male, age 22

Presenting Problem: The subject came to a counseling clinic with an alleged personality problem. During the first session with the psychologist, the subject revealed that he had "unnatural affection for male friends."

Personal and Family History: The patient had one younger sister and no brothers. His mother was an aggressive, dominant person who made most of the decisions in the home. The father was a weak individual who allowed his wife to dominate the family.

During childhood, the boy had few friends except two girl playmates who lived next door. During high school, the subject first experienced an interest in the bodies of boys in gym class. Later he left home and attended college where he began having homosexual activities with younger high school boys whom he met in the neighborhood.

Treatment

Since the homosexual's difficulties arise in connection with an inability to relate properly to others, it is important that the counselor provide an accepting, non-critical atmosphere for the counselee. The homosexual has had inadequate relationships with significant adults in his environment. One of the major factors which will assist him to overcome his misdirected sexual drives will be the formation of a clearer role concept based upon his new relationship with the therapist. As the homosexual begins to relate to the counselor he can gradually form correct attitudes toward his sexual role. Since it may take many months for the counselee to develop this type of relationship with the therapist, counseling with the homosexual is usually a long-term process.

The counselor helps the homosexual to understand the dynamics of his disorder. Together they can discuss the conditions in the person's background and family environment which have caused him to turn to this deviate behavior. As the homosexual begins to see the forces which have led to his abnormal behavior, these impulses begin to lose their power.

In addition to a full understanding of the dynamics of his personality development, the client needs to be assisted in re-establishing wholesome attitudes toward sex and marriage. A discussion of the body's functions and the place of God-given heterosexual relationships will assist the individual.

Some therapists have had excellent success by using group therapy as an adjunct to individual counseling. As a homosexual begins to gain insights and make progress in individual therapy, the counselor may have him join a group therapy session. These group sessions help the homosexual to focus on social and interpersonal relationships. Since the homosexual is a person who has difficulty relating to the opposite sex, the opportunity to engage in social interaction in a mixed therapy session is very valuable. In these sessions the homosexual can gain confidence in his ability to deal with members of the opposite sex. As new self-confidence and role conceptions are formed, the previous homosexual urges begin to lose their hold.

A strong program of spiritual development for the believer and a genuine conversion for the unsaved are of utmost importance in overcoming serious sexual disorders. Experienced Christian counselors know that many homosexuals are not seriously concerned about their problem until they have been spiritually converted. The typical homosexual may say, "This is the way I was born and I like it. I don't want to change." But after he trusts in Christ as his personal Savior, he is convicted by the Holy Spirit for his homosexual activities and he knows his actions are not pleasing to God. This usually causes him to be concerned about his condition and prompts him to seek professional help.

Spiritual growth not only convicts a man of his homosexual activities; it also enables him to overcome them. This recovery is clearly spoken of in God's Word: "Do you not know that the unrighteous *and* the wrongdoers will not inherit *or* have any share in the kingdom of God? Do not be deceived (misled); neither the impure *and* immoral, nor idolaters, nor adulterers, nor those who participate in homosexuality." In the 11th verse we find that those people spoken of in the 9th verse overcame their sin problems. "And such some of you were (once). But you were washed clean [purified by a complete atonement for sin and made free from the guilt of sin]; and you were consecrated (set apart, hallowed); and you were justified (pronounced righteous, by trust) in the name of the Lord Jesus Christ and in the (Holy) Spirit of our God" (I Corinthians 6:9, 11, Amplified Bible).

When Christ controls a persons's life, he controls his sexual appetite as well. He keeps men from lusting after women and He prevents men from lusting after other men. This demonstration of the power of the Holy Spirit to control the life of a believer is often apparent when evaluating the psychological tests of a homosexual. When two people with equally disturbed psychometric test results are compared, it is sometimes found that one is actively engaged in overt homosexuality while the other is not. The distinguishing factor is often found to be the fact that one of the individuals is unsaved, while the other is able to control his drives by the power of the Holy Spirit.

Christian psychologists who have worked widely with homosexuals on a deep spiritual basis, taking into account all of the basic factors discussed above in this section, have been unusually successful. When a person with homosexual tendencies gains basic understanding of his problem and progresses in his Christ-centered therapy, he will achieve a satisfactory adjustment.

27. Hostility

Description
Hostility is a strong emotion which usually results from a threat to the status, esteem or physical well-being of an individual. Among adults hostility is often shown by outbursts of temper and shouting. While most people occasionally become frustrated and react with aggressive behavior, some develop consistent patterns of reacting to stress situations by fits of anger and rage.

The hostile individual is difficult to get along with. If he does not get his way or is engaged in severe competition, he becomes very unpleasant. He frequently has marriage and family difficulties. He may argue with his wife constantly and scold and punish his children. In church and other social situations the hostile person often disrupts the plan of activities. He becomes engaged in personality conflicts with group leaders and seeks to have his views become the center of attention.[1]

Etiology
A person harboring hostility may use aggression when attacking a frustrating situation or when attempting to remove an unpleasant object. Hostile behavior is a reaction to the thwarting of one's goals. When an individual's sense of security or personal well-being is threatened, he may react with anger and hostility.

Hostile, angry behavior originates primarily from the subject's childhood relationships with his parents. The hostile person is one who has developed feelings of insecurity and now tries to protect his weak self-concept by attacking others.

Several factors are important in considering the origin of hostile behavior.

Discipline. Unnecessary, inconsistent, and harsh discipline are contributing factors to the development of hostility. Severe

---

[1]Some individuals are fearful of directly expressing their feelings of aggression. Instead, they turn this hostility toward themselves. For a discussion of this dynamic of introverted hostility, see GUILT and DEPRESSIVE REACTIONS in this volume.

discipline usually makes the child feel unwanted, unloved and resentful. Because he has been the victim of harsh treatment at the hand of his parents, he believes that the world is a hostile place and that stressful situations are to be met with anger and hatred. Since he had to suffer, he unconsciously attempts to punish others with verbal remarks and overt behavior.

Overdependence. The overindulgent parent attempts to supply his child with his every whim. He is overprotective and cautious to the extreme, not allowing the child to develop his own independence. As the overprotected child grows older he feels bound and helpless because of his extreme dependence upon his parents. He wishes to be an individual who can stand on his own two feet, but he is unable to throw off his parental control and involvement. Because of such restriction, he becomes hostile and resentful.

Improper Training. Frequent expressions of anger may also be the result of improper training. If a child is able to gain attention and get his own way by exhibiting temper tantrums, he may frequently turn to this type of behavior in other situations when he wants his way.

Parental Inconsistency. Hostile attitudes are often incurred by parents who are inconsistent. This may occur in two ways. One or both parents may vacillate from loving acceptance to angry rejection of the child, or the parents may present opposite viewpoints toward his training and behavior. The father, for example, may be a strict disciplinarian, while the mother goes to the other extreme in leniency. She may even openly criticize the husband for his harsh rules and "unreasonable" demands. In such situations the child is insecure because he does not know what to expect from his parents. As a result he becomes confused and irritated.

Imitation of Parents. Many children who express their disappointments and frustrations with outbursts of anger are merely imitating their parents. When parents fail to control their temper, children often grow up accepting these expressions of anger as normal. Consequently, they exhibit their own emotions in the same way.

Physical Causes. Sudden outbursts of temper are sometimes

associated with brain injury. A child with brain damage is often hyperactive and restless and may show wide fluctuation of performance. He may be quiet and likeable at one moment but an instant later show aggressive and hostile behavior. The overall physical health of an individual also plays an important role in cases of anger and hostility. Although not a basic causative factor, the person who suffers from poor health is more likely to be easily upset and frustrated.

Illustration

Identification: White male, age 35
Presenting Problem: Patient's inability to get along with others.
Personal and Family History: The patient was the only child born to parents of upper middle-class status. The mother was concerned for her son's welfare. She did not allow him to play with neighborhood children often for fear they would take advantage of him. She supplied his every wish, and when he gave indication of physical discomfort, she put him to bed and often called a physician.

The father was extremely concerned that his son be a "model" child. He used harsh discipline to make certain that the boy would be obedient and respectful. After the client had graduated from college, he took a job with a large corporation. He married at the age of 27. During college and at work the patient had difficulty working closely with others. He often became upset if he did not get his way and found it difficult to cooperate with others. In the office he frequently became irritated with the secretaries and scolded them for petty inefficiencies.

His hostile behavior also seriously affected his family life. He argued with his wife and often shouted at the children to be more obedient and respectful.

Treatment

Children: In dealing with hostile children, parents should be assisted to see the importance of a peaceful, noncritical atmosphere in the home. Consistent attitudes and discipline are also essential in the development of a well-adjusted child.

When a child throws a temper tantrum it is important that

the parents do not become upset, angry or unduly attentive to him.[2] Giving in to the child in order to silence his anger only increases the likelihood of undesirable behavior in the future. Parents should attempt to understand why their child is upset and the episode should be dealt with calmly.

Parents must also see that by providing a good example they will instill the concept of the rights of others. In this way, children will learn that it is not always possible to have their own way.

Medical examinations are likewise important. Some children are harboring rather severe physical problems which are unknown to them, their parents or their teachers. Upon correction of these problems the hostile behavior is alleviated.

Adults. The first step in counseling with a hostile adult generally centers upon ventilation of the hostile feelings. Before therapy can delve deeply into all of the causes of his disturbances, he must get his feelings of anger and hostility out in the open so he can discuss and evaluate them. Following this, the therapist needs to focus upon the person's concept of himself. The hostile individual needs to come to the realization that his angry reactions are actually a method of trying to defend his own self-concept against various threats and frustrations.

Spiritual factors are of utmost importance in dealing with hostile individuals. Since the person is insecure he is easily threatened and often reacts with hostility. If, however, he can develop a new self-concept and a new sense of security, the basic source of his hostility will be removed. This new sense of personal adequacy and security comes through (1) an understanding of the previous experiences which have caused him to become hostile and (2) through the development of a new sense of security in the Lord. The believer in Jesus Christ can come to a full understanding of God's love and His eternal watchcare over the individual believer. When a person realizes his true position in Christ and the fact that God is in control of his life,

---

[2]For a discussion of Temper Tantrums see the author's book, *Young Children and Their Problems.*

there need be no remaining fear and insecurity.[3] Freedom from these feelings removes the necessity of protecting oneself against imaginary attacks by outbursts of hostility.

If feelings of hostility are the result of physical problems, professional medical care should be sought. In many cases a physical examination reveals hidden ailments which are influencing the person's behavior. The alleviation of these physical conditions may bring significant release from hostile impulses.

[3]For a discussion of methods of overcoming this problem, see INSECURITY in this volume.

28. Hypochondriacal Reaction

Description

Hypochondria is a neurotic condition characterized by excessive preoccupation with one's health without accompanying organic pathologies.[1] Although hypochondriacs claim they are suffering from various aches and pains, the physician can find no organic basis for their complaints. Hypochondria is in many ways similar to neurasthenia. The principle difference is that the hypochondriac complains of a disorder in a specific organ, whereas the neurasthenic complains of a more general loss of health and vigor.

Hypochondriacs often spend much time reading medical journals, health magazines and newspaper articles on disease. They are quick to ascribe to themselves physical illnesses ranging from cancer to heart ailments.

Some hypochondriacs are also extreme food faddists. They follow the latest trends and developments in health foods and keep their kitchens well-stocked with supplies of such commodities. These individuals are often characterized by instability and immaturity, especially in their approach to problems.

Etiology

Hypochondriacal symptoms are customarily the *result of childhood experiences*. Early in life an unwanted or insecure child learns that physical illness usually brings him sympathy and attention. Future hypochondriacs often show undue preoccupation with health matters, even at a very young age.

Some people manifest hypochondriacal symptoms *in order to control others*. A sudden illness or an intense pain may often be enough to discourage a previously planned group activity and to center attention on the person showing symptoms of physical distress.

The parents' role in the development of hypochondria in

---

[1]For a discussion of this disorder, see Kisker, George W.: *The Disorganized Personality*, McGraw-Hill, New York, London, 1964.

their children cannot be overemphasized. If the child's mother or father is prone to hypochondriacal tendencies, it is only natural that the child will also place an exaggerated emphasis on bodily health. *When parents exhibit extreme concern over every slight physical ailment,* children soon learn that illness can be advantageous. They grow up with the subconscious realization that when difficult or threatening situations arise they can rely upon physical illnesses as a way out.

When an individual has had *numerous illnesses in his childhood* which have met with much sympathy and overconcern, he may unconsciously retreat to a similar situation in adulthood as a means of demanding attention.

Another major cause of hypochondria is a *feeling of failure and disappointment.* The person who reaches for unrealistic goals which he is unable to attain may seek an excuse to justify his failures. Physical illness seems to be a logical explanation. By hiding behind hypochondriacal symptoms, he escapes the stigma attached to failure and gains the spotlight that would have been warranted by success.

Feelings of guilt, especially those related to moral behavior, may also be causal factors in the development of hypochondriacal reactions.[2] If a person is concerned over his past behavior, he may constantly look for signs of the punishment which he feels is due him. To such a person physical illness is easily interpreted as retribution for past sins.

Illustration

Identification: White male, age 35

Presenting Problem: The patient has seen several medical doctors during the last two years. He complains of severe stomach pains and headaches and has an intense fear of cancer.

Personal and Family History: This man is an only child. His father died of cancer when the boy was eight years of age. His mother was very protective and concerned about her son's physical welfare. Financial pressure made it necessary that she return to work. Consequently, she was unable to spend much

[2]For a discussion of this dynamic see GUILT in this volume.

time with her son. At the age of ten the boy had a prolonged illness and the mother was forced to quit her job in order to care for him.

During his school years the patient had difficulty in forming close interpersonal relationships. He did well academically, but he failed to participate in many social activities. He married shortly after graduating from high school in an effort to escape his mother's overprotectiveness. However, his childhood experiences prevented him from being mature enough to cope with adult problems. Therefore, he subconsciously turned to illness as a crutch and has seen medical specialists almost continually since he was married.

His medical history reveals complaints of minor pains and illnesses without any known physical basis. His condition is becoming increasingly severe. He now fears that he is suffering from incurable cancer in addition to numerous other physical maladies.

The patient has recently suffered a serious financial setback and is upset and worried over this failure.

Treatment

In counseling with the hypochondriac, it is necessary to come to an understanding of the emotional needs which the individual is attempting to fulfill by means of physical complants. If the subject is basically an insecure person seeking for affection and attention, his childhood experiences should be examined in order to determine the basis of these feelings.[3] He needs to realize that his security should be based upon his absolute position in Christ rather than upon the acceptance which his friends might give him. Through counseling the client can see that his feelings of insecurity are based upon childhood experiences. As he gains an understanding of the causes of his behavior and beings to see his true position and total acceptance in Christ, the person is freed from the need to seek attention through the exhibition of physical symptoms.

Closely tied in with feelings of insecurity are the instances

[3]See the discussion of INSECURITY in this volume.

when a person turns to hypochondriacal symptoms in order to have an excuse for failures. Here again attention should be turned to the ineffectiveness of this type of behavior and consideration of the basic emotional causes for the actions. The person needs to understand the reasons for his excessive goals and learn to more realistically evaluate his potential. Since this person is experiencing feelings of failure due to his insecurity, the counselor needs to help him overcome these attitudes.

An individual turning to physical complaints because of severe feelings of guilt and need of punishment must be helped to fully express his feelings of worthlessness and guilt. Then, gradually, he can be led to a deep understanding of the complete forgiveness of sins through the blood of Christ. "In whom we have redemption through his blood, the forgiveness of sins, according to the riches of his grace" (Ephesians 1:7). As he comes to comprehend and assimilate the new life he has in Christ, he will accept and act upon the fact that "As far as the east is from the west, so far hath he removed our transgressions from us" (Psalm 103:12). He will then gradually lose the need to turn to physical illnesses for the punishment he feels he deserves.[4]

---

[4]See the discussion of GUILT in this volume.

29. Impotence and Frigidity

Description

Frigidity is a condition of the female marked by a lack of sexual desire or the inability to experience orgasm. The severity of frigidity may range from the woman who has slight sexual desires to the woman who has strong feelings of disgust toward sex. It is also important to realize that some women have adequate sexual desire but are unable to receive gratification because of emotional conflicts.

A male condition similar to frigidity in women is impotence. The impotent man may either lack sexual desires or he may be unable to achieve sexual gratification through intercourse. As in the woman, the severity in the man may range from very little desire for sexual relations to extreme thoughts of repulsiveness regarding sexual matters.[1]

Feelings of guilt and inadequacy over sexual impotence and frigidity often result in other emotional symptoms such as anxiety and depression. Since sexual adjustment is a major area of one's total personality pattern, problems such as impotence and frigidity are likely to affect general feelings of adequacy.

When considering problems of sex, it is important to realize that there is a wide range of normality in sexual drives and responses. Differences which vary from the norm, therefore, should not necessarily be considered as maladjustments. For example, some married couples desire sexual intercourse only once or twice a month while others may enjoy coitus several times a week. Similarly, a person may respond sexually in a normal fashion in certain instances, but be unable to experience the same reactions at other times. Such differences do not necessarily signal special problems.

Etiology

In some cases of impotence and frigidity there is a *physical* factor leading to decreased sexual functioning. In most in-

[1]For a discussion of related sexual maladjustments, see EXHIBITIONISM, HOMO-SEXUALITY, INCEST, MASTURBATION and SEXUAL DEVIATION in this volume.

stances, however, the underlying causes are of an emotional nature. Some of the most common causes of frigidity and impotence are the following:

Feelings of Sexual Inadequacy: Some people have experiences which have caused them to develop strong feelings of inadequacy in their sexual roles. They are shy and afraid of showing this inadequacy in sexual relations. Such an attitude of fearfulness is responsible for some cases of impotence and frigidity.

Unwholesome Sexual Attitudes: When parental emphasis has been on the dirtiness and evil of sex, boys and girls may experience difficulty in making normal sexual adjustment when they reach adulthood. They enter marriage with years of experience which points to the shame and disgust associated with sex. It is then, of course, very difficult to immediately discard these distorted viewpoints and replace them with wholesome attitudes so necessary to satisfactory sexual adjustment.

Latent Homosexuality: Men and women who have not developed normal heterosexual relationships throughout life frequently experience difficulties in sexual adjustment. Some individuals have homosexual tendencies but are not aware of them. Whether known or unknown, these feelings may prohibit the development of normal heterosexual relationships within marriage. A man, for example, who was raised by an overprotective, overindulgent mother may have identified so closely with her that now, as a grown man, he thinks of all women (including his wife) as mother figures. Therefore, normal sex relations in marriage are repulsive to him.

Repressed Hostility: Deep feelings of hostility and resentment toward the parent of the opposite sex are another possible cause of impotence and frigidity. For example, a woman may harbor strong feelings of resentment toward her father, which she projects onto other men. Since she has these feelings she is unable to achieve sexual gratification in marriage. Similarly, a man may hold resentments, either consciously or unconsciously, toward his mother, stepmother or some other female authority figure. This, too, interferes with his feelings toward his wife and he does not want normal sexual relations with her.

An Inconsiderate Sexual Partner: A woman may experience difficulty in achieving sexual satisfaction because her husband is concerned only with his own gratification. He may be hasty and rude during intercourse, thus making it a very unsatisfying experience for the wife. This can also occur when the wife assumes an aggressive role in the family and in sexual intercourse. The husband may finally come to perceive of himself as an inadequate, passive person, quite overwhelmed by his dominant, aggressive wife. To him, his only recourse is to withdraw from sexual relations and thereby no longer expose his weakness to his wife.

Lack of Emotional Closeness to the Sexual Partner: A man and wife who do not have an emotionally secure marriage with sufficient natural display of affection may experience difficulty in achieving sexual gratification. A lack of love, daily quarrels and other upsetting feelings cannot be discarded at will. If people are to have a good sexual adjustment in marriage, an atmosphere of love and emotional security is essential.

Illustration
Identification: Male 28 years of age
Presenting Problem: The patient's wife first brought the problem of her husband's impotence to light when she talked to her family physician. After a brief discussion the physician encouraged the wife to talk to her husband about coming to see the doctor.

The husband was reluctant to seek professional help, but after months of insistence by his wife, he did see the family doctor. It soon became evident that the causes for the patient's impotence were very deep, stemming from experiences during childhood. The patient was then referred to a Christian psychologist who saw the man once a week for several months.
Personal and Family History: The patient was raised in a middle-class home of average income. He had two sisters older than he. The father was regularly employed at a moderate salary as a bookkeeper in a small firm. The mother was a homemaker who worked intermittently as a waitress in a nearby cafe.

The patient told the psychologist that his relationship with his father was always distant and strained. But he revealed that he felt close to his mother. Further discussion pointed up the fact that his closeness to his mother was unhealthy inasmuch as she was overindulgent and possessive.

The patient was married at the age of twenty-five, but was unable to have satisfactory sex relations because he felt guilty over sexual matters. Finally, he turned to alcohol. He learned that by becoming intoxicated he could forget his true feelings and have somewhat satisfactory relations with his wife. This, however, led to increased guilt feelings after he had become sober and had reflected on the whole procedure.

Since his wife did not understand the problem, she accused her husband of immorality with other women and openly ridiculed him. This naturally made the situation worse. Through several months of therapy the patient became sufficiently well-adjusted to have normal sex relations.

Treatment

After a thorough physical examination, treatment of individuals suffering from impotence and frigidity must center upon the emotional conflicts causing the disturbance. The counselor should help the client understand the reasons for the problem, then encourage complete ventilation. As the person comes to understand the causes of his problem, then discusses them fully, the troublesome impulses will begin to diminish. In time he will develop normal sex feelings.

If the basic causes are related to immorality and other sinful experiences, the counselor will not only lead the client to deep insights, he will also encourage him to ask God's forgiveness through confessing his sin. When Christ comes in He cleanses the heart and gives release from guilt and sin.[2]

The development of socialization, first with family members and then with peer groups, is an important consideration in evaluating a persons's sexual adjustment. A client can begin to see himself and the causes for his maladjustments as he real-

---

[2]See the discussion of GUILT in this volume.

istically looks at his relationships with his family and his acquaintances.

Any unconscious feelings such as hostility need to be examined and discussed in the light of present emotional adjustment. In the case of an inconsiderate sexual partner, it is necessary for the counselor to work closely with both parties in order to fully evaluate the total marriage relationship as well as the sexual adjustment.

Reeducation of attitudes toward sex is nearly always necessary. The counselor needs to help the person develop a wholesome understanding of the body's sexual functioning and the importance of healthy attitudes toward sexual intercourse and reproduction. Specific suggestions concerning coitus may also prove beneficial.[3]

Counseling sessions devoted to the Biblical teachings regarding sex will help a client to see that sex in marriage is right and wholesome and ordained of God. This basic understanding can become one of the most significant factors in helping to reduce frigidity and impotence.

[3]Many married couples have found the following book helpful: Lewin, S. A. and Gilmore, John: *Sex Without Fear*, The Medical Research Press, New York, 1962.

30. Incest

Description
Incest refers to sexual relations between family members or close relatives. Among the most common forms of incest are sexual relationships between brothers and sisters, and fathers and daughters.[1]

Etiology
One of the major factors contributing to incestual relationships is an *overcrowded living condition*. When a brother and sister are forced to share the same bed or bedroom because of inadequate living space, they may engage in sexual experimentation, especially during the adolescent period.

Incestual relationships are found more commonly among *families of low moral standards*. Homes with no Christian influence and a lack of moral and spiritual integrity are more likely to produce this sexual deviation.

A *personality maladjustment in an adult* may also lead to incest. For example, a father who is immature, insecure, cruel or mentally ill may force sex relations upon his daughter. One who is withdrawn and who is isolated from social contacts is more likely to turn to incestual relations.

A *desire for information regarding human reproduction and sexual functioning* may also contribute to a minor's involvement in the incestual relations. In an effort to learn more about sex, an adolescent, for example, may engage in sexual relations with a brother, sister or another member of the family.

Illustration
Identification: White male, age 34
Presenting Problem: The subject was suspected of having had incestual relations with his fourteen-year-old daughter after she had talked to a social worker about her pregnant condition. In a subsequent interview, the girl admitted having had relations

[1]For a discussion of related disturbances see SEXUAL DEVIATION in this volume.

with her father. At the time of his apprehension by local law authorities, the father admitted his guilt.

Personal and Family History: The subject and his daughter lived in an economically deprived home in an isolated rural area. She was the oldest of six children. Her mother, a cripple, suffered from chronic illness. The father was a poorly educated farmer, unable to make an adequate living for the family. People in the area described him as "peculiar" and "alone."

The father introduced the daughter to sexual relations when she was only nine years of age. She told authorities that her father continually warned her not to tell anyone, otherwise they would both be taken away from their home.

The girl made poor grades in school until she finally dropped out in the sixth grade at the age of thirteen. She had few friends at school or elsewhere in the community.

Treatment

Through a number of counseling sessions a person involved in incestual relations can come to see the unnaturalness and wrongness of his actions. If crowded living conditions are largely responsible for the beginning of the difficulty, they should be corrected. Adolescent brothers and sisters should not be left alone without supervision. Parents who are away from home many evenings or for extended periods of time should see that their children have adequate supervision.

Therapy for such a person needs to be directed toward a better self-understanding and a recognition of the factors which led to the perversion. He can then be helped to develop an adequate self-concept and a realistic appraisal of himself and his behavior. Sex education is also helpful, especially to young people who are involved.

After understanding the immorality associated with incestual relationships, the person can come to a knowledge of God's complete forgiveness for his misdeeds. Subsequent Christian activities will help him grow in every way, thus becoming a more adequate, responsible person.

31. Inferiority

Description
The person with an inferiority complex is characterized by feelings of incompetency and a lack of personal adequacy.[1] Most people experience inferiority feelings occasionally, but some are plagued by them throughout their daily experiences.

Among the most common symptoms of inferiority feelings are:

Attention-getting behavior: The individual continually seeks to gain the attention of others.

Self-consciousness: The subject is easily embarrassed and upset.

Over-sensitiveness: The person cannot stand criticism or comparison with others.

Enviousness: The subject is jealous or envious of the personal qualities or possessions of others.

Perfectionism: The individual is afraid that his performance is unsatisfactory.

Domination: The person may attempt to lord it over those who are inferior to him.

Seclusiveness: The individual does not like to engage in social activities, but prefers to remain alone.

Compensation: The person hides his feelings of inferiority by concentrating on developing one trait which will gain the attention and respect of others.

Criticism: The subject may habitually criticize others in an effort to create and maintain a more adequate self image.

Etiology
Feelings of inferiority develop when one believes that he does not measure up. This may stem from comparing himself with others, thinking he is not equal to them. They may also result from things he feels he cannot accomplish. Real or imagined

---

[1]For a related discussion see INSECURITY in this volume.

deficiencies of either mental or physical functions may result in feelings of inferiority.

Most self-depreciation concepts stem from early childhood. Among the adult attitudes responsible for the development of inferiority feelings in children are:

Rejection. When parents make a child feel that he is unwanted and unloved, he frequently develops the attitude that he is unworthy and that his behavior does not measure up to the standards of others. Parental rejection is often a causative factor in feelings of inferiority.

Frequent punishment. Some individuals develop serious feelings of inferiority because they have undergone constant punishment which was not appropriate to the misbehavior. When a child is punished too frequently and too severely his parents are in essence saying, "You don't live up to what is expected of you. You don't suit us." Such punishment tends to establish a basic personality pattern characterized by feelings of personal inferiority.

Teasing: Calling a child by undesirable nicknames and generally making fun of him is also damaging to one's self-concept. This dynamic is often found among people who themselves feel insecure and ill at ease.

Negative correction: When parents humiliate a child by severe scolding and ridicule, especially in the presence of others, they instill in him an attitude of his own unworthiness. Continued over a period of time this parental behavior can cause serious personality maladjustments.

Unfavorable comparison: Some parents continually compare the actions and accomplishments of one sibling with those of another. They do not understand that people are different; or, perhaps they use comparison to "shame" a child into changing his behavior. When parents make unfavorable comparisons between children, they cause the child to feel inadequate, inferior and insecure.

Oversolicitude: Another basic cause of feelings of inferiority is the refusal of parents to let a child make his own decisions and learn to assume responsibility. When parents closely guide every activity of their child they instill in him the feeling that he must rely upon others for help. Eventually he feels incapable of doing things by himself. Unless this attitude is corrected he will go through life leaning on others.

Perfectionism: By requiring especially high and unrealistic standards parents are laying a foundation for feelings of inferiority in a child. Being unable to reach the excessive expectations, the child feels inadequate and inferior.

Disappointing experiences: Experiences of failure in later life often serve as precipitating events for strong feelings of inferiority. When a person is basically insecure, the trauma and feelings of inadequacy associated with a failure to perform one's duties capably may bring about increased feelings of inferiority. Marital conflicts and acute financial reversals are examples of these experiences.

Illustration

Identification: White female, age 27

Presenting Problem: The subject finds it difficult to engage in social activities because of extreme feelings of inferiority. In a situation which calls for comparisons or competition she becomes uneasy and sensitive. Although she likes people and wants to be with them, she becomes upset because of her feelings of inferiority and inadequacy.

Personal and Family History: The patient is the youngest of three children. In school her oldest sister was academically superior. The subject's parents frequently pointed out that she was not showing the abilities and talents of her older sister. Even as a child she was encouraged to perform each task "perfectly." Her school assignments had to be superior and all of her household duties "just right."

The subject had no close friends as a child. She was alone most of the time. During school she did not participate in extracurricular activities, but spent much time studying. After a year of college she married and now has three children. She is unhappy and complains of being a failure and not being able to do anything right.

Treatment
Children: If a child has developed general feelings of inferiority, steps should be taken to *provide him with experiences in which he feels comfortable.* Success, no matter how small, builds up his self-confidence. Situations which demand undue competition should be avoided.

Parents and teachers should show confidence in the child's abilities. It is important that he be given sufficient praise and opportunities to excel in those areas in which he has interest. He should be encouraged to attempt simple tasks and as his confidence increases he can be given more complex ones.

When an adult spends *time with a child it is usually interpreted by the child as personal affection and appreciation.* In time, the child will come to feel that he is adequate because he is accepted and loved by adults.

When parents *respect the rights of a child* they are helping him to develop adequate self-concepts. Encouraging a child to talk and express his views signals to him that he is significant. When a child is helped to make his own decisions he comes to think of himself as worthwhile and competent.

Adults: Treatment in adults is more difficult. The client must investigate with the counselor the *factors in childhood which have led to the development of feelings of inadequacy.* As the client begins to see these forces and their effect upon him, he can learn to evaluate his true capacities and abilities. Thus, he can adjust his goals more realistically.

Naturally, *the counselor's acceptance of the client* helps to instill confidence and feelings of worthwhileness. With this beginning the therapist can help the counselee take the next steps toward a more desirable self-image.

When counseling with clients who have inferior feelings, *spiritual aspects are especially important.* Through the Bible the counselor can help the counselee to thoroughly understand his position in Christ. God's love, watchcare, guidance and provision can also become a vital part of the client's inner re-sources. A further aspect of spiritual counseling concerns God's will and God's provision of talent to accomplish this will. As the person begins to gain a clear understanding of his worthi-ness before God through Christ, he can develop a more healthy concept of his own abilities.

32. Insecurity

Description

A basic psychological phenomenon which is common to most types of mental and emotional disturbances is the feeling of insecurity. Hostility, depression, and many of the psychotic disorders have insecurity as the common element.

The insecure individual is a person lacking in feelings of self-confidence. He feels inadequate, unwanted and unloved, and as a result is vulnerable to constant emotional conflict. The insecure person is often a nervous individual susceptible to constant worry and apprehension.

A well-adjusted person has the confidence and self-reliance to meet the stresses and strains of daily living. When a conflict or frustration arises the normal person has a "defensive structure" which is sufficient to handle the situation. He is not overwhelmed by difficulties. Instead, he is able to work through the situation to a solution and thereby maintain the necessary feelings of personal adequacy.

The insecure individual is unable to do this. When a frustration or conflict arises he feels overwhelmed. Rather than being able to calmly deal with the situation and resolve the frustration, this person feels unable to stand up to the stress. He is fearful and does not have the needed confidence in himself to cope with the problem. The well-adjusted person, on the other hand, has adequate defenses to handle such conflicts. Being open to attack by nearly every frustration and conflict, however minor, the insecure person may then develop one of the many forms of emotional and mental illness.

Etiology

There are innumerable experiences throughout life which may cause a person to develop feelings of insecurity. The most frequent of these are discussed below.

Parental rejection and lack of love. If a person is to grow into adulthood with a wholesome self-concept and with feelings of personal worth and adequacy, it is important that his early home environment provide him with a free interchange of love and affection. Some parents, however, because of their own emotional maladjustment, are unable to meet their children's needs for love. In some cases the parental rejection may be very obvious, as in the case of a mother who does not want her newborn baby and therefore fails to pay adequate attention to him. In other instances the child may interpret as rejection the fact that his parents both work during the day and spend little time with him in the evening. Many times, for example, a child will run up to a parent to show a new school project or to ask a question, only to be told, "Go on now, I'm tired and want to rest for awhile." If this parent-child pattern continues over a long period of time, it is only natural that the young person will develop serious feelings of insecurity.

Domineering parents. Other children develop feelings of insecurity because of the overbearing manner of their parents. Some parents regulate every aspect of a child's development. They allow the child no deviation from their expectations. He may be told what to wear, where to go and what to do, with little or no opportunity to express his own feelings. In these cases the parents are lacking in understanding of the child and are being inconsiderate of his feelings. Sometimes parents strictly manage their children because of their own insecurities and their fears that the child may get out of their control. This makes the young child feel that he is incapable of doing anything on his own. Since his parents do not allow him any individuality and freedom to make decisions, he is likely to enter adulthood with the same attitude and be unable to handle situations himself. When placed in a frustrating environment, he does not feel capable of standing on his own, since as a child he was never allowed to do this.

Perfectionistic and overly critical parents. Human beings often learn and develop by making mistakes. Some teachers and parents, however, fail to realize that children are not miniature adults. An insecure parent will feel compelled to see that his children are functioning at the peak of efficiency. Even in very early childhood, parents often set unrealistic goals of accomplishment for their children. For example, as a child begins to develop speech some parents continally correct him to make sure he will learn "correct" speaking patterns. When the young child is given a small task about the home, the mother may be quick to point out all of the flaws in his performance and to tell him how he could have done better. As the child begins school he is continually criticized for failing to achieve top grades. If he brings home a "C" on his report card, it should have been a "B." If he brings home a "B," it should have been an "A." In this manner the parents are continually telling the growing child that they are dissatisfied with his performance. He is seldom praised and complimented; only corrected and criticized. As this person enters adulthood he will have a firmly established feeling of failure and insecurity. Even though he may have superior ability, obtain excellent grades, and hold a top executive position, he cannot throw off the feelings of insecurity. Pointing out the fact of his superior ability and accomplishment does not overcome the problem. The years of parental criticism cannot easily be remedied without a process of therapy which gives understanding of how the feelings developed.

Unstable home situation. Other cases of insecurity develop from an early home environment characterized by instability. Immature parents who drift from job to job and city to city and who fail to give stability and security to the home usually raise children who are laden with feelings of insecurity.

Adults feel much more secure and confident when they know what to expect in the days, weeks and months ahead. This is even more important to a child. If the young person feels unsure about the future; if he does not know what to expect by way of either economic or emotional support, he will likely develop feelings of insecurity and inadequacy.

Cruel and harsh discipline. In some families patterns of parental rejection go to severe limits. In these cases parents may inflict serious physical punishment upon their children, varying from excessively severe discipline to instances of unmerciful beating. This type of treatment is sometimes at the hands of alcoholic parents or those with severe emotional disturbances. Discipline can be firm and effective without being of a harsh physical nature. A child grows much more healthily from love and understanding than he does from fear of parental punishment.[1]

Negative correction. Some parents attempt to channel their child's behavior by verbal lashings which humiliate and belittle him. They may point out the child's mistakes by calling him "stupid" or "ignorant," or by teasing and giving him degrading nicknames. Such parental behavior readily instills into the young child the feeling that he is "no good" and unworthy. If parents continually call the child "stupid" or "ignorant," it is only natural that he may consider himself to be just that. Although these statements may shame the child into complying with the parent's wishes for the time being, in the long run they only serve to create serious personality problems.

Parents may also try to discipline their children by threatening them with frightening experiences like "throwing you in a hole," "burning your fingers," "giving you away," "sending you to a reform school," "cutting off your tongue," "giving you to the black people (or Indians)" or other such threats.

Instead of this, parents should correct or punish the child in a thoughtful manner, pointing out the wrongs he has done and showing him how to do better. This type of correction maintains an excellent relationship between the parents and the child and aids healthy emotional development.

Overindulgent parents. Some parents, mothers in particular, almost totally squelch the young child's emotional development. A boy or girl grows into a heathy, well-adjusted adult by gradually learning to meet life's situations for himself. But some mothers, for example, continue to dress their children until they are several years old. Instead of gradually teaching the child to dress himself as much as possible, she feels she must be sure that she completely dresses him to get everything "perfect." When the child goes out to play the mother watches nearly every move he makes. She hesitates to let him play with neighborhood children for fear he may be physically harmed. When the child wants to try a new task in the home, such as

---

[1]For a more complete discussion of the problem of discipline, see the author's book *Discipline in the Christian Home.*

pouring his own milk, the mother says, "No, you had better let me do that." Every time the child tries to step out on his own and say to himself and the world, "I can do something myself," the mother is there to say, "No, you can't, I'll do that for you." As this child grows older he feels incapable of making his own decisions. Since for years he has been indulged by his mother and has not been allowed to make his own decisions, it is now impossible for him to feel capable of standing on his own and meeting the daily frustrations of life.

Unfavorable comparisons with siblings. Comparison of one child with another is another common cause of feelings of insecurity. Some parents attempt to motivate a child to do better in school or to improve his behavior by saying, "Why can't you be like Mary?" Such statements are detrimental to a young child. In essence, the parent is telling the child, "You have failed; Mary has not. I like Mary, but I don't like you." In this way the child grows up feeling that he is inadequate as compared to the sibling. He feels insecure and fearful because he has been continually told that he does not measure up to the other child.

Parental inconsistency. A child is happier when he knows what to expect. Some parents, however, are inconsistent in their methods of dealing with a child. This inconsistency may be one of two kinds. One parent, for example, may vacillate from a kind, loving, and permissive attitude on one day to a much more strict and severe reaction on another. In such a situation the child does not know what to expect from his parents day to day. This leads to feelings of insecurity. Another situation which yields uncertainty is when the two parents differ greatly in their methods of discipline. One parent may be lenient with the children while the other is much more strict and severe. There may even be open conflict between the parents as to which type of discipline should be used. In these cases the children are torn between the two parents. They do not know to whom they should look for guidance or what they might expect as a consequence of their behavior. Such uncertainty is a basic cause of insecurity.

Fearful and insecure parents. When a child's parents are

themselves fearful and insecure, it is natural for the child to develop similar patterns. In recounting her childhood, one lady, for example, told her counselor how her mother would grab her in fear during a thunderstorm and crawl under a table or bed. Had the mother reacted in a normal way this child would not have become so fearful. But because she was continually exposed to fearful situations, she developed into a shy and fearful person who had serious adjustment difficulties in later life. One of the basic reasons was the parent's continued fearful behavior.

Absence of parents. Some children are raised without one or both parents, yet they achieve a satisfactory personality adjustment. In such cases there are usually adults, possibly other family members, relatives, teachers, or men and women in the community, who serve as important adult figures. But with many children, the absence of one or both parents mitigates against excellent personality development. When a boy or girl has no parents, he is prone to wonder if there is a warm, secure place for him in the world.

If a child has only one parent he may be neglected or even overindulged. He may also wonder what would happen to him if his one parent should die. As one woman told her counselor, "My father died when I was very young and my mother did her best to make up for the lack. I became very close to my mother, but I often wondered what would happen to me if she died. I used to think about which relative I might have to live with or whether I would be sent to an orphanage. In fact, in kindness my mother talked with me about what relative I should ask for in case she should pass away. I don't know; maybe what she did was best, but I grew up feeling very insecure."

Traumatic experiences. A person sometimes suffers an extremely upsetting and traumatic experience. The fear and emotional upset associated with such an event may become deeply imbedded in the personality structure of an individual and cause serious feelings of anxiety and insecurity for years to come. One adolescent girl, for example, was in an automobile accident in which her mother and brother were seriously injured. This girl had a close relationship with them and the sudden shock of the tragic accident proved very disturbing. After a number of months, however, the girl seemed to overcome the serious depressive reactions which were a result of the accident. Years later, while undergoing therapy for emotional disturbances, it was found that one of the basic causes of her feelings of insecurity was the traumatic car accident. Even though the woman felt she had overcome it, the unconscious effects of this traumatic experience had continued to plague her for years. As a child no one helped her to resolve her deep feelings, and consequently their residual effects lingered on.

Situational circumstances in adulthood. Some people with adequate childhood experiences develop feelings of insecurity in their adult years. Although these are often of less severity than long-standing personality disturbances, they can be very distressing. A woman in her forties, for example, saw a psychologist because of marital difficulties. Testing revealed that she did not have any serious personality maladjustments, but that she was currently experiencing a high level of anxiety and strong feelings of insecurity. During counseling it became apparent that much of her difficulty was arising from the inadequate relationship with her husband. He was suffering from serious emotional difficulties and he frequently took his feelings out on his mate. He began drinking heavily a few years after their marriage and often criticized and physically abused his wife. Many years of this treatment resulted in her feelings of insecurity and fearfulness.

The lack of a genuine conversion and inadequate spiritual understanding. Many cases of insecurity are compounded by a lack of spiritual growth and understanding. The person outside of Christ is unaware of the security, confidence, and peace of mind which can be imparted fully only through the acceptance of Jesus Christ as Savior. When we trust in Christ, God becomes our Father and we become His sons. "But as many as received him, to them gave he power to become the sons of God, even to them that believe on his name" (John 1:12). God also says that we are "heirs of God" and "joint heirs with Christ."

Such Biblical knowledge, however, must be internalized and

become a part of one's daily living. Even Christian leaders with years of seminary training can know the Scriptures and yet not assimilate them into their very existence. They cannot actually say, "For me to live is Christ . . . in him I live and move and have my being."

The realization that as Christians we are in Christ is a tremendous source of confidence and security. The insecure person needs to realize that he is in the Father's hand: "And I give unto them eternal life; and they shall never perish, neither shall any man pluck them out of my hand. My Father, which gave them me, is greater than all; and no man is able to pluck them out of my Father's hand" (John 10:28, 29). Without this assurance of eternal life and God's constant watchcare, a person is much more vulnerable to feelings of insecurity and inadequacy.

Treatment

Counseling with the person suffering from feelings of insecurity and fearfulness is especially rewarding. It is a great satisfaction to see a person with lack of self-confidence gradually develop into a mature and secure adult with an increased sense of adequacy and a new joy and zest for living. In some individuals with less serious feelings of insecurity much progress may be made in only eight or ten sessions. In most cases, however, therapy needs to continue over a number of weeks if the person is to thoroughly resolve his attitudes and replace his feelings with new and improved adjustment.

The first step in counseling with the insecure individual is to allow him to express freely the fears, hesitancies and insecurities which are interfering with his personal happiness. The very opportunity to discuss these feelings is an important aspect of therapy. In many instances the counselor is the first individual with whom the person has ever felt free to discuss his innermost feelings.

As the counselee begins to discuss his current feelings, the counselor will want to initiate the second basic stage in therapy. This is an evaluation of the experiences in the subject's background which have caused him to be this way. By skilled questioning the counselor can lead the person to discuss the early relationships with his parents, teachers and other significant figures. As this is done the person must begin to see the relationship between his early experiences and his present feelings. It is not enough to merely discuss past experiences. Only as the person understands the relation of these childhood experiences to his current attitudes will his feelings lose their hold. A question the trained counselor will often raise is, "How do you feel this experience has affected your emotional adjustment through the years?" or "When this happened to you, how did it make you feel?" This process of gaining insight is the core of therapy and usually requires a number of counseling sessions. All of the possible causes of insecurity listed above will want to be carefully considered to see which ones give clues to understanding the specific problem which the counselee presents.

As the person begins to gain relief of symptoms from discussing his problem and receives insight into the causes of his behavior, the counselor will bring into the heart of therapy the client's spiritual growth and understanding. Experience indicates that clients who make the most significant and lasting progress are those who have been led into a thorough understanding of their position in Christ. Genuine spiritual conversion and a close walk with God are of utmost importance in overcoming feelings of insecurity.

The insecure individual is in need of love, understanding and stability. The Word of God speaks with authority to these very problems. The Scriptures teach of our need of the Savior and of His continued guidance. As the believer begins to understand the wonderful dealings of God with man he gains a new sense of confidence and joy which is impossible outside of Christ. The whole process of human life and existence comes into focus when one comes to grips with the full teachings of the eternal Word of God.

Confidence is bright for those who are in Christ and who know that with His soon coming they will be transformed into His risen likeness. One of the greatest sources of encouragement and growth for the insecure individual is the great truth spoken by the Apostle Paul, "For I am persuaded, that neither death, nor life, nor angels, nor principalities, nor powers, nor things present, nor things to come, nor height, nor depth, nor any other creature, shall be able to separate us from the love of God, which is in Christ Jesus our Lord" (Romans 8:38, 39). Indeed, life in Christ brings security.

33. Involutional Psychotic Reaction

Description

Involutional psychotic reaction is a depressive reaction that has its onset during the involution period—that is, when physical, mental and sexual functioning begin to decline. This period varies greatly in individuals but it may begin as early as 40 to 55 in women and about 50 to 65 in men. The chief symptoms are depression, worry, restlessness and apprehensiveness. The two major types of involutional reactions are (1) the depressed and (2) the paranoid.

Depressed: The depressed individual exhibits symptoms of sadness, apprehensiveness, restlessness and fatigue. He may express his uselessness and worthlessness to those about him and may have sudden spells of weeping. He may feel he has committed some unpardonable sin or that he is unworthy of living and may even contemplate suicide.

Paranoid: In addition to the usual symptoms of the depressive, the paranoid exhibits delusional thought processes. His delusions are usually of a persecutory nature such as fears that others are attempting to minimize him, ruin his business, harm his family or take his life.

Etiology

Involutional psychotic reaction develops out of a combination of physical and emotional factors. In understanding the origins of these disturbances it is important to consider (1) the individuals premorbid personality structure, (2) physiological changes associated with the involutional period, and (3) psychological factors associated with this period.

Premorbid personality structure. One of the most significant factors in understanding the dynamics of involutional psychotic reaction is a knowledge of the person's previous personality patterns. It is extremely rare that a well-adjusted person suddenly develops a severe emotional disturbance during middle-age, even in response to dramatic physical changes. Instead, these reactions occur in an individual who has had minimal adjustment throughout life. The person may not have experienced any previous severe personality difficulties, but finds that added stresses of the involutional period undermine his past defenses and leave him vulnerable to mental illness.

The premorbid personality structure of the person suffering from an involutional psychotic reaction is generally one of anxiety and insecurity. Throughout life this person has been susceptible to emotional conflicts and may have evidenced a self-critical attitude and an intropunitive manner of handling hostility. Because he has had adequate defenses, however, and has not been placed under severe stress, the person has gone through life without any serious adjustment difficulties.

Physiological precipitating factors. When an individual with a basic personality structure of insecurity enters the involutional period, various physical changes begin to lower his resistance to emotional conflicts. One of these physical factors is an increasing decline of bodily functions and an overall diminishing of physical energy. Other important physiological factors are hormonal changes with a resultant disturbance of body chemistry. The full effect of these physiological changes is not yet known, but clinical evidence has consistently demonstrated the effect of these changes on personality functioning. Any combination of these physical conditions may lower the person's total resistance. This allows emotional conflicts (which may in the past have been handled adequately) to overpower the individual, resulting in serious personality disturbances.[1]

Psychological precipitating factors. A significant consideration in understanding involutional psychotic reactions is the effect of the person's psychological attitudes toward this period of life. During the involutional period, an individual who is basically insecure begins to realize he is nearing the end of his life span. He evaluates past achievements and begins to stress his failures. He sees experiences which he could have handled

[1]For a medical discussion of the relationship between physical and emotional stress, see: Selye, Hans: *The Stress of Life*, McGraw-Hill Book Company, New York, 1956.

more efficiently. He also looks into the future and, due to his insecurity, sees no hope for increased achievement. He may fear the loneliness of life without children in the home, and he may worry over financial insecurity. Sexual decline may also concern him. All of these factors are likely to combine to dim the person's outlook on life and bring about a change in behavior.

Illustration
Identification: White female, age 51

Presenting Problem: The patient came to the psychologist because of periods of severe depression. She complained of being unable to continue many of her activities because of her worry, depression and fatigue.

Personal and Family History: The patient is one of three children born into an upper middle-class home. During the subject's childhood the mother was employed and the child was frequently left with a baby sitter. She reports that her father died when she was ten years of age.

The patient had many normal childhood experiences. However, since her mother was employed, she spent much time away from home, playing with neighborhood friends. She graduated from high school and lived with her mother until she married at the age of 25.

The subject has had a good marriage, with two children. The youngest daughter, who had been living at home, moved to another city to take a different job. The patient now finds herself alone most of the time. A few months after her daughter left home her own mother died and the subject began to experience the present symptoms of depression.

Treatment
Therapy for involutional psychotic reactions should include both medical and psychological care. Since this person may be undergoing physiological changes, it is of utmost importance that a complete medical examination be given. Shock therapy is widely used in severe cases of depression to relieve initial symptoms and to get the patient to a point where individual or group therapy may be initiated.

After proper medical examination and treatment these individuals need psychotherapy directed at (1) their premorbid personality adjustment and (2) current situational stresses and emotional frustrations. A major portion of counseling with these individuals is directed toward the resolution of basic personality disturbances such as insecurity and depression.[2] The childhood experiences which have caused these individuals to have marginal adjustment and be susceptible to later emotional stresses must be discussed and resolved. The individual needs to be freed from feelings of guilt and to develop a more adequate sense of personal worth.

In addition to therapy directed toward past experiences, the person suffering from an involutional psychotic condition needs much help in resolving current emotional stresses and conflicts. The effect of separation from loved ones is often an important therapeutic consideration. Often parents whose children have grown and married develop feelings of loneliness and rejection. These attitudes need to be carefully discussed and alleviated. Fears of personal inadequacy and uselessness because of increasing age must also be resolved. Such clients need much reassurance and support in developing increased feelings of adequacy.

It is also important that they are occupied in part-time work or with various hobbies. These activities help to give a person a better sense of usefulness and may be of much encouragement.

Spiritual factors are also very important. These individuals need to find their sense of security and meaning in life through a faith in the Lord Jesus Christ. As they study His Word and continue to grow spiritually, they gain a renewed interest and confidence in life. By taking an active part in church activities a person can also invest his time in a worthwhile manner.

A total therapy program based upon a consideration of these physical, emotional, situational, and spiritual factors can bring great improvement and increased feelings of joy and satisfaction to the person suffering from involutional disturbances.

---

[2]See the discussion of these disturbances in this volume.

34. Jealousy

Description

Jealousy may be defined as an attitude of envy or resentment toward a more successful rival. Feelings of jealousy are usually the result of frustration in attempts to achieve a desired object. The jealous person exhibits numerous forms of behavior which reveal his true feelings. He is at odds with his environment. He may be suspicious and stubborn. He frequently attacks the individual who is the object of his envy by making slanderous statements or, in some cases, by actual physical assault. The jealous person is often irritable, high-strung and nervous. He feels that he cannot measure up to the standards and expectations of others. However, by slandering and downgrading those with more apparent ability, he attempts to enhance his own self-esteem.

In children some feeling of jealousy or sibling rivalry is universal. Parents should expect a certain amount of competition for success and recognition among children. Wholesome competition is an essential part of development. It is when attitudes of jealousy become fixed and very intense that they are symptomatic of emotional difficulties.

In addition to the usual characteristics of jealous behavior, more complex cases frequently exhibit other symptoms of maladjustment. These may be manifested in various types of sleep and eating disturbances. A child or an adult, for example, who is overcome with feelings of jealousy may refuse to eat regular meals, or, on the other hand, he may turn to continual eating as a substitute solace. Similarly, he may show his problem by not sleeping well or even by escaping into excessive sleep.

Etiology

Basic to most cases of jealousy is the *parental handling of early childhood relationships.* As already noted, some competitive behavior and jealousy is to be expected among all children. The parental handling of these initial experiences in competition is of utmost importance in the development of healthy attitudes of security and well-being. If parents help their children to develop healthy interpersonal relations and a respect for the rights of others, feelings of jealousy can often be avoided.

A common cause of jealousy in a child is the *coming of a baby* brother or sister. When a new baby enters the family he becomes the center of attention. The older child feels left out and is often resentful of the new arrival because it requires attention which was previously centered upon himself. Children who have been overprotected and have had excess attention lavished upon them are particularly vulnerable to feelings of jealousy when a new member is born into the family.

Excessive competiton may also stimulate jealousy. Parents who challenge their children to outdo each other in play and school accomplishments usually create a situation that is unwholesome. Making unfavorable comparisons with brothers or sisters is a common cause of jealousy.

Parental favoritism is another source of jealousy. If parents center their affection and attention on one child, it is only natural that others in the family will become jealous of the favored sibling.

Underlying jealousy may be strong *feelings of insecurity and inadequancy.*[1] The person who is very insecure is frequently envious of others. Such feelings result from childhood ridicule, rejection, criticism, severe punishment and disappointments.

In some instances jealousy is the result of *severe emotional disturbance.* One of the major symptoms of paranoid reactions, for example, is excessive suspicion and distrust of others.[2]

A *lack of spiritual development* may also be an influential factor in feelings of jealousy. Since all people have a sinful nature they are prone to many types of envy, lust and jealousy. "For from within, out of the heart of men, proceed evil thoughts, adulteries, fornications, murders, thefts, covetousness, wickedness, deceit, lasciviousness, an evil eye, blasphemy, pride, foolishness: All these evil things come from within, and defile the

---

[1] For a discussion of the causes of these attitudes, see INSECURITY in this volume.
[2] For the relationship of jealousy to severe cases of mental illness, see the discussion of PARANOID REACTIONS in this volume.

man" (Mark 7:21-23). When a person's thoughts are not controlled by Christ, he tends to compare his situation with that of others and then becomes envious and jealous.

Illustration

Identification: Negro female, age 26

Presenting Problem: This woman and her husband came to a marriage counselor for therapy. She accused her husband of unfaithfulness in marriage and he firmly denied this accusation.

Personal and Family History: The subject was one of seven children born into a family of low socioeconomic status. She had undergone many physical and emotional deprivations in childhood due to a poor home environment. Both of her parents had to work in order to support the family and there was no spiritual influence in the home.

In school this subject received above-average grades. She was highly competitive and when she did not get her way often became easily angered. During high school she began to blame others for her failures and was critical of her friends.

The subject married at eighteen after a short courtship. Her husband is receiving a good salary and they now have three children. Early in her marriage she showed strong feelings of jealousy. Any time her husband was seen talking with another woman she became angry and accused him of not loving her. This pattern of jealousy continued until it became so extreme that she accused her husband of being unfaithful. Finally the two agreed to seek marriage counseling.

Treatment

In treating jealousy the counselor must understand the basic causes that have produced the feelings of envy and inadequacy. In the case of children the parents should seek to remove favoritism and to terminate unnecessary comparisons between siblings. Assuring a child that he is loved and arranging for pleasant times alone with him also do much to minimize feelings of envy and jealousy. Parents will do well to examine their own feelings toward their children to make sure they are not showing favoritism.

When current causes for jealous feelings are absent, it is evident that the jealous individual is suffering from personality disturbances. Such a person needs a series of counseling sessions to determine the causes of his feelings and to come to the realization that his present feelings are not based upon objective information but rather on distortions arising from his past experiences.

The person with accompanying feelings of inferiority and insecurity must be led to an understanding of the forces in his life which have caused him to develop feelings of inadequacy. As he comes to a better self-understanding he will be able to accept the true nature of his abilities and capacities and to develop an adequate self-concept. It is important that the jealous person come to know and accept his personal limitations. Otherwise, he will likely strive for unrealistic goals and, in turn, be jealous of those who have different ability or more talent.

Spiritual factors are of vital importance in working with jealous individuals. In the case of the unsaved person or the immature Christian, the counselor should emphasize the new nature which Christ provides through salvation. The Bible challenges all to "put off the old man with his deeds; and . . . put on the new man . . . after the image of him that created him" (Colossians 3:9, 10). A person may be jealous because he has been frustrated in his attempts to gain acceptance, prestige or unusual accomplishment. These desires are often contrary to the Lord's will, but the person continues to pursue his quest for outstanding recognition. In such cases, the individual needs to realistically consider his attitudes and responsibilities toward God. I John 2:15-17 points out the utter futility of seeking the things of the world: "Love not the world, neither the things that are in the world. If any man love the world, the love of the Father is not in him. For all that is in the world, the lust of the flesh, and the lust of the eyes, and the pride of life, is not of the Father, but is of the world. And the world passeth away, and the lust thereof: but he that doeth the will of God abideth forever." Spiritual growth and understanding will enable the person to develop a Christ-centered rather than a self-centered motivation. As the client comes to see the importance of serving the Lord and seeking eternal values, his need to gain approval and to compete for worldly desires will begin to lessen. Then he will not tend to covet things out of his reach and he will rejoice in the challenge of being his "own" best for Christ.

In counseling with adults who are married it is important to work with both husband and wife. Since the jealous individual is basically a very insecure person, the spouse needs to understand the emotional needs involved. As the husband or wife of a jealous person gains insight into the causes of this behavior, he can assist his mate's personality growth by giving increased compliments, praise and affection.

A total program directed toward an understanding of the basic emotional and spiritual causes and an improved family relationship can bring significant changes in the life of an insecure and jealous individual.

35. Lack of Faith

Description
This is the condition of the person who has an apparent desire to know God in a personal way and to experience peace of heart and mind, but somehow seems to be unable to place faith in God. Outward motions such as public commitments at church, praying at the altar, and other efforts may be many, but all of this action leaves the person feeling empty and devoid of real faith. His prayers seem to go no higher than the ceiling and salvation always appears out of grasp, much like the mirage that fades into the distance. This individual may make an effort toward God, but somehow he never seems to achieve a vital contact.

Etiology
Lack of faith may be the result of *not seeking God according to the Bible*. A person may desire faith in God but not according to the teachings of the Word of God. It is reported that the noted evangelist, Dwight L. Moody, frequently prayed that God would increase his faith until one day he came face to face with the Scripture in Romans 10:17, "So then faith cometh by hearing, and hearing by the word of God." Immediately he recognized the spiritual truth: immersing oneself in the Bible is the means by which faith is communicated to the soul rather than beseeching God to grant faith through some mystical manner.

A distorted view of the Bible, as well as ignorance of the Word of God, may keep a person from having faith in God. Some see the Bible as merely a wonderful collection of literature—the best of the writings of men. They decide they will accept only what appeals to their fancy and reject the rest; then they wonder why a vital faith in God and peace of soul elude them. God, of course, has chosen to impart saving faith through His Word, so if it is viewed as only the product of great men, the vital connection between God and man is short-circuited.

Outright disbelief and skepticism of the Scriptures will most naturally result in a lack of faith. God has deliberately shut Himself up in His Word as far as communicating to man the conditions by which he may know and experience the reality of God. The witness of any born-again Christian is the result of a life transformed by the Word of God, inspired by the promises of God, burdened with the condition of the lost revealed by the Word of God, and evidencing spiritual power from much time spent in God's Word.

Not only are there spiritual causes for a lack of faith, but there are also a number of emotional or psychological causes which have a bearing on a person being unable to lay hold of God by faith.

Prominent in the psychological causes for lack of faith are *feelings of unworthiness.* This is often the result of having been made to feel that one is never quite good enough to satisfy his parents, teachers, friends and others. The person who could never quite match up to the expectations of those closest to him may eventually generalize these feelings to God Himself. It may seem only logical to conclude that, having never really pleased any human being, surely it is presumptuous to feel that one can please God or claim Him as the object of living faith.

The opposite of feelings of unworthiness are *feelings of pride.* A person who is puffed up with a sense of his own importance may be reluctant to admit his true condition. It is little wonder that such a person never seems to be sure of faith in God, for "God resisteth the proud, and giveth grace to the humble" (I Peter 5:5b). Inseparably linked to faith is repentance; and it is impossible where pride reigns. A proud spirit is, of course, partly a spiritual condition, but it may have been psychologically induced by overpermissive, indulgent parents or an environment devoid of limits or disciplines.

A general mood of *depression* or *frequent periods of discouragement* may stand in the way of a strong, healthy faith. Bizarre and irrational thoughts will hinder faith. Depression is an emotional mood that tends to infect every other area of one's being. God seems unreal, and the way to God may seem cloudy and confused. Depression breeds fear, timidity and extreme self-blame. A lack of success in any undertaking usually causes such a person to blame himself and conclude that all is hopeless. In such a condition even Bible reading may seem to carry only a message of condemnation and judgment.

Unresolved guilt and sin in a person's life may keep him from taking hold of God by faith. Thoughts and actions that are contrary to God's laws may prevent a person from feeling genuinely accepted by God. The person who refuses to say the same thing as God about sin will find God refusing to speak peace to his mind and heart: "If I regard iniquity in my heart, the Lord will not hear me" (Psalm 66:18).

A person who has experienced *rejection* in a number of areas of life may find this a very real barrier to faith. One who has always been rejected in human relationships may not be able to comprehend the meaning of love on the human plane, let alone the wonder of the love of God. Most people who suffer from a feeling of rejection have had little or no meaningful love in their childhood. Many say, "No one ever loved me; I don't really know what love is; therefore, how can I be sure that God loves me?" Disillusionment with people makes confidence in God the more difficult. Disappointment in people seems to cause many to build an outer shell of cynicism and unbelief to prevent getting hurt psychologically.

Severe mental illness usually affects adversely what little capacity there is for faith to exist. An extreme neurotic condition or a psychotic state in which one is out of touch with reality may seriously incapacitate a person. He may be unable to reach out and accept God's love and forgiveness.

Even *fatigue and physical illness* may bring a certain inability to place confidence in God. Such spiritual giants as Abraham, Moses, David, Elijah and even the Apostle Paul seem to have had their times of poor health, discouragement and anxiety; but God was gracious and tender in His dealings with them. We, too, would do well to be patient as we counsel with precious souls who struggle to come to grips with the living God.

Treatment

In helping people who want to know God but who seem to be unable to do so, the counselor may tend to look at the problem too narrowly. He may think that the only thing necessary is to tell the person to believe. Then, by substantiating his statement with a few Scripture verses, he feels he has done all that is necessary. But this is seldom true. Indeed, the counselor needs to rely heavily upon the Bible, inasmuch as the Scripture itself leads a person to faith: ". . . the holy scriptures, which are able to make thee wise unto salvation through faith which is in Christ Jesus" (II Timothy 3:15). But getting through to a counselee so that he feels ready to yield himself to the Lord may be more complex than one realizes. Misunderstandings, strong feelings, unconscious attitudes and other factors may need to be considered before a person is ready to accept Christ and follow Him.

If a person indicates that he is not worthy of God's love, the counselor should encourage full ventilation of feelings. In this way, he can get to the basic cause of his feelings of unworthiness and help to minimize them. Although it is true that none of us is actually worthy of salvation, God does look upon all human beings as worthy of regeneration and sonship in His family. "Come unto me, all ye that labor and are heavy laden, and I will give you rest. Take my yoke upon you, and learn of me; for I am meek and lowly in heart: and ye shall find rest unto your souls. For my yoke is easy, and my burden is light" (Matthew 11:28-30). To be effective with a person who has such feelings of unworthiness, the counselor may need to devote several sessions to this consideration. Very often these feelings stem from experiences in childhood—possibly serious criticism or even neglect by those who were nearest to him. As these feelings are brought to light and discussed, they will tend to disappear so that God's love can be appropriated.

Some clients, on the other hand, feel overwhelmed by their own importance and righteousness. If a person fails to admit his true condition as a sinner, the counselor will want to humbly point him to the Word of God which poignantly describes his condition. "For all have sinned, and come short of the glory of God" (Romans 3:23). "He that covereth his sins shall not prosper: but whoso confesseth and forsaketh them shall have mercy" (Proverbs 28:13). "Let the wicked forsake his way, and the unrighteous man his thoughts: and let him return unto the

Lord, and he will have mercy upon him; and to our God, for he will abundantly pardon" (Isaiah 55:7). Until a man senses his need, he will not seek a remedy.

When counseling with a person who is deeply discouraged and who shows definite depressive reactions, a counselor will want to thoughtfully consider his approach.[1] The client's unhealthy and bizarre feelings may block out his attempts to trust in the Lord. God may seem unreal, and trust in Him would seem out of the question. Such a client may blame himself and feel there is no hope left. All of his attempts to read the Word and to find God may end tragically in discouragement and judgment. In such cases, the counselor will want to bring comfort as indicated in the following Scripture, "Who comforteth us in all our tribulation, that we may be able to comfort them which are in any trouble, by the comfort wherewith we ourselves are comforted of God" (II Corinthians 1:4). The counselor's concern will bring a ray of hope. He may point out that God understands the feelings of men and that He does not willingly want His creatures to suffer: "For he doth not afflict willingly nor grieve the children of men" (Lamentations 3:33). Such portions of Scripture, when properly brought to the attention of the counselee and when discussed in detail, will help him to understand that God is not to blame for feelings of discouragement. Experienced professional counselors know, also, that little by little they must introduce the fact that God is sovereign and has a right to deal with both believers and unbelievers as He deems best. The counselee may then reach the point where he is able to trust the Lord and accept the sovereignty of God.

When counseling with one who is outright skeptical of the Scriptures, it usually does little good to tell him that he should or must believe. Instead, the counselor will be wise to help the client to uncover his hostile or other deep-seated feelings and attempt to resolve them before expecting a total commitment to the Lord Jesus Christ. In time, the counselor will want to challenge the skeptic to systematically read the Word of God. Since it is quick and powerful it will pierce through to the

[1]See the discussion of DEPRESSIVE REACTION in this volume.

unbeliever's mind and heart: "For the word of God is quick, and powerful, and sharper than any two-edged sword, piercing even to the dividing asunder of soul and spirit, and of the joints and marrow, and is a discerner of the thoughts and intents of the heart" (Hebrews 4:12). In the reading of Scripture, God reveals to the earnest searcher the nature of Biblical doctrine: "If any man will do his will, he shall know of the doctrine, whether it be of God, or whether I speak of myself" (John 7:17). Not to be minimized is the counselor's own abiding faith in God and the Bible. His own spiritual integrity and maturity will speak quietly but eloquently to the man or woman who disbelieves. Many outstanding Christians can point to the time when they did not believe in Christ, but were brought face to face with Him because of the godly life and bearing of a devoted Christian counselor.

In summary, when a person feels he cannot lay hold on God personally, the counselor should view the problem broadly, considering the medical, psychological and spiritual aspects. As he does, he will uncover dynamic mitigating forces, some of which may be on an unconscious level. In this way the client will be freed of feelings which bind him and he will be better able to yield himself to God who sent His Son to die for all mankind. "For God so loved the world, that he gave his only begotten Son, that whosoever believeth in him should not perish, but have everlasting life" (John 3:16).

36. Lying

Description and Etiology

Lying is defined as the telling of a falsehood with the intent to deceive. Children's lies may be divided into several categories.[1]

Fantastic lies. Since fairy tales are read to children, it is not unusual for them to occasionally invent imaginative stories. These pose no problem as long as the child is shown that his stories are only imaginative. Sometimes, however, children will resort to a world of fantasy in order to gain pleasure and satisfaction which they do not receive from their environment. If the child begins to turn to this imaginary world to gain satisfactions, professional help should be sought to overcome his disturbances.

Imitative lies. A parent who falsifies information to make events more interesting is setting an example for his child to follow. Since the boy or girl observes his parent's untruthfulness, he may develop the belief that lying is acceptable. Parents should be careful to avoid lying if they expect their children to be truthful.

Lies of exaggeration. Children often exaggerate information. Such exaggerations in the form of bragging are usually not cause for deep concern, but the child should be helped to understand that his statements are inaccurate and that it is desirable for him to tell the truth.

Social lies. Closely akin to imitative lies are social lies. The child whose mother sends him to the door to tell the visitor she is not home or that she is ill is likely to grow up with the belief that the falsifying of information is acceptable.

Defensive lies. Probably the most common type of untruth is the defensive lie. Faced with the possibility of punishment, a child often turns to lying to avoid the consequences of his behavior. When a child is punished if he admits his guilt, and

---

[1]These classifications are delineated in the following book: Bakwin, H. and Bakwin, R.: *Clinical Management of Behavior Disorders in Children*, W. B. Saunders Company, Philadelphia, 1953.

is not punished when he conceals the truth, it is only natural he will continue to use this means of avoiding an unpleasant situation.

Compensatory lies. If parents place great importance on academic achievement or other skills, the child may feel that he is justified in giving false information in order to impress his teachers, parents or friends.

Antagonistic lies. When a child becomes aggravated at another member of the family for continually disturbing him, he may make up lies in order to be left alone. For instance, if the child is busy playing with his toys and the mother asks him repeatedly to do an errand, he may reply that he is feeling ill and is unable to perform the task.

Vengeful lies. A child who is upset with his parents because he feels they treat him unfairly may turn to lying to get revenge. He may even invent stories of his evil deeds in order to shock and "get even" with his parents.

Pathological lying. This is a condition of chronic lying in which the individual appears to gain nothing from his falsification. This type of lying is sometimes accompanied by various forms of delinquency and it is indicative of severe emotional conflict.[2]

Lying in adulthood may be a sign that the person is *unable to accept himself* as he is. When a person has an adequate self-concept he does not need to falsify information in order to defend himself or to impress others with his worth. The person who feels inferior, however, may turn to lying in an attempt to demonstrate to others that he is successful.

Another basic cause of lying is the *lack of an adequate relationship with the Lord.* "The thoughts of the righteous are right: but the counsels of the wicked are deceit" (Proverbs 12:5). The person who is not walking in fellowship with Christ is controlled by his old nature. He has no desire to live a righteous and honest life. Instead, he is concerned with obtaining nearly everything he can to satisfy his own wants.

A regular pattern of lying in adulthood may also be related

[2]See the discussion of DELINQUENCY in this volume.

to a more *general personality disturbance* such as a SOCIO-PATHIC PERSONALITY.[3] In these cases the dynamics of the total maladjustment must be understood.

Illustration

Identification: White male, age 12

Presenting Problem: The mother of this boy sought help from her pastor because the boy continually lied and seemed to be unable to tell the truth.

Personal and Family History: The subject is somewhat smaller than most boys his age, although he is in good health. He lives with his mother and stepfather in a modest apartment in a large city. His natural father died when the boy was six, and the mother remained unmarried for three years after the death of her husband.

The mother reports that her son has had problems ever since he entered school. Finally, in the fourth grade he was referred to the school psychologist because of low achievement and constant lying. Tests revealed that he was slightly below average in intelligence and that he was extremely insecure and apprehensive. The parents were advised to seek professional counseling, but they felt it was unnecessary, thinking the boy would probably grow out of it.

He has never accepted his stepfather who feels subject is spoiled and needs stronger discipline. The mother disagrees openly with her husband but punishes the boy in order to satisfy the stepfather and because the subject will not tell the truth.

No form of punishment has been successful in helping the child to stop lying. During the past year he has turned to falsehoods when telling the truth would have been more advantageous to him. Lately he has lied many times and has told his mother that he didn't know why he did it but that he couldn't stop.

[3]For a discussion of this problem see SOCIOPATHIC PERSONALITY in this volume.

Treatment in Children

In dealing with a child who frequently lies it is important to realize that this behavior is only a symptom of his real difficulty. Lying is usually an attempt by the child to adjust to his environment. The counselor must seek the underlying conditions which give rise to the child's behavior.

Parents of lying children should examine their behavior to see if their "white" lies and poor examples are the cause of the difficulty.

The child who feels neglected, insecure or inferior will often develop lying as a means of gaining attention. Parents of such a child should concentrate on improving family relationships in order to give him more attention and to develop feelings of security which are important to successful adjustment.

The practice of punishing a child when he admits guilt and not punishing him when misbehavior is concealed by lying should be changed. If the child realizes that by telling the truth his parents will attempt to assist him in his difficulties rather than punishing him, he will be encouraged to be more truthful.

If the parents know of a child's misbehavior, they should confront him with the information rather than attempting to draw the information from the child and thus giving him the opportunity to avoid an unpleasant situation by lying.

Pathological lying usually necessitates prolonged therapy aimed at resolving the deep-seated emotional conflicts which give rise to the behavior. Frequently, the child who is a pathological liar has severe feelings of inferiority and insecurity.[4] In these cases the counselor should arrange for a series of sessions when he can work both with the child and his parents. During the time with the child, the counselor will need to spend some time getting acquainted and gaining the friendship and confidence of the young person. After establishing a good relationship with the child, the counselor can gradually turn the discussion to the child's feelings. Topics such as relationships to parents, siblings and peers should be considered. By encouraging the child to tell of some of the happiest times he has

[4]For related discussions, see INFERIORITY and INSECURITY in this volume.

had and also unhappy times, the counselor frequently gains helpful insights into the child's emotional world.

By spending an interesting hour a week with an understanding counselor, a child's feelings of security and worth can be increased.

In addition to working with the lying child, the counselor needs to have regular sessions with the parents. These sessions should help the parents gain insight into the thoughts, feelings and actions of their child. The parents' own adjustment difficulties may also need to be considered. With this understanding parents can make changes in the family relationships which will fulfill the unmet emotional needs causing the pathological lying.

Treatment in Adults

Studies of adults who lie compulsively reveal that in most cases habits of lying were developed in childhood. Consideration, therefore, should be given to the roots of the problem, exploring the early beginnings as indicated in the first part of this discussion.

The counselor may need to allow for several sessions before the adult client will feel comfortable to talk freely and truthfully to the counselor. If the client finds a non-threatening environment in the presence of the counselor, he will more likely face his true feelings and, in time, be able to discuss them honestly.

Much time is required for a client to thoroughly explore the childhood beginnings of his problem, then gain insight into how they have developed into compulsive tendencies to lie. With full exploration of these basic causes, the client will usually come to see that he is leaning on unreliable crutches and that his problems can be solved only as he accepts himself and tells the truth. With patience, the counselor can help the client to develop a new sense of security and personal worth. With this new adjustment the person can be freed from the necessity to put on a false front to others.

Through spiritual conversion and dynamic Christian growth, the Holy Spirit can motivate a client to change, then enable him to become a well-adjusted man of God.

37. Manic-Depressive Reactions

Description

Manic-depressive reactions are a group of psychotic disturbances characterized by moods of elation and depression. These periods of excitement and depression may last from a few days to many months.

This disorder may be divided into three major types: (1) Manic Reactions, (2) Depressive Reactions, and (3) Mixed and Circular Types.

Manic Reactions: The major symptoms of manic reactions are periods of elation and hyperactivity. The individual is extremely excited and energetic and may also be very irritable. Manic reactions are usually divided into three categories, ranging from mild to severe manifestations of manic behavior.

Hypomania is the mildest type of manic reaction. Persons suffering from hypomania are talkative and overactive. They are aggressive, enthusiastic and often jovial and lighthearted. These individuals do not exhibit signs of severe psychotic disorders such as delusions and hallucinations, but rarely do they have insight into their own maladjustment.

Acute mania is a more severe manifestation of manic reaction. This disorder is characterized by intense irritability, flight of ideas, incoherent speech and elation. The person suffering from acute mania is easily provoked to anger and may become quite destructive. His speech may wander from subject to subject with no logical connection between one phrase and the next. He is also extremely excited and overactive.

Hypermania is the most serious of the manic reactions. With this the individual exhibits extreme forms of overactivity. He is unusually aggressive, excited and violent. His speech is incoherent. He is confused and disoriented. He may pace the floor like a "wild man," singing, shouting and laughing. The hypermanic may also experience hallucinations.

Depressive Reactions: Depressive reactions are characterized by symptoms which are primarily opposite to those occurring in manic states. The depressed individual feels dejected and sad. Depressive reactions may also be divided into three major categories.

Simple depression is characterized by a general loss of enthusiasm and energy and an accompanying state of dejection and gloom. The individual is easily discouraged and life seems to be a tremendously difficult experience. Daily living does not seem to be worth the effort expended. This person may possibly have thoughts of suicide.

Acute depression is a more severe manifestation of the symptoms exhibited in simple depression. The individual is listless in mental as well as physical functioning. He thinks himself completely worthless and may begin to blame himself for the illnesses and difficulties of others. He may refuse to eat and communicate. A person suffering from acute depression may not be properly oriented to the happenings going on about him. He may withdraw from social contacts, experience many delusions and hallucinations, and seriously consider suicide.

Stuporous depression is the most severe of the depressive reactions. A person suffering from stuperous depression may become totally unresponsive. When spoken to he may not react at all. Such a person is usually bedridden and so inactive that he may have to be fed. He is not oriented properly to time and place. He may experience severe hallucinations and delusions.

Mixed and Circular types: Some individuals suffering from manic-depressive reactions will alternate between moods of depression and periods of elation and overactivity. These cases are known as *circular reactions.*

Occasionally a person will suffer a *mixed reaction,* exhibiting symptoms characteristic of both depression and mania simultaneously. In this type of reaction a person may experience great elation and excitability but his motor activity may be listless and immobile.

Etiology

The underlying cause of depression and mania appear to be quite similar. The extremely opposite symptoms stem not from opposite causes but rather from the individual's method of adapting to his frustrations and conflicts.

Parent-child relations play an important role in the development of manic-depressive reactions. Although we cannot give a concrete parental pattern which leads to these reactions, it is apparent that rigid standards and severe discipline are found in the childhood of many suffering from such illness. The inability to fulfill excessively high parental ambitions may cause the child to feel inadequate and guilty. These feelings may then lead to the development of manic-depressive reactions.

The person who develops manic symptoms is often aggressive, sociable, extroverted and very ambitious. When his unrealistic vocational goals are frustrated, he may develop manic patterns in order to escape his failure. By becoming active in many other projects and by constantly telling others of his "big ideas," he avoids actual feelings of failure. Another person may react by becoming severely depressed. He blames himself for his failures and turns toward a life of dejection and discouragement rather than substituting numerous activities with which to hide his past failures.

Hostility toward parents may also give rise to manic-depressive reactions. The manic will act out his hostilities while the depressive suppresses his anger and directs it toward himself by developing feelings of guilt and inadequacy.

Illustration
Identification: White male, age 26
Presenting Problem: This subject was admitted to a private psychiatric hospital with diagnosis of manic-depressive psychosis, acute mania.
Personal and Family History: This man was the oldest of five children. His mother reported that he seemed to have a normal, healthy childhood. She did state, however, that he was always overactive.

The subject's father died when he was nine, and his mother continued to work to provide for the family. She was rather quiet and apparently well-adjusted.

The patient's grades in school were average, although he did experience some difficulty in mathematics. He left high school shortly before graduating. Later, he became a salesman for a lumber company and talked continually about "really getting ahead." He was dismissed from his sales job because he "did too much talking." He did not seem to be affected by losing his position and he continued to tell friends that he was "moving right up the ladder." Not long after the dismissal, his mother noticed that he became confused and even more excitable. He would lose his temper and become incoherent. "We became afraid of him," the mother reported.

Upon being hospitalized, the subject talked incessantly and usually incoherently. He also became very angry and often destroyed furniture and his own clothing.

Treatment

Manic-depressive patients usually respond well to therapy, but it is often necessary for them to be hospitalized for a period of time. Proper medical care is vital to the treatment of these persons. Since individuals suffering from manic-depressive reactions may refuse to eat, or may be so active that they neglect their health, every effort must be made to see that such persons are in good physical health.

Manic patients are encouraged to direct their energy into constructive labors and an attempt is made to quiet them by the use of drugs. Shock treatments and prolonged narcosis (drug-induced sleep) are often used to rid the patient of his hyperactivity. Psychochemotherapy (the use of drugs to treat mental disorders) has significantly lessened the use of electroshock therapy in these types of psychoses.

Shock therapy is also used in treating depressed individuals. As soon as the initial symptoms have been removed, whether by shock treatment, medication or narcosis, psychotherapy must be started if lasting improvement is to be shown. Therapy is directed at exploring the client's past experiences which have led to the development of these reactions. He needs help to construct a more realistic opinion of himself and an improved ability to handle stress situations.

When a persons's disturbance is connected with conflicts

over excessively high levels of aspiration and consequent feelings of failure, spiritual factors are of vital importance. In these cases the counselor needs to assist the person to evaluate the experiences which have led to his conflicts. He can then be shown in a Biblical light what the Lord expects of each of His children. A realization of the fact that God understands both our assets and liabilities and that we are only held responsible for those talents which He has given is a comforting thought for distressed individuals. Scriptures such as the Parable of the Talents in the twenty-fifth chapter of the book of Matthew are especially beneficial.

In addition to a more realistic evaluation of one's potential and a clearer understanding of what the Lord requires of His people is the importance of understanding God's forgiveness. Clients will need to come to the realization that all humans fall short of the Lord's desires, but that He stands ready to forgive and to give strength to serve Him better in the future. These spiritual insights are comforting thoughts for the person suffering from depression and discouragement.[1]

---

[1]For a more complete discussion of this problem see DEPRESSION in this volume.

38. Masturbation

Description

Masturbation is the self-stimulation of the sex organs, resulting in an orgasm. In adolescence new hormonal activity begins, producing sexual tension and desires which can be relieved through masturbation.[1]

Contrary to some popular belief, masturbation does not cause mental illness or a host of other symptoms attributed to it. However, cultural and social taboos may lead to feelings of guilt and anxiety which threaten one's emotional adjustment. Some individuals, whether children, adolescents or adults, turn to excessive and almost compulsive masturbation. When this occurs it is usually a symptom of a disturbing emotional problem.

Etiology

Occasional self-stimulation of the genitals during childhood and masturbation during adolescence is common. Each person goes through periods of sexual experimentation in which he may engage in masturbation. It is not uncommon for unmarried individuals to gain some sexual satisfaction and release by this means. Individual differences in sex drives as well as sexual stimulation and response account for a variety of patterns in masturbation.

Insecure, unhappy children will often attempt to gain gratification and relief from tension through masturbation, just as some turn to nail biting or thumb sucking. When parents criticize unduly and hold up unrealistic standards of behavior, their children are more likely to turn to self-stimulation. When a child masturbates compulsively there is usually an underlying disturbance which is causing this behavior.[2]

Another dynamic frequently underlying chronic masturbation is the feeling of sexual inadequacy. People who do not have satisfactory heterosexual relationships may feel a need to

[1]For a related discussion, see SEXUAL DEVIATION in this volume.
[2]See the author's book, *How To Tell Your Children About Sex.*

prove that they are sexually adequate. By masturbating they consciously or unconsciously attempt to prove to themselves that they are capable of normal sexual functioning.

When young people enter adulthood and continue to masturbate excessively rather than to develop normal heterosexual behavior, it is usually a sign of maladjustment. They may be withdrawn and insecure, fearing close relationships with the opposite sex. Consequently, they continue to rely on masturbation for release of sexual tension. If they are to develop normal heterosexual relationships, they must come to an understanding of the factors influencing their feelings and behavior.

Illustration
Identification: White female, age 25
Presenting Problem: Chronic masturbation since the age of five.
Personal and Family History: The subject is a married woman who is in good physical health. Her husband is a youth director in a large church where he receives an adequate salary. They have no children but they are expecting a baby in seven months. Although she has wanted help before, the impending birth of a child and the contemplated visits with a physician have prompted her to seek assistance.

The subject began masturbating when she was a small child, shortly after the death of her mother. She was raised in a home where there was no spiritual instruction or help. However, during high school she listened regularly to a Christian radio broadcast and in time made a definite profession of faith in Christ.

"When I masturbated as a child," she told her therapist, "I'd do it in secret, usually thinking about what I wanted to be when I grew up. It was when I was feeling sorry for myself."

She was married at the age of twenty-two and reports that she has been fairly happy but she has never been able to give up masturbation.

Treatment
Counseling with individuals who masturbate excessively should be directed toward understanding basic factors which have led

to this type of behavior. Merely telling a person who masturbates frequently that the habit is bad or sinful is no solution. What is needed, rather, is an understanding of the cause of the problem. This may require several counseling sessions.

The introverted, insecure person who has turned to masturbation must come to an understanding of the factors responsible for his lack of confidence and his feelings of insecurity. As he begins to comprehend and discuss them, he will develop increased confidence and he will be better able to develop normal sexual patterns.

Sex education is another important consideration in counseling with individuals who masturbate frequently. These persons may have various misconceptions concerning sexual functioning. The counselor needs to help them develop normal, wholesome attitudes toward the human body if he is to enable them to overcome their sexual maladjustments.[3]

A counselor may help young people with such problems by discussing school life, home environment, friends, hobbies, part-time jobs, church activities, dating and other common interests. In this way, the counselor can ascertain their daily routine, their successes and failures, and various factors which might have a bearing upon their problem of masturbation. As young people understand that masturbation is a reflection of a broader personality problem, they can more easily set up plans to achieve a better adjustment.

Wholesome social and physical activities are also helpful to one who masturbates excessively. Counseling, then, may include discussions about making friends and participating in various activities. If there are severe feelings of guilt, they should be brought to light, discussed and resolved in order to build a foundation of future self-respect and feelings of worthwhileness.

In the case of a married person who masturbates, the therapist should consider (1) the total personality adjustment of the counselee, (2) the attitudes and adjustment of the spouse, and (3) the specific sex factors in the marriage. Experienced coun-

[3]In counseling young people regarding problems of masturbation, a counselor may suggest that they read the author's book on a Christian view of sex, *Life and Love.*

selors know that a husband, for example, may never have achieved sufficient adjustment in his own personality development to allow him to have normal heterosexual relationships. As a result, he practices masturbation to avoid intimate sexual relations with his wife. In such instances, the counselor should focus therapy on helping the client to achieve a good personality adjustment. Some husbands, on the other hand, are basically well-adjusted, but their wives suffer from personality disturbances and do not want to have normal sex relations with their husbands. Or, as in the case of some couples, the wife is an aggressive, domineering person with whom the husband feels uncomfortable. This, in turn, may cause him to practice masturbation. In these instances the counselor will want to work with the wife to help her achieve a total personality adjustment. In addition, the counselor should help the husband to understand his wife's problem. In still other cases, the husband, or wife, or both, may need specific instruction regarding sexual functioning, accompanied by insight regarding procedures and techniques to improve their intimate relationships.

39. Menopause

The menopause is the termination of the menstrual cycle (the monthly flow period). This natural cessation of menstruation usually occurs between the ages of 45 and 55. The menopause is also referred to as the "female climacteric." The word "menopause" is derived from the Greek "men," meaning month, and "pause," meaning cessation.[1] In addition to the natural cessation, an artificial menopause can be produced by surgical removal of both ovaries or by stopping ovarian function through radiation treatments.

Menopause is not a "change of life," as it is often called, because the changes usually consist only of cessation of menstruation, followed by the inability to become pregnant. It is not a time to be anticipated with fear and apprehension resulting from believing bizarre tales that have no scientific support or medical foundation. On the contrary, it should be regarded as a natural phase of female life which continues with joys previously known plus the addition of new ones.

There is considerable variation in the duration of the menopause. In most cases it lasts for about one year. Some women have an abrupt cessation; others, a gradual lessening in the amount of flow over consecutive months. Still others have a "dodging period" which involves skipping one or more periods from time to time until complete cessation of the period is realized. There is no definite pattern regarding the time this period will stop and start, or its duration. There are no medical means of predicting or measuring these factors.

No two women are alike in the symptoms they manifest. The "hot flush or flash" is the one unique symptom, along with periods which decrease in frequency, duration and amount of flow. Anything contrary to this should be checked by a medical doctor. There are some women who do not have the hot flush

[1]For this section, the author wishes to acknowledge the contribution of Robert D. Carpenter, M.D., physician and surgeon, and full-time medical consultant on the staff of the Narramore Christian Foundation.

or flash. Many experience the menopause without difficulty. Still others would similarly glide smoothly through the menopause if they were properly informed as to what to expect. Additional common symptoms are: transitory dizziness and headache, irritability, excitability, nervousness and a worn-out feeling. At the same time, it should be remembered that other conditions can produce these same symptoms. Those who have had menstrual difficulties such as cramping, may find that such discomforts will diminish as the normal pattern of the menopause takes place; that is, fewer periods, decreasing in flow and duration. Again, it should be noted that augmentation or exaggeration of any phase of the menstrual period is not normal and should be brought to the attention of a physician. Comparing notes will usually confuse and frustrate a woman if she feels her symptoms should be like another's. When she hears of a "new" symptom, she may develop it shortly.

Some of the discomfort that women experience may be attributed to anticipation. If one thinks she is going to have certain symptoms, she may very well begin sensing them.

A medical doctor can give proper pre-menopausal education regarding the basic physical and emotional approach and, in some cases, a woman can benefit from professional psychological counseling either before or during this period. The doctor can give replacement hormonal therapy to relieve or minimize the embarrassing and bothersome hot flashes.

Good exercise is helpful for many physical-psychological problems and the menopausal period is no exception. Proper exercise keeps the body in good tone. This, in turn, bolsters the forces needed to handle various problems. In I Timothy 4:8, we read: "Bodily exercise profiteth little; but godliness is profitable unto all things, having promise of the life that now is, and of that which is to come." In essence, bodily exercise *does* profit during one's lifetime.

Sometimes the question is asked, "Do men have something similar to the menopause?" Men do experience the "male climacteric" and it usually takes place unnoticed because there are not specific symptoms or signs which would signal the occurrence. For the men, the ability to procreate ceases and sexual activity decreases in varying degrees depending upon the individual. Usually this takes place later in life for the male than does the menopause for the woman.

It is no easier to conceive during the menopause than under normal nonmenopausal circumstances. However, a woman may think that since she is not having periods, there is no possibility of pregnancy. But this is not true, because a woman can still ovulate (form eggs) for several months to even a year after her last period has occurred. What likely happens is that usual precautions are no longer observed, thus making it easier to conceive. In a similar manner, many women have become pregnant some months after delivery even though they have not menstruated. To reiterate, it is possible for a woman to ovulate even though there are no apparent periods.

The menopause may affect a married woman's attitude toward sexual intercourse. For example, a wife may have increased desire following the completion of the menopause because the fear of pregnancy is gone and she becomes more relaxed. On the other hand, a woman may have a decreased desire for intimate relations because she feels that intercourse is solely for procreation. This latter attitude, which is difficult to support Biblically, can lead to many personal and marriage problems. A wholesome, Scriptural concept of sex can be of inestimable value to a woman before, during and after the menopausal period.

The term "menopause," should not be a "wastebasket" or diagnostic "catchall" for complaints and ailments totally unrelated to the true menopausal pattern. Unfortunately, the menopause is frequently referred to when a woman is actually suffering from other causes quite unrelated to the menopausal syndrome. A person who is plagued with emotional disturbance, for example, might be erroneously told that she is "passing through the menopause," when actually her troubles are stemming from very different causes. The menopause is sometimes blamed for almost any kind of problem in that age group.

Professional counselors can make a significant contribution to the emotional and mental well-being of a client who is erroneously blaming her personality conflicts and spiritual immaturity on the menopause. Through psychodiagnostic measures, as well as skillful interviews, such a woman can come to understand her need for therapy.

A Christian counselor can assist a woman greatly through spiritual counseling. She can be helped to devote her life more completely to Christ. Thus, the normal changes in life can be anticipated and experienced with normal satisfaction. The earlier she develops mature, Christian attitudes the less likely she will be to have problems later in life.

40. Mental Deficiency

Description

Mental deficiency is a condition marked by low intelligence which prevents a person from properly caring for himself without supervision. When a person's intelligence quotient is below approximately 70, he is considered mentally defective.

Mentally deficient or feeble-minded individuals comprise approximately two and one-half per cent of the population and are generally classified in three major catergories: idiot, imbecile and moron.

Those with an I.Q. of less than 25 are classified as *idiots*. Individuals in this category are the most severely retarded of the feeble-minded. They are unable to learn even simple tasks and are completely dependent upon others for their care. Many are incapable of dressing themselves. In adulthood they reach the mentality of an average two-year-old, and need continuous supervision. Accompanying mental deficiency is a high frequency of physical handicaps and susceptibility to disease.

Individuals having I.Q. scores between 26 and 50 are classified as *imbeciles*. In adulthood they may reach the mental level of a five or six-year-old child. These people are unable to profit from formal education but they can usually learn to perform a few simple tasks. They may develop limited speech ability but few can be taught even simple reading and writing. Although they are unable to make their own living, they are often able to protect themselves against common physical dangers. Such persons must be cared for under the close supervision of their families or an institution.

Morons are the highest grade mental defectives. These have I.Q. scores ranging from 51 to 70 and are considered educable. They usually profit from the first few grades of elementary education. Their reading and writing skill is limited. Because of their meager resources many morons become juvenile delinquents, prostitutes and criminals. When given proper training and supervision, many of these retarded individuals are able to make satisfactory adjustments. Most of them can be taught to perform routine types of labor and are capable of earning at least a portion of their living.

Individuals with intelligence quotients between 70 and 80 are generally classified as *borderline defectives*. Most of these persons are able to profit from modified classroom instruction. Some give indication of neurological impairment while in others the major retardation factor appears to be heredity. When working with these individuals it is important to evaluate each one's abilities and limitations. Few borderline defectives need to be institutionalized. However, they do require careful guidance in order to earn a living and make adequate social adjustments. If they do not find a satisfactory place for themselves at school or in the community, they may turn to antisocial behavior.

Persons classified as *dull normal* include those with intelligence quotients ranging from 80 to 89. They comprise approximately 15 per cent of the entire population of the United States. As children in school, they are known as slow learners. Since their mental abilities do not measure up to those of their classmates, they are often not interested in academic achievement. They may have reading difficulties and sometimes are required to repeat elementary grades because of poor achievement. Physically and socially these individuals are often equal to others their age. They can compete quite well in athletics and may have relatively few handicaps in their social adjustments. As adults they may marry and earn their own living in simple types of employment. It is important that adults working with children of this intelligence level understand their mental capacities. Teachers should offer them special encouragement and assign tasks which are interesting but not too complex. When the emotional needs of these children are met, they are usually socially well-adjusted and are able to live happy, productive lives. If, however, the difficulties associated with their limited intellectual capacities are compounded by emotional disturbance, serious problems may arise. The successful adjustment of these individuals, just as with all others, is largely dependent upon the family and school environment. Parents must provide an atmosphere of acceptance where the child feels secure and loved. They should avoid forcing him into academic performance beyond his capabilities. Criticism should be kept at a minimum. Instead, parents and teachers should encourage the slow learner in areas where he is successful and in which he shows interest and ability.

It is important that these children have the benefit of a stable, spiritual environment. A personal acceptance of Christ as Savior and instruction in the Word of God will do much to assist the child of dull normal intelligence. Many of these individuals have placed their faith in Christ and have lived happy, useful lives.[1]

Etiology

The causes of mental deficiency are generally divided into primary (endogenous) sources and secondary (exogenous) sources. Primary sources of mental deficiency are thought to be the result of heredity while secondary mental deficiency is the result of brain pathology.

Primary Mental Deficiency: The two most common types of primary mental subnormality which are presumed to follow the Mendelian laws of heredity are (1) familial mental deficiency and (2) amaurotic family idiocy.

A diagnosis of *familial mental deficiency* is generally made when no apparent organic or environmental cause for the retardation can be found but when there is a history of mental deficiency in the patient's family.

Amaurotic family idiocy is a congenital disorder which differs from other types of mental deficiency in that at birth and during early life the person appears to be developing normally. Symptoms of this disorder may begin to emerge any time from infancy to adolescence. First evidences are muscular weakness and deterioration, visual disturbances and mental deterioration. This disease becomes progressively worse. Blindness results in many cases, speech disturbances develop, and more severe mental deterioration is noted. At present there is no known

[1]Various organizations are publishing Sunday school materials for slow learners. For specific information write Shepherds, Inc., P. O. Box 1261, Milwaukee, Wisconsin.

treatment for this disorder and deterioration of the nervous system continues until death results.

Secondary Mental Deficiency: Mental retardation resulting from organic damage to the brain is known as secondary mental deficiency. There is usually no history of mental retardation in the subject's immediate family. Secondary mental deficiency is associated with endocrine disturbances, brain inflammation, brain injury (either during or after birth), degenerative brain diseases and diseases which secondarily affect brain tissue.

Prenatal Disorders: Among the most common prenatal disorders associated with mental deficiency are mongolism,[2] cretinism, microcephaly, macrocephaly and hydrocephaly.

Macrocephaly is characterized by an excessive enlargement of the head. This enlargement is due to an abnormal growth of the glia cells which form the supporting structures of the brain tissues. The abnormal growth of these cells prevents normal development and function of the brain tissues, thus causing mental deficiency.

Formal education is of no value with these individuals, but some may be trained to perform simple tasks and to take care of their personal needs.

The cause of the accelerated growth of glia cells is not known but is due to pathological factors during the prenatal period. No effective means of treatment has been found for this disorder.

Microcephaly results from the failure of the cranium to develop properly and a corresponding inadequate development of cerebral tissue. The major physical characteristic of this disorder is, as the name implies, a small head. The circumference of the microcephalic individual's head may be as much as five inches smaller than the normal size of twenty-two inches. The patient's skull is cone-shaped with a receding forehead. The face is usually normal size in contrast to the underdeveloped head. Most mircocephalics are classified in the idiot and imbecile ranges of intelligence. Occasionally one will achieve a moron rating. Speech difficulties are common. Many do not learn to talk and those who do use simple language and lack

[2]MONGOLISM is discussed independently in this volume.

clear pronunciation. Emotionally these individuals are usually good-natured. They are often restless and hyperactive but are affectionate and even-tempered. Many can learn to perform simple tasks and some may even become self-supporting if closely supervised.

The precise causes of microcephaly are unknown. However, it appears that prenatal conditions such as encephalitis, toxins, and chemical imbalance play an important role in creating this disorder. There is, at present, no successful method of treating victims of microcephaly. Treatment is limited to teaching them how to care for their personal needs.

Hydrocephaly is an abnormal accumulation of fluid within the cranial vault, producing an unusually large head. The pressure caused by this excess cerebrospinal fluid results in damage to the brain and enlargement of the cranium. Physical characteristics frequently accompanying the enlarged head include handicaps such as harelip, cleft palate and clubfoot. However, these conditions do not necessarily relate to one's mentality. In hydrocephaly, motor coordination is generally poor and the person is awkward and clumsy. Intellectually these individuals are usually idiots or imbeciles. Occasionally, a hydrocephalic is found in the moron level. Emotionally, they are usually affectionate and good-natured. The abnormal accumulation of cerebrospinal fluid is due to the lack of free passage of this fluid from the brain into the spinal canal. The exact causes for this blockage are as yet unknown. It is believed that acute inflammation results in the formation of tissue which interferes with the natural flow of cerebrospinal fluid. Treatment of hydrocephaly is primarily medical. Surgery is being used in attempts to relieve the abnormal intracranial pressure and in controlling the progression of the disorder.

Cretinism is a congenital deficiency of thyroid secretion with resulting deformity and idiocy.[3]

Postnatal Disorders: Postnatal causes of mental retardation include all factors operating upon the child after birth. These include infections, common childhood diseases such as measles

[3]For a related discussion, see ENDOCRINE DYSFUNCTION in this volume.

and mumps, nutritional deficiencies, endocrine imbalances and head injuries. Contrary to widespread opinion, however, head injuries after birth do not play a major role in mental deficiency. In a study of 1,000 institutionalized mental defectives, Bolt[4] found that only 1.5 per cent could be attributed to head injuries after birth.

Two childhood diseases which may cause damage to the brain are (1) epidemic encephalitis and (2) epidemic cerebrospinal meningitis.

The inflammation of the brain tissue caused by epidemic encephalitis results in the destruction of cortical nerve cells. During the acute phase of this disease the patient is typically very drowsy and runs a high fever. He may sleep throughout the day, awakening only for short periods. As a result of these symptoms the disease is commonly known as sleeping sickness. The lethargic state may be followed by symptoms of insomnia and hyperactive behavior. These individuals are overactive, excitable and irritable. There is generally little intellectual deterioration associated with epidemic encephalitis in adults. Instead, the patient may exhibit progressive personality deterioration. He may become nervous, depressed and dejected. A serious case of epidemic encephalitis in early childhood may result in encephalitic mental deficiency. A previously normal child may become hostile and hyperactive. His intellectual functioning is impaired and he has difficulty integrating perceptual experiences in a normal manner. Treatment of epidemic encephalitis is primarily medical but damage to the brain cells is irreparable.

Epidemic cerebrospinal meningitis is caused by a microorganism called meningococcus which attacks the coverings of the brain and spinal cord. The inflammation has an adverse effect on adjacent brain tissue. They may be temporary or permanent, causing impairment of neural function or even destruction of nerve cells. If the disease is present during infancy or early childhood, severe mental deficiency may result. The older

---

[4]Bolt, W. H.: "Postnatal Trauma as an Etiological Factor in Mental Deficiency," *American Journal of Mental Deficiency*, vol. 103, pp. 247-267, 1948.

the child, the less severe will be the disease and the less likelihood of mental deficiency. Symptoms associated with this disease are severe headache, irritability, vomiting, fever and convulsions. In severe cases the patient may also become confused and delirious. Certain medications have proved helpful in treatment; however, undesirable aftereffects may result.

Understanding and Guiding the Mentally Deficient

To better understand persons who are mentally retarded, several areas should be considered.[5] Actually, there is no cure for mental deficiency. In cases of neurological handicap certain drugs are often used to alleviate distressing symptoms, but they cannot repair brain tissue damage. It is important that parents of mentally handicapped children learn to accept such limitations and abilities. A child who is severely retarded will always be in need of care, either at home or in an institution.[6] Most mentally deficient persons can be trained in personal habits and are able to gain some proficiency in speaking. Today there are numerous opportunities available in special education for retarded children.[7] Many states have made provisions for teaching the mentally deficient. There are also private institutions and organizations that specialize in training mentally handicapped individuals.

It should be kept in mind that a person's score on only one intelligence test should not necessarily be used as a final criteria for his future. In working with the mentally deficient it is necessary to consider a person's physical, emotional, social and vocational capacities along with his tested mental ability.

In families where there are children other than the retarded child it is important that the deficient child receives his share of attention. But it is equally important that the other children are not neglected. Some parents will lavish attention on the

[5]For further information on this topic, see Levinson, Abraham: *The Mentally Retarded Child*, John Day Company, New York, 1952.
[6]Recent information on a variety of aspects concerning mental deficiency is available at nearly all medical offices, hospitals and public health offices.
[7]For a discussion of educational arrangements for retarded children, see: Cruickshank, William M. and Johnson, G. Orville (Eds.): *Education of Exceptional Children and Youth*, Prentice-Hall, Englewood Cliffs, N.J., 1958.

retarded child at the expense of the other siblings, while others may reject the retarded child and focus all their attention on the one with greater capacities.[8]

In working with the mentally deficient it is essential to realize that the primary goal of training is not scholastic improvement as much as personal adjustment. Whether in special classes, at home or in an institution, five major areas of learning and training should be considered for each mentally deficient individual: (1) personal health and hygiene, (2) basic education, (3) personal and social development, (4) vocational training, and (5) spiritual training.

Nearly all mentally deficient children can learn to feed and dress themselves and to control basic body functions. Depending on the degree of retardation they can also be taught habits of cleanliness and learn to avoid physical danger.

Teaching retarded children a few practical matters is also important. All who are capable should learn to recognize signs such as exit, walk, fire, stop and go. Many children of low mentality can be taught to write their own name and to do simple counting.

Emphasis should be placed on good character and acceptable social behavior. As parents provide a loving, relaxed home atmosphere, they can teach such characteristics as honesty and friendliness. Retarded children can also be taught to participate in activities around the home and playground.

Parents should see that mentally deficient children have the opportunity to develop vocational abilities equal to their potential. Many who are retarded can learn to perform simple vocational tasks. Vocational training for the mentally deficient not only aids in their support but, even more important, it keeps the individual occupied and provides him with a sense of accomplishment. When he is busy and happy he is not likely to engage in socially unacceptable behavior.

In working with retarded individuals it is well to remember that their ability to think in abstract concepts is extremely lim-

---

[8]For a discussion of parent counseling, see the section on Treatment in the chapter on CEREBRAL PALSY in this volume.

ited. Anything that is taught must be kept simple and be repeated over and over. If the child is to learn cleanliness, for example, he must be taught each act separately, by repetition—to brush his teeth, to comb his hair and to wash his face.

Institutionalization is generally recommended for all cases of idiots. Since individuals of this mentality are unable to learn even simple tasks of personal cleanliness, they are usually better cared for in an institution which is equipped to meet their needs.

In communities which do not provide adequate training and leisure time activities for the retarded or when the family is unable or unwilling to care for such a one, institutionalization is also recommended.

41. Mongolism

Description
Mongolism is a form of mental deficiency which is characterized by facial features somewhat resembling the Mongolian race.[1] The person with this type of retardation has slanting, almond-shaped eyes; a long, thick tongue; thin, dry lips; short, stubby hands; and small, irregularly-spaced teeth. He is shorter and generally smaller than the average person.

The speech of the mongoloid usually does not develop properly. Some may never learn to talk, others are extremely slow in speaking and many have an unusually deep voice.

Accompanying these physical symptoms is a high susceptibility to physical ailments. Circulatory disorders and respiratory infections such as tuberculosis and pneumonia are common in mongoloids.

The life span of the mongoloid is usually short. The widespread use of antibiotics has increased the life expectancy of the mongoloid, but a great number succumb to physical illnesses by late childhood.

Although often called mongolian idiots, the mongoloid child is usually found in the imbecile range of intelligence. The majority of mongoloids have an intelligence quotient between 25 and 50. This is in contrast to the moderately retarded child whose I.Q. ratings are usually between 50 and 75, and the normal I.Q. rating which is approximately 100. Mongoloids account for about one per cent of all mental defectives.

Etiology
Mongolism has long been considered the result of heredity, but recent research suggests that this hypothesis is unsound. Clemens Benda, in a study of over 500 families,[2] concluded that "hereditary factors are of no importance." Recent research gives indication that mongolism may be due to a pathological con-

---

[1]See the discussion of MENTAL DEFICIENCY in this volume.
[2]Benda, Clemens,E., M.D.: *Mongolism and Cretinism*, Grune and Stratton, New York, 1949.

dition of the mother during pregnancy. Adrien Bleyer, in a study of 2,822 mongoloid children[3] found that over fifty per cent of the mothers were more than ten years beyond the average maternal age.

Benda's findings led him to the belief that mongolism is likely due to a glandular imbalance in the mother during pregnancy. It is probable that a malfunctioning of the pituitary, or "master gland," affects the other glands of the endocrine system, resulting in the abnormal development of the child.

Illustration

Identification: White female, age 5

Presenting Problem: The patient was first seen by the school psychologist during the "kindergarten roundup" when parents of the community brought their children to school in the spring to enroll them for the following fall term. The child was accompanied by her mother who "wondered" if she could enroll the girl in kindergarten.

The mother indicated that her daughter was slow but that she was "real smart" in some ways. When asked by the school psychologist whether the mother thought that her daughter would benefit from kindergarten experience, the mother insisted that she would and that being around other children and under "stricter discipline" would also help the child. In further discussion with the psychologist the mother stated that she was afraid the school would not accept her daughter. Actually, the object of the mother's visit was to learn whether the girl would be permitted to enter kindergarten or whether a special class was provided for retarded children.

Personal and Family History: The parents had moved to the community only a few months before seeking to enroll the girl in school. At the time of the girl's birth the parents were in their late thirties. They had no medical records to show the school, but stated that they "did not know anything was wrong" with their daughter until she was nearly two years of age. Since

[3]Bleyer, Adrien: "The role of Advanced Maternal Age in Causing Mongolism," *American Journal of Diseases of Children*, vol. 105, pp. 79-92, 1938.

the nature of the problem had evidently never been adequately explained to the parents, the school psychologist met with them on two occasions to help them understand the child's limitations.

The patient had the usual intellectual, physical and emotional traits of mongolism. She was slow in learning to speak and at the age of five was still very difficult to understand. The parents reported severe respiratory illnesses and general poor health. They also admitted that in recent months neighbors had begun to notice the child's condition.

Treatment

At the present time there is no adequate means of treating mongolism. Attempts have been primarily concerned with endocrinology but little success has been found.

Prevention of this disorder appears to lie largely in the use of precautionary measures during pregnancy. Steps should be taken to insure proper diet and glandular functioning, especially in older mothers.

Care of the mongoloid child is improving in the home, in institutions and in public schools. As people throughout the community understand mongolism better they tend to create a more favorable environment for the mongoloid child who is living with his parents. Public schools, too, are beginning to provide training classes for such children. In some states classes for the severely retarded are compulsory, in others they are optional. But in either case special state apportionments are usually available to districts which do provide classes for the severely retarded.

State hospitals have also improved their care and training of both children and adults who are mongoloid. In addition to more appropriate medical care, much is being done to provide beneficial training. Undoubtedly the greatest strides in the future will focus upon eliminating mongolism through better care of the mother before and during pregnancy.[4]

Another important consideration in dealing with a mongoloid

[4]For a comprehensive treatment of the problem of mongolism, see Benda, Clemens E., M.D.: *The Child With Mongolism (Congenital Acromicria)*, Grune and Stratton, New York, 1960.

is the attitude of the parents toward the child. Several counseling sessions are usually required to thoroughly evaluate these parental attitudes and to assist the parents in developing a realistic outlook toward their child.[5]

[5]For a discussion of the major areas to consider in counseling with parents of a handicapped child, see CEREBRAL PALSY in this volume.

42. Neurodermatitis

Description

A person's skin is frequently an indicator of various physical and emotional disturbances. Since it is influenced both by the autonomic nervous system and by the endocrine system, unique reaction in either of these may result in an inflammation or disorder of the skin. Some individuals who are nervous and tense may compulsively rub or scratch certain portions of their body. This, too, can result in a cutaneous disturbance. Inflammation of the skin due to emotional factors is known as neurodermatitis. Other related disturbances include pruritus (itching of the skin), hyperhidrosis (excessive sweating), and atopic dermatitis (allergy or hypersensitivity of the skin). As a diagnostic group these various disturbances are known as psychophysiologic skin reactions.[1]

Etiology

As with other psychosomatic disorders, skin disturbances are often due to bodily changes resulting from emotional disturbances. Whereas some individuals express emotional conflicts through neurotic or psychotic disturbances, others develop physiologic dysfunctions. In such cases, the individual is suffering from a high level of anxiety but does not allow these feelings to be expressed emotionally. Instead, he attempts to repress emotional conflicts and frustrations and unconsciously channels the anxiety into bodily symptoms.

Some investigators suggest a *constitutional predisposition* which plays an important role in psychosomatic disorders. Although they agree that the basic etiological factors are emotional, they point out that this type of physical manifestation of emotional conflict appears to be partially influenced by the constitutional makeup of the individual.

It is well known that *emotional reactions such as fear, guilt*

[1]For a discussion of psychophysiologic disorders, see Gregory, I.: *Psychiatry: Biological and Social*, W. B. Saunders Company, Philadelphia and London, 1961.

and hostility have physiological influences in all human beings. The individual with a psychophysiologic skin reaction exhibits either an overraction of this autonomic nervous system response or a continued physiological disturbance due to chronic stress, frustration and anxiety.

Strong feelings of hostility which are denied conscious awareness lie at the base of some psychosomatic skin reactions. An insecure individual with a need for dependency is afraid to vent his feelings of anger because this may result in rejection or rebuttal. Rather than giving his feelings emotional expression, he turns them inward, creating a high level of anxiety. This chronic anxiety may then influence the autonomic nervous system and cause various skin reactions.

The person who develops a psychophysiologic skin reaction is frequently found to have suffered from *continued stresses and emotional deprivations during childhood.* He may have felt a strong need to achieve in order to be accepted and frequently was very competitive in his relations with others. As a child and youth he was continually anxious about being accepted and he had a high level of striving. These feelings all combined to create a persistent anxiety which finally found expression through visceral means.

In adulthood a *relentless pattern of stress or frustration* may underlie various skin disturbances. When a person's marital and family relationships are unsatisfactory, the resulting chronic tension may give rise to various skin problems. Undue concern about finances, education, vocational matters and other factors tends to aggravate the condition.

Treatment

In treating psychophysiologic skin reactions it is important to give consideration to both physical and emotional factors. Complete medical examination by a physician, especially a dermatologist, is helpful to rule out the possibility of organic causes as well as to treat the disturbing symptoms of the skin disorder.

After medical attention has been received, a process of counseling can be initiated. Many times the initial stages of therapy with a person suffering from a skin reaction are very difficult because of his inability to accept the fact that there is an emotional basis for the disturbance. His personality is characterized by denial and repression. The very emotional reactions which precipitated the cutaneous disturbance make it difficult for the patient to admit to a psychogenic factor in his problem. In these cases the counselor must often proceed slowly, gradually helping the person to gain insight into his feelings. A number of sessions may be required before the client begins to see any relationship between his emotional adjustment and the physical symptoms. As the counselee gains insight and develops emotionally, the disorder will gradually disappear.

The actual process of therapy should be centered upon the subject's emotional mechanism. He needs to evaluate his inability to freely express emotions and feelings. Ventilation and emotional catharsis are especially important for the person with a psychophysiologic disorder. Many times this person is afraid to express his inner feelings because he has never done so. Too, he may unconsciously think he will harm or even destroy another person. He feels he must repress his strong, hostile feelings in order to avoid such irrational behavior. For this reason, the counselor should exercise care and patience in bringing unconsicous feelings of hostility to light. Only after a close relationship with the client has been established should these threatening areas be examined in depth. When the counselor proceeds step by step, the client can learn to accept and deal with his threatening, unconscious feelings.

The counselor will also want to discuss with the client the major areas of stress and frustration in his life. Since it is these conflicts which often underlie the disturbance, they should be deliberately considered and resolved if the physical symptoms are to be alleviated. As the person gains an improved self-concept and as he develops feelings of adequacy and security, he can meet life's daily frustrations and conflicts without succumbing to distressing anxiety which often results in skin disorders.

Since neurodermatitis is due to emotional factors, it is imperative that the counselor not overlook spiritual aspects of the problem. Personal faith in God and daily commitment to Christ afford guidance and peace which is not known otherwise. Spiritual insight and maturity are helpful in alleviating feelings of stress and frustration.

43. Obesity

Description

Overeating is a problem which is common to all ages. As a counselor deals with various emotional problems, he will soon be confronted with both children and adults who are suffering from overeating and the resulting obesity.

The problem of overweight is rarely found without accompanying symptoms. Many obese individuals, for example, suffer from a lack of physical energy and vitality. The overweight person is often moody, with some feelings of depression. Contrary to the stereotype of the rotund individual as jovial and happy-go-lucky, most overweight people are just the opposite. Many individuals who consistently overeat also exhibit lack of concern for their physical appearance. Some overweight women, for example, dress very untidily and have little interest in being neat and well-kept.

Obesity frequently brings other adjustment difficulties. The overweight individual often is ashamed of his physical appearance and because of this fails to take part in group activities. Having a low self-concept and poor physical appearance, he frequently has few close friends. The overweight high school girl, for example, feels out of place in many social activities. The obese teen-age boy is usually unable to participate in athletic activities. Because of these limitations, social relationships are seriously handicapped.

Etiology

The causes of overeating are multiple. Some are *physical problems such as hormonal and metabolic disturbances.* Improper diet and nutrition are other physical causal factors. Daily schedules which demand overwork without sufficient exercise may also lead to overeating.

In the majority of instances of overweight, however, the source of the difficulty can be traced to emotional factors. *The emotionally deprived person may turn to eating to fulfill his need for love and affection.* Feeling unloved and uncared for, some individuals subsitute the pleasure gained from eating for the needed emotional gratification of love and acceptance. Having an excessivly strong need for love, the person symbolically replaces this need with excessive overeating.

Research studies show that *a large proportion of obese children are unwanted.* The mothers of such children may react in one of two ways: Some overtly reject the child by criticizing, condemning and failing to show affection. In these cases the child may be forced to eating as a subtitute measure of gaining some feeling of pleasure and satisfaction. Other mothers with strong feelings of hostility and rejection toward their children react in an oversolicitous manner. Rather than directly expressing her feelings of rejection, this mother attempts to conceal her displeasure with the child by being overindulgent and oversolicitous. The mother refuses to let her child grow up. She continues to treat him as an infant and supplies his every need. She lavishes food upon him in an effort to show her love and cover her feelings of hostility. In this situation the child often reacts by taking all possible food offered by the mother in an attempt to remain in her good graces. By eating, the child is complying with the mother's wishes and thus gaining her approval. The above maternal behavioral patterns demonstrate two common dynamics in overeating. In the case of the openly rejecting parent, the child is *eating to compensate for unmet emotional needs.* In response to the oversolicitous mother, the child is *attempting to gain parental approval.*

Feelings of hostility underlie some instances of overeating. When a person (especially an adolescent) has strong hostile feelings toward parents, he may turn to overeating as a way of punishing the parents. This type of person is often afraid to openly disagree with parents or express his feelings of hostility. He does know, however, that the parents will be upset by overeating and obesity. The adolescent may then choose this method of expressing hostility toward his parents.

A very *inadequate self-concept* is common among overweight indivduals. These persons often feel unworthy of love and acceptance and unconsciously are driven to overeating in order to prove to themselves this unworthiness. It at first seems strange that a person would unconsciously attempt to prove his own unworthiness, but the person with a low self-concept often feels he is in need of punishment and rejection and thus compounds his own pathology.

In a limited number of cases of obesity *the basic cause is a psychophysiologic disorder.* The normal person, when placed in a stressful situation, is able either to verbalize his conflicts or engage in some physical activity to release the tension. Some individuals, however, are fearful of expressing their feelings. When faced with frustration and conflict they are unable to release the built-up tension. When this pattern of reacting is continued, the tension which is denied verbal or emotional expression seeks release through physical sources and the effective functioning of an organ may be hindered.[1]

Some people turn to excessive eating as an *unconscious means of avoiding involvement with the opposite sex.* When a girl harbors strong feelings of hostility toward men or is very fearful of sexual involvement, one of the best ways to avoid becoming involved with a man is to make herself so unattractive that men will not desire her acquaintance. In this way obesity serves an emotional need to avoid close relationships with the opposite sex. In some cases this dynamic is also associated with an overly-dependent parental relationship. A young woman in her early twenties, for example, may have an especially strong attachment to her mother. Not wanting to leave this relationship through a possible marriage, she overeats to reduce the likelihood that someone will date her and attempt to take her from her mother.

Illustration

Identification: Latin-American female, age 26
Presenting Problem: This young woman was referred for psychological care by her medical doctor who found no physical cause of her overeating.
Personal and Family History: This subject is the second of two

---

[1]For further discussion of this type of psychophysiologic reaction, see HEADACHES, NEURODERMATITIS and PEPTIC ULCERS in this volume.

children born to an upper-class home. Her father is a business executive and her mother is active in community social affairs. The subject's older brother has serious emotional disturbances and has been in difficulty with the police for theft and other antisocial behavior.

During therapy this woman began to discuss her childhood experiences. She reported that her father worked long hours and her mother was so engaged in church and social activities that she spent little time with the children. The subject states that she has been overweight "as long as I can remember." An interesting question by her therapist gave much insight into the cause of her compulsive eating. During the third interview, the counselor asked the woman to do some "homework during the week." He requested her to make a list of the times when she seemed to have a special desire to eat. When these occasions were discussed in the next session, it was apparent that her desire for food became greater when she was in a frustrating situation or had experienced rejection from a friend. One day, for example her husband became angry and stormed out of the house. After a time of crying she went immediately to the refrigerator to substitute pleasure associated with eating for the emotional needs her husband had failed to meet. Another time the subject felt a strong desire to eat after she had been reprimanded by her boss for a poor quality of work on her part-time job.

Treatment

The first consideration in dealing with an overwieght person should be a physical examination. Although endocrine and metabolic disturbances are not found to play causative roles in the majority of cases, it is important that this possibility be ruled out before attempting psychotherapy. If a person is suffering from a serious hormonal problem, many months of counseling therapy will not relieve the symptoms.

In some instances a medical specialist will prescribe medication to relieve excessive appetite. Although this alone is generally ineffective, when combined with insights into the causes for one's overeating, it is a helpful adjunct to therapy.

After physical considerations have been dealt with, the counselor should begin a program of therapy directed toward understanding and resolving the basic conflicts which are causing the person to turn to excessive eating. Practical concerns, such as regulating one's schedule to avoid overwork and having sufficient exercise, must be dealt with. Substitution of food with low caloric value is also important. Dynamics such as the substitution of food gratification for emotional support, or the relationship of hostility to overeating need to be explored and resolved.

The unmet emotional needs of the subject must be considered. The causes of the person's emotional deprivation and the effects of these on his personality adjustment are of utmost importance. As the client begins to gain insight into his behavior, the counselor can lead him into spiritual understanding which will fill the emotional void. The love of the Lord and knowledge of His daily provision offer such a person real comfort and security which cannot be realized outside of Christ.[2]

When a child is overweight, the counselor can help parents learn to provide for his emotional as well as his physical needs. If the child is lacking love and affection, these needs must be supplied. If he has inadequate social relationships with peers, he should be assisted in developing interpersonal skills. The child with feelings of inadequacy and inferiority needs much help to overcome these detrimental feelings. He should be complemented and encouraged by his parents. They should provide the child with tasks suitable to his developmental level and see that he has wide interests. This new sense of accomplishment and encouragement will assist him in overcoming feelings of inferiority which are at the base of his overeating.

[2]For a discussion of the application of spiritual concepts to a person's emotional adjustment, see the subject INSECURITY in this volume. Also, see the author's book, *This Way to Happiness.*

44. Obsessive Compulsive Reactions

Description

The obsessive-compulsive individual is usually characterized by extreme doubt, unreasonable fears, undue worry, lack of confidence, and the tendency to repeatedly perform some act or thought. He feels it is necessary to perform certain acts without regard to rational considerations. For example, he may be forced to count objects, touch certain things, avoid stepping on a crack in the sidewalk or wash his hands excessively. If he fails to do these, he feels uncomfortable; if he does them, he is forced to rationalize and justify his acts. All people perform such compulsive acts to a limited degree but their lives are not controlled by them.[1]

Obsessive thinking is commonly accompanied by anxiety. The person may be so tense and anxious over the content of his thoughts that he is unable to function effectively and thus feels useless. Or he may be anxiously obsessed with an idea that something terrible is about to happen. This individual may also be forced to think things which do not in themselves cause apprehension but may later produce severe anxiety. For example, compulsive counting itself produces little apprehension but he may worry so much over his inability to stop counting that he will develop further anxiety.

Etiology

Studies reveal that obsessive thoughts may be functioning *to keep unpleasant ideas from entering the consciousness*. Thus a person who has a fear of furry objects, for example, may become obsessed with the thought, "I am not afraid of furry objects."

Obsessive thoughts may also include the *expression of hostile*

---

[1]For a discussion of Obsessive Compulsive Reactions in children see: Finch, S. M.: *Fundamentals of Child Psychiatry*, W. W. Norton and Company, Inc., New York, 1960.

feelings. In this reaction a husband or older sibling may be obsessed with thoughts of injuring a new-born baby. These thoughts may be an expression of angry feelings to the baby because it deprives the husband or older child of the mother's affection and attention.

Such thoughts may also serve as a *reaction formation to hidden desires or impulses.* In this reaction a mother may be obsessed with thoughts of concern over her child. These obsessions are sometimes an indication of the mother's attempts to hide true feelings of hostility or aggression toward the son or daughter.

Another cause of obsessive reactions is *extreme feelings of guilt.* An individual who feels guilty over past misdeeds may have obsessive thoughts concerning condemnation which might befall him.

A person who finds *life's dealings threatening and dangerous* may develop obsessive thoughts of various forms in order to escape concentration on uncomfortable situations or experiences. By keeping his mind occupied with obsessive ideas, a person is able to avoid facing threatening reality situations.

Compulsions may result as *defense reactions to certain thoughts and fears.* An individual who constantly washes his hands or bathes, for example, may be performing this behavior in an unconscious attempt to cleanse himself from immoral thoughts or actions.

Compulsive behavior may also *reflect a past traumatic experience.* For example, a person may exhibit a particular motion which is symbolic of his attempt to avoid a car accident in which a close friend was seriously injured.

Illustration
Identification: White female, age 31
Presenting Problem: The patient is obsessed with thoughts concerning the safety of her children. She works during the day and feels compelled to frequently call the nursery where her children are kept.
Personal and Family History: The patient is one of three children. Her father is in professional work, and her mother is also well-educated. Both parents were oversolicitous with the pa-

tient when she was a child, not allowing her to develop adequate independence.

The patient did well in school, but did not learn to take initiative. She continued the pattern of dependence begun in childhood. She was married soon after graduating from high school and her first child was born several years later.

After diagnosis and several counseling sessions, the therapist believes that the client is attempting to cover her hostility toward her children. They emphasize responsibility which she is unable and unwilling to take. Rather than consciously taking out her aggression on her children, she has developed obsessive thoughts concerning their welfare. These thoughts enable her to avoid her true feelings toward her children.

Treatment

If the obsessive-compulsive behavior has resulted from a particular incident in the person's past, the counselor should explore this experience and lead the individual to an understanding of the development of the obsession or compulsion.

If the irrational behavior is a result of an accumulation of the individual's past experiences and personality development, an extensive personality evaluation may be necessary. The therapist should help the client to explore his irrational fears and compulsions. The client's behavior usually begins to take on new meaning when it is understood in relationship to earlier experiences and personality development.

As therapy progresses, the counselor can help the client immeasurably by introducing spiritual content into the sessions. Since people are spiritual beings with a capacity for God, they can benefit from the power which Christ offers through knowing Him personally and maturing as a Christian. This spiritual understanding, however, must be patiently integrated in therapy so that it affects one's thinking and eventually his behavior. Excessive doubt, extreme fears, undue worry and lack of confidence—these and other feelings which are frequent symptoms of the obsessive-compulsive client, can be minimized through spiritual guidance.[2]

[2]For a discussion of the application of spiritual concepts to neurotic disturbances, see DEPRESSIONS and INSECURITY in this volume.

45. Paranoid Reactions

Description

Individuals suffering from paranoid reactions are characterized by extreme suspicion and delusions. There are two basic manifestations of this disorder, each having many similar dynamics. The first of these is a *paranoid state*, distinguished by paranoid delusions and often accompanied by hallucinations. The person suffering from a paranoid state may show confused thought processes and some extreme forms of maladjustment. He does not exhibit, however, the extremely bizarre personality deterioration of the schizophrenic.

The second major paranoid reaction is known as *paranoia*, which is characterized by logical, well-systematized delusions. The paranoiac rationalizes his own thinking and believes that those who oppose or differ with him are wrong. A person suffering from paranoia does not usually exhibit any other abnormal psychological symptoms. He may appear to react normally in all of his activities except in the area of his delusions. Paranoia may be divided into four major categories.

Persecutory Paranoria. This is the most frequent of the four forms of paranoia. Individuals suffering from persecutory paranoia are characterized by delusions of persecution. They are firmly convinced that some person or group is against them and is plotting to do them harm.

Grandiose Paranoia. These individuals believe that they are endowed with extraordinary gifts and ability. Grandiose paranoia most frequently manifests itself in those who consider themselves religious prophets, social reformers and ingenious inventors.

Jealous Paranoia. The jealous paranoiac may seize upon any type of behavior or act, then attribute it to infidelity on the part of his spouse or loved one. If the jealous paranoic's wife has her hair set at the beauty parlor, it is because she has found another man. If a husband is late getting home from work, it is because he has special interests in his secretary.

Erotic Paranoia. These persons entertain the false belief that various individuals are falling in love with them. A friendly smile or a casual remark may be interpreted as meaning that the individual has a romantic interest in the paranoiac. He may then begin to send gifts and letters to this new lover. If his show of affection receives no response, he may merely consider this a test of his love.

Etiology

The development of paranoid reactions stems primarily from childhood. The future paranoiac reveals many signs of his disturbance even as a young person. His early life is usually characterized by *extreme frustrations and emotional conflict* which cause him to become over-anxious and insecure. *The home atmosphere is often stern and authoritarian.*

The parents may be very domineering and critical, frequently accusing the child of misdeeds. Such an environment produces *feelings of rejection and insecurity* in the child. As a result, he becomes suspicious, distrustful, and resentful. As he grows older he becomes seclusive and has few close friends in whom he will confide. When he does not get his way he becomes irritable and moody. In adolescence he may become overconfident, self-assertive, critical and aggressive.

By calling attention to the undesirable motives and actions of others, the paranoiac sometimes attempts to camouflage his own feelings of rejection and insecurity. He does this to relieve the focus on his own deficiencies but in so doing he may become suspicious of others and develop feelings of persecution.

Guilt feelings may also give rise to paranoia. A person who feels he has transgressed some moral or ethical law may convince himself that he deserves severe punishment for his misdeeds. As he thinks about it, he begins to believe that his punishment is being plotted in the minds of some of his acquaintances.[1]

A dynamic frequently found among paranoid individuals is that of projection. In this mechanism the individual harbors

---

[1]For a discussion of paranoia, see: Gregory, Ian: *Psychiatry: Biological and Social*, W. B. Saunders Company, Philadelphia, 1961.

strong unconscious feelings which are threatening and unacceptable. For example, a person may have extremely hostile feelings which he has managed to repress from consciousness. If he allowed these feelings to come to awareness he would be terribly upset and threatened. Since these feelings are strong, however, he is unable to keep them completely repressed and he unconsciously projects them onto others. By believing that others are angry and hostile the subject can take a condemning attitude to the very feelings he unconsciously harbors. Instead of seeing these unpleasant thoughts as part of his own personality structure, he views others as being controlled by these feelings. Rather than being the hostile person in need of condemnation, the paranoid person then thinks of himself as the persecuted one who is in need of sympathy and protection.

Illustration

Identification: White female, age 35

Presenting Problem: The patient is experiencing delusions of persecution. She first became suspicious of her husband and is now growing progressively worse. She is afraid to leave her home for fear neighbors will enter the house and poison her food. She keeps the doors and windows locked and the shades drawn most of the time.

Personal and Family History: The patient comes from a highly rigid, authoritarian home. As a child she was made to conform to an extremely strict code of behavior and her parents threatened her with stories of evil which would befall her if she was a "naughty girl." Throughout school she was timid, and took little part in social activities. To her teachers she was a model child, never disturbing the class and always acting in a polite and courteous manner.

The patient was married at twenty-five and now has two children. Shortly after marriage she began to develop guilt feelings about her behavior. These thoughts became increasingly severe until she now feels that she deserves severe punishment for her misdeeds. She fears that her neighbors are plotting to injure her and poison her family.

Treatment

Therapy for persons suffering from paranoia is admittedly difficult. Most paranoiacs resist psychological help. They feel that they have been conspired against if they are sent to a therapist. Unless they seek therapy of their own will, little progress will be made.

The essence of therapy with a paranoiac is to provide an atmosphere of acceptance in which the patient can discuss his feelings and delusions. The key to success with these individuals often hinges on total acceptance by the counselor. The therapist cannot take a critical position if he is to gain the confidence of the paranoid individual. As the paranoiac comes to understand that the counselor accepts him as he is with no thought of condemnation or persecution, he begins to gain confidence in the counselor.

It frequently takes a number of months of therapy before the paranoid person can begin to genuinely trust his counselor. Only when this relationship is established can the counselor initiate apparent corrections of the client's distortion of reality.

As the paranoid individual begins to place his trust in the therapist, a major step is accomplished. It is likely that the counselor is the first person in the client's lifetime who has totally accepted him as he is. It is often the first relationship of genuine trust and assurance. As the client begins to experience the phenomenon of trust and confidence in the counselor, he can gradually begin to generalize this newly discovered trust to his family members, then to others in his environment. Through this gradually widening circle the paranoid slowly replaces suspicion and distrust with confidence and assurance in his interpersonal relationships.

An important consideration in dealing with these individuals is the question, "From whom is the person receiving his emotional cues?" The paranoid is a person who is extremely sensitive to what others think of him. His total life has been distorted because of this overraction to the supposed desires and actions of others. If the paranoid person is to recover from his suspicion he must come to the point of realizing that his acceptance and worthiness do not come from pleasing those in his environment. Instead, he needs to gradually grow in the understanding that his source of security and worthiness comes from the Lord. He is accepted by God without having to live up to certain standards. Even though his parents may have been critical and condemning, the Lord is not. "To the praise of the glory of his grace, wherein he hath made us accepted in the beloved" (Ephesians 1:6). With repeated discussion of these concepts the paranoid individual can gradually be freed from the necessity of ordering his life according to the believed pleasure of others. He can build into his personality structure a new sense of identity which is based upon the total acceptance he finds in Christ.

46. Peptic Ulcer

Description

A peptic ulcer is a psychophysiologic disorder which is characterized by an open sore in the lining of either the duodenum or the stomach.[1] If located in the duodenum, it is called a duodenal ulcer; and if in the stomach, a gastric ulcer.

Stomach distress before meals, relieved by eating, is the typical symptom pattern of peptic ulcers. Untreated, these can cause vomiting, obstruction and hemorrhage.[2]

Etiology

The exact mechanism for the production of a peptic ulcer is not clearly known. On a physiological level, *excessive acid secretion of the stomach's digestive juices* and the overactivity of the stomach and the duodenum play major roles. When the secretion is disturbed over a period of time, it may result in an ulcer.

The cause of this oversecretion and overactivity is no longer believed to lie solely in the diet of the individual. Research studies show that *chronic emotional stress* can disrupt the normal functioning of the autonomic nervous system. This, in turn, influences the secretion of gastric juice which is a basic casual factor of the ulcer. Elements which may interfere with the normal functioning of the autonomic nervous system include *overwork, nervous tension, worry and emotional strain.*

Many attempts have been made to identify a basic personality type which is most susceptible to peptic ulcers, but these studies have been contradictory and inconclusive. Some ulcer patients, however, are characterized by *insecurity, strong dependency needs, aggression, guilt and anxiety.* In many instances the person is a very *busy, competitive and hard-driving*

[1]For a discussion of the medical aspects of ulcers, see: Harrison, T. R. and others (Eds.): *Principles of Internal Medicine*, McGraw-Hill Book Company, Inc., New York, 1962.

[2]For a discussion of ulcers and related psychophysiologic reactions see: Coleman, James: *Abnormal Psychology and Modern Life*, Scott, Foresman and Company, Chicago, Atlanta, Dallas, Palo Alto, Fair Lawn, 1964.

individual. He is continually *under pressure to achieve.* It is sometimes found that this strong desire for achievement is an attempt to overcome underlying *feelings of dependency* by proving one's adequacy and successfulness. The continual tension this individual faces results in improper bodily functioning and creates the ulcer.

Spiritual factors are influential in the cause of some ulcers. When a person is convicted of sin, but refuses to yield to God, the anxiety over this battle may tie with a general pattern of anxiety which results in the formation of an ulcer.

Illustration

Identification: White male, age 42

Presenting Problem: The subject reported to a family physician for complaints of "stomach trouble." He related the fact that he had suffered from stomach difficulty for several years but that it had become worse during the past six months.

Upon his first visit to the physician for severe stomach pains and vomiting, the subject suspected an ulcerous condition. "Doc," he was reported as saying, "would you give me a complete examination to see if I have an ulcer?"

Personal and Family History: The subject was about 45 pounds overweight. He was the president of a growing and successful new manufacturing company. He was aggressive, having moved to three new communities during the last eight years, each community and home representing an advancement economically.

After medical treatment was begun, the subject was referred for simultaneous psychological evaluation and conseling. Four months of combined therapy proved helpful in alleviating both the symptoms and cause.

Treatment

Effective treatment of peptic ulcers lies in a combination of medical, psychological and spiritual care. Medications, proper diet, and/or surgery may relieve symptoms of pain, bleeding and chronic distress.

If the individual is to avoid recurrence of this disorder, it is usually necessary to combine counseling with medical treatment. Psychotherapy is directed toward enabling the patient to better handle stress situations. As a person becomes more secure and is able to solve his daily difficulties, he will experience a lessening of the psychosomatic reaction.

In the case of the individual who is carrying an extra heavy workload, or whose daily schedule does not permit sufficient relaxation, practical solutions are necessary. The counselor may direct the client's attention toward (1) understanding conscious or unconscious drives, (2) establishing more reasonable goals, (3) setting up a desirable daily schedule, (4) gaining needed relaxation, and (5) developing appropriate eating habits.

When an individual is driving himself in an attempt to prove to others his adequacy, the counselor needs to lead him to an understanding of this dynamic. As the person begins to accept himself as he is, the need for this overwork and excessive strain will diminish.

If the causes of ulcerous conditions are mainly emotional in origin, the patient will benefit from spiritual help. In addition to surrendering one's life to Christ, the individual should be encouraged to establish a program for spiritual development. This may include the establishment of daily devotions, reading Christian literature, fellowshiping with believers, witnessing for Christ and regular church attendance. As he grows spiritually and finds satisfaction in living a humble, serene life in Christ, the symptoms of emotional disturbance will diminish.

An important consideration in developing into unconscious material in psychosomatic illnesses is the fact that occasionally the physical reaction is the person's means of defending against an underlying psychotic condition. In these cases the individual may be harboring strong hostile impulses or other unconscious thoughts which, if accepted into consciousness, would be too threatening to bear. If the counselor uncovers this threatening material too rapidly, he may precipitate the underlying psychotic condition and cause much more severe disturbance. Consequently, it is wise to work gradually when bringing unconscious dynamics to the attention of clients suffering from psychophysiologic disorders.

47. Phobic Reaction

Description

A phobia is a fear of some object or situation which, in itself, poses no actual danger to the individual.[1] The person suffering from a phobia usually recognizes the irrational nature of his fear, but he is unable to simply reason his feelings away. He may exhibit a phobia for any object or situation. The following are some of the most common fears which trouble people:

Acrophobia—fear of high places
Agoraphobia—fear of open or public places
Aichmophobia—fear of sharp or pointed objects
Algophobia—fear of pain
Anthropophobia—fear of men or a particular man
Astraphobia—fear of thunder, lightning or storms
Claustrophobia—fear of closed places
Ereuthophobia—fear of blushing
Gynephobia—fear of women or of a particular woman
Hematophobia—fear of blood
Hydrophobia—fear of water
Monophobia—fear of solitude
Necrophobia—fear of dead bodies
Nyctophobia—fear of darkness (night)
Ochlophobia—fear of crowds
Pathophobia—fear of disease or some particular disease
Pyrophobia—fear of fire
Thanatophobia—fear of death
Toxiphobia—fear of poisons (or of being poisoned)
Zoophobia—fear of animals (or some particular animal)

Persons suffering from phobias will go to great extremes to avoid objects which bring about fear reactions. The intensity of fear associated with an object may range from irritating concern to serious distress and attacks of extreme anxiety.

In addition to irrational fear, individuals suffering from pho-

[1]For a discussion of Phobic Reactions, see: Thorpe, L., Katz, B., and Lewis R.: *The Psychology of Abnormal Behavior*, The Ronald Press Company, New York, 1961.

bia may exhibit physical symptoms such as backaches and other pains, nausea, dizziness and skin rashes.

Etiology

Many times a phobia is the result of a *sudden traumatic experience in the early life* of the individual. Among the more common fears is that of dogs, which often arises when a child is attacked by a dog and is unable to overcome the fear associated with this experience. For years after the incident the person may not be able to come near a dog without reacting with deep anxiety and fear.

Phobias may also arise as a *displacement of anxiety.* In these cases the fear object is symbolic of a certain experience or event which the person found unbearable. The extreme dread is attached to the newly substituted fear object. Displacement of anxiety may also occur when a person transfers free-floating anxiety to a specific object. In this way he experiences anxiety only when in the presence of the fear object. At other times he is freed from previously distressing anxiety.

Phobias may also come about through the *influence of parents.* A mother or father who has an extreme fear of lightning, for example, may pass this on to the children by hiding every time there is an electrical storm and warning of the great danger involved.

Other phobias can develop from *guilt feelings.* If a person feels extremely guilty and believes that he deserves punishment for some past action, he may develop a fear of the punishment he anticipates.

Another cause of phobia is an *attempt by the person to avoid situations in which he might exhibit otherwise repressed aggressive or erotic impulses.*

For example, a housewife may develop aichmophobia (fear of sharp objects) because she is afraid that when she handles a sharp object she may use it to destroy her children or her husband.

Illustration

Identification: White female, age 30
Presenting Problem: The patient has an abnormal fear of water.

When she is near a swimming pool or other body of water, she becomes panic-stricken and often faints. If she hears water running in the house, she also becomes nervous and upset.

Personal and Family History: The patient was one of three children born into a middle-class home. She had a normal, happy childhood with the exception of one traumatic experience. While on a weekend outing at a nearby lake the family was attempting to teach the girl to swim. When she refused to get into the water, one of her older brothers shoved her in. Although she was pulled out of the water, she was terrified by the experience and has been unable to overcome the anxiety and fright associated with it.

Treatment

Treatment for phobias arising from past traumatic experiences may be dealt with by the process of desensitization. The patient is encouraged to talk out his fear, discussing the particular event which is responsible for his phobia. He is gradually led to approach the fear object so that he can overcome the feelings of anxiety associated with it.

If the phobia has been displaced to some object other than the original fear-provoking one, the process of therapy may need to be more extensive. Such cases often involve a deeper personality maladjustment and so require a longer period of time before the individual is able to overcome his ungrounded fears.

The counselor can help the fearful person understand that most phobias grow out of a passive personality which reacts submissively and fearfully rather than realistically.[2] To phobic individuals, it is easier to fear a stress situation than to cope with it. The patient needs to analyze the dynamics in his life which cause him to react as he does. As he learns to recognize the unconscious emotional forces that have brought on his phobic reactions, he will begin to objectify his fears and think differently about them.

[2]For therapy with related problems, see ANXIETY RE-ACTION and INSECURITY in this volume.

Additional reinforcement is available to the patient when he considers his relationship and responsibility to God. As he puts trust in Christ and claims the power and victory which are at the disposal of the child of God, new confidence and serenity flood his life. The promise, "For God hath not given us the spirit of fear; but of power, . . ." (II Timothy 1:7) becomes a reality, and he knows that he need never walk alone.

48. Pica

Description
Pica is a disorder sometimes found in children or in adults who have psychotic disorders marked by severe regression. In this disturbance the person apparently gains enjoyment from eating dirt, paper and other debris. Some individuals have been known to eat paint, clothing and human feeces. This condition is often accompanied by poor health which results from digestive disturbances caused by foreign material taken into the stomach.[1]

Etiology
All children occasionally eat materials which are not conducive to good digestion. But such behavior is usually temporary and disappears naturally or with the attention of parents. In the case of seriously distorted eating habits, however, the person is suffering from serious personality disturbances.

Pica is found most frequently among children of *below average intellectual ability*. The lack of mental ability and the emotional frustrations associated with this limitation appear to play important roles in the formation of this disturbance.

Another basic casual factor is an inadequate home environment characterized by *low moral and economic status*. Children who suffer from malnutrition associated with serious physical and emotional deprivations are more susceptible to this disorder.

Some children who are normal in intelligence but who are severely emotionally disturbed have been known to eat dirt to "get even" with parents, siblings or playmates. Some have said that they did so to "kill themselves." Thus, the problem of pica may be associated with *deep-seated hostility*.

Feelings of rejection and excessive anxiety and tension are common to individuals with perverted appetites. Individuals raised in homes which foster these emotional disturbances are more likely to evidence this type of behavior.

[1]For a discussion of pica and other eating disturbances, see Kanner, Leo: *Child Psychiatry*, Charles C. Thomas, Springfield, Illinois, 1960.

Illustration
Identification: White male, age 4
Presenting Problem: The subject was brought to the physician by a neighbor lady who complained that she had often seen the child eating dirt. The lady stated that the boy's mother was expecting another child soon and that she not only seemed unconcerned about the problem but was unable to bring the child for help.
Personal and Family History. The subject is one of five children, all under ten years of age. The father is a day laborer and neither parent went beyond the ninth grade in school.

Neighbors have reported that they have seen the child eating dirt since he was old enough to crawl. The child has been ill much of his life, and his general development has not been normal.

The physician's examination revealed that the child was suffering from malnutrition. In addition it was suspected that he might have below average intelligence. Arrangements were made for the child to be seen several times at a community mental health clinic. There he was given intelligence tests and it was learned that his intelligence was at the dull normal level.

Treatment
Pica usually disappears rapidly in children of average intelligence when acceptable food is given and the child is supervised so that he is not permitted to eat improper objects.

Treatment with mental defective lies primarily in supervision to see that they are unable to eat those things which might be harmful to their health. If this condition continues into later childhood, professional help should be sought. Any prolonged continuation of this disorder is usually indicative of severe emotional disturbance. In these the total family is important in order to provide a better emotional environment in the home. In the case of adults suffering from this problem it is likely that the perverted appetite is only one symptom of a psychotic condition.[2]

[2]See the discussions of PSYCHOTIC DISORDERS and SCHIZOPHRENIA in this volume.

49. Postpartum Psychoses

Description

Many women suffer from acute attacks of emotional disturbances connected with childbirth. These reactions may occur any time during pregnancy and throughout the first year following birth of the child. The most common feature of postpartum emotional disturbance is generally depression. This may range from an exaggeration of usual feelings of worry to a severe condition. The mother may become exceedingly irritable and especially vulnerable to emotional frustrations. In some cases there is a psychotic condition related to the disturbance.[1]

Etiology

Postpartum emotional disturbances do not differ grossly from other forms of emotional and mental illness. Instead, almost any form of emotional disturbance may be manifested in connection with childbirth. The circumstances surrounding pregnancy and childbirth serve not as casual factors, but merely precipitate the disturbance in an individual who is already predisposed to emotional difficulties. A woman may go along through life with a borderline level of adjustment until she becomes pregnant. At that time the added stress and strains may bring to light the personality maladjustment which she had been able to deal with under normal circumstances. She may have had one or more pregnancies before experiencing this one that precipitated depression.

Both *physical and emotional factors* are important in the etiology of postpartum disturbances. The emotional factors are the same as for other difficulties, with some new considerations. The mother's *fear or dread of pregnancy,* for example, may cause excess worry and influence her adjustment during pregnancy and childbirth. Attitudes toward the expected child are also important. In some cases *the mother does not want the*

---

[1]For a discussion of other psychoses see PSYCHOTIC DISORDERS and SCHIZOPHRENIA in this volume.

child and rejects the new baby. She may also experience *feelings of guilt over this hostility.* This combination of factors is sometimes associated with postpartum disturbances.

The birth of a new child also brings *connotations of added responsibilities.* The woman who has a borderline level of adjustment has all she can handle emotionally without caring for a new baby around the clock. The pressure of these new responsibilities is another casual factor in emotional disturbances associated with birth.

The attitude of the father toward the new child is also important. If the father is negative or even passive, this can cause the mother much worry and concern. Continued rejection or passivity from the father may result in serious conflicts for the new mother.

Some *mothers view the new baby as competition for the affection of their husbands.* When this happens, the mother may be thrown into much turmoil as she sees her husband giving the child affection which she needs so desperately herself.

Physical factors often play an important role in postpartum depression. In addition to the *general physical strain of pregnancy and childbirth,* there are sometimes *metabolic factors* which compound the woman's adjustment. *Difficult births and excessive hemorrhaging* may drain the woman's strength and leave her more susceptible to emotional disturbances. The exact part that chemical imbalances play is still not clearly understood.

Illustration
Identification: Negro female, age 39
Presenting Problem: This woman was referred to a psychologist by her medical doctor for postpartum depression. She began experiencing severe feelings of depression two months after the birth of her third child. The medical doctor had treated her physical complaints and felt that a major portion of the woman's difficulty was emotional.
Personal and Family History: This subject was reared in a middle-class home. Her father was professionally employed and her mother did not work outside of the home. All family mem-

bers were born-again Christians and there was no history of mental or emotional disturbances among other family members.

The woman states that she has been a nervous person "most of her life." She has had occasional periods of "the blues," but has never seen a doctor or counselor for these symptoms.

During counseling it was found that this woman's third child was unplanned. The subject and her husband had two children, ages eleven and thirteen, and were hoping to be able to spend more time with each other, being free from the continual care of the children. The unexpected baby caused the mother much frustration as she found her schedule filled with responsibilities to the child when she desired, instead, to spend more time with friends and more time out of the home. These problems were compounded by relatives and friends who frankly told her they were surprised that she wanted another baby. "You and your husband are both too old to be starting in again, having babies," they chided. These stresses, plus the physical hardships of pregnancy, had combined to cause this subject's tension and feelings of depression. She responded well to medication and intensive therapy and in time was functioning effectively.

Treatment

Treatment for the woman suffering from postpartum depression should combine both physical and emotional factors. It is of utmost importance that a thorough physical examination be given in order to remove any organic causes of the disturbance. After proper medical diagnosis and treatment, counseling may be started. Therapy with these individuals follows the same pattern as other disturbances discussed in this volume, with the exception that consideration should be given to unique aspects associated with childbirth. These include the mother's attitudes toward the new child, her feelings concerning her new responsibilities, and any misconceptions about pregnancy and childbirth. In many cases long-term therapy is required to resolve serious, unconscious personality conflicts.[2]

[2]See also DEPRESSION, especially the section on Treatment, in this volume.

50. Profanity

Description

Swearing or profanity denotes the use of vulgar, obscene or blasphemous language. In the Scriptures we are admonished to "let no corrupt communication proceed out of your mouth, but that which is good to the use of edifying, that it may minister grace unto hearers" (Ephesians 4:29).

Although the professional counselor rarely has a client come with the presenting problem of profanity, he does deal with many individuals whose total spiritual and emotional maladjustment includes a pattern of profanity. In other cases a wife or husband may come to a counselor because of the vile and upsetting language of his or her mate. In still other instances, parents may bring a child for counseling because he is suffering from emotional disturbances including vulgar language.

Etiology

The use of obscene language in a child can usually be traced to *imitation of the parents or other significant adult figures.* When a child is brought up in an environment where vulgar language is the accepted pattern of speech, it is only natural that he adopt this as his own.

Another frequent cause of obscene language among children is the *encouragement he gets from parents.* Some mothers and fathers react to an occasional profane word from their child with smiles and laughter. They think this behavior is "cute," coming from such a small child. In this way, the child may begin to use vulgar language to become the center of attention.

Obscenity of speech may also be *a means of aggression.* The hostile person who has heard others swear when frustrated may turn to profanity in order to express his aggressiveness. In these cases the profanity may be a part of a broader pattern of maladjustment found in the sociopathic personality.[1] In some instances, a young person will develop vulgar speech *in order to*

[1] See the discussion of SOCIOPATHIC PERSONALITY in this volume.

shock his parents and to express feelings of hostility toward them. One thirteen-year-old girl who did not have a good relationship with her parents started using vulgar language. This behavior began as she was entering her adolescent years and the parents did not allow her any freedom to join in extracurricular activities and spend time with her friends. In order to "get back" at her parents, this girl associated with many undesirable teen-agers and soon began droping an occasional swear word at home. The major factors here included the poor parent-child relationships, the influence of the girl's adolescent friends, and her lack of devotion to the Lord.

Some individuals make constant use of swearing because *they have low intelligence and lack a wide vocabulary with appropriate means of expression.* Whereas the cultured and refined person has learned a broad and acceptable vocabulary, the person of low intelligence or with inadequate education may feel a necessity to turn to profanity in order to give special emphasis to what he is attempting to say.

The unsaved individual and Christians who are not living in close fellowship with the Lord are much more likely to express themselves with vulgar and profane language. The person whose life is controlled by Christ usually keeps his speech honoring to the Lord unless he has some rather serious personality disturbances.

The heart of the unregenerate man is filled with sin and corruption. "A good man out of the good treasure of his heart bringeth forth that which is good; and an evil man out of the evil treasure of his heart bringeth forth that which is evil: for of the abundance of the heart his mouth speaketh" (Luke 6:45). The vile language that comes from so many unsaved individuals is an indication of the inner impurity and evil of their own lives.

Illustration

Identification: Spanish male, age 34
Presenting Problem: This man came to his pastor complaining of difficulty in "controlling my tongue."
Personal and Family History: The subject is a factory worker who is married and has three children. His early home back-

ground was very poor. His parents divorced while he was young and he was shifted from one foster home to another. During his adolescent years the subject spent some time in juvenile camps for deliquent activities. Two months before coming to his pastor with the problem of swearing this man had accepted Christ as his Savior. He had come to realize that his speech was not pleasing to God and he had prayed often that this would be removed.

It took this man a number of weeks to make significant progress in developing cleaner speech. Since he had been accustomed to using vulgar language for over twenty years, it was not easy to alter this pattern of reacting. With increased understanding of the factors which caused him to use vulgar language and with added spiritual growth, including daily Bible readings, this man gradually overcame his difficulty.

Treatment

When counseling with parents of children who are developing improper speech, the most important consideration is usually the environment which the parents are providing for the child. If they subtly encourage his profanity by smiling at his speech, or if they are setting him an example of poor speech, this should be corrected.

If the young person is turning to profanity to vent his hostile feelings toward his parents, the counselor will need a number of sessions to work with the entire family. Some of the sessions will be spent with the teen-ager alone; others will be devoted only to parents. Several sessions will also be shared by the entire family. In this way the young person and his parents can gain understanding of each other. In most cases, there is inadequate communication between parents and child. The parents often feel that the child is "ornery and defiant." The young person may feel that the parents "either don't care or can't understand." By sharing a number of counseling hours each family member can come to understand the reasons why other members react the way they do. As the family develops better communication, they will be able to resolve their difficulties and gain a much more rewarding life which comes from increased family unity.

Because the pattern of profane speech is usually of long standing, working with adults often takes considerable time. When a person has been accustomed to using one type of language, he becomes conditioned to these words. He finds it difficult, therefore, to drop ingrained habits and initiate the opposite behavior immediately.

In dealing with this individual the counselor will want to guide the person to an understanding of the reasons for his profane speech. The counselee needs to see if this is an expression of his hostility, if it is due to past environmental factors, or if it is basically a spiritual problem. As the person gains insight into the causes of his behavior, the counselor can help him to gradually replace old behavioral patterns with new and wholesome speech.

When an unsaved person or a carnal Christian is living in sin and his life is centered upon evil thoughts, his speech patterns will usually not change unless his heart condition is improved. As the counselor leads his client into a closer walk with the Lord many inward changes will take place which will be evidenced by improved speech. When the person develops a love for the Lord and begins to serve Him, amazing changes will take place. One's total life should become Christ-centered. As Paul wrote to the Philippians, "Finally, brethren, whatsoever things are true, whatsoever things are honest, whatsoever things are just, whatsoever things are pure, whatsoever things are lovely, whatsoever things are of good report; if there be any virtue, and if there be any praise think on these things" (Philippians 4:8). When the believer allows the Lord to work this miracle of dedication in his heart, the problem of filthy communication as well as many other sinful actions will disappear.

51. Psychotic Disorders

Description
Psychotic disorders are severe forms of mental illness characterized by loss of contact with reality.[1] A common term for these serious personality disturbances is insanity. The psychotic person lives partially in a world of fantasy. He has difficulty distinguishing between external reality and subjective experience. In addition he may experience hallucinations and delusions. Such an individual is unable to relate effectively to those about him.

The severely psychotic individual frequently loses orientation to his environment and is unable to carry on his work. He may also become dangerous and difficult to manage. Serious disturbances such as these may require hospitalization for prolonged periods.

Etiology
Psychotic conditions may arise either from organic or functional causes. Certain organic conditions cause damage to brain tissue which brings about severe mental disorder. Among the most prominent of these organic factors are encephalitis (infection of the brain), continued intoxication from drugs and alcohol, traumatic injuries to the brain, and arteriosclerosis (hardening of the arteries, usually associated with advanced age). Some research also indicates the importance of bodily chemical imbalances in psychotic states.

Psychological factors appear to play a major role in most psychotic conditions. The psychotic individual is unable to adequately meet daily frustrations and conflicts. Throughout his early life he has developed methods of escaping from problem situations until he finally becomes so accustomed to retreating from reality that he is unable to function normally.

One of the most common factors in the childhood experi-

[1]See also the discussions of INVOLUTIONAL PSYCHOTIC REACTION, MANIC DEPRESSIVE REACTION, PARANOID REACTION and SCHIZOPHRENIC REACTION in this volume.

ences of psychotic patients is insecurity in early family relationships, caused by parental rejection, severe discipline and overprotection. Any number of parental patterns can cause a child to grow up with inadequate emotional strength to meet life realistically.

As a child the psychotic individual did not learn to properly handle stress situations. Factors such as insecurity or parental overprotection caused the child to feel incapable of meeting difficult situations. Whereas normal children gradually gain their independence and learn to meet common frustrations, the psychotic person has not developed this ability. As a result, he turns to excessive daydreaming and fantasy to escape unpleasant experiences and to achieve the success he cannot find in reality.

Treatment

Because of the severity of psychotic disorders an individual suffering from these disturbances must often be hospitalized. This is necessary to protect both himself and society since the psychotic may not be able to control his actions and may become dangerous. During hospitalization, a combination of medical and psychological therapy is provided. Psychiatric therapy may include shock treatment and chemotherapy. In rare instances brain surgery is used to alleviate disturbing symptoms. The hospital provides the patient with a structured environment where he can have freedom to adjust to a routine and a relatively non-threatening situation. While the patient is hospitalized he may also receive either group or individual psychotherapy. Opportunity to discuss one's adjustment difficulties is of utmost importance if the person is to actually overcome the basic personality problem. Various psychiatric treatments may bring relief of the severe symptoms, but they generally have only minimal effect on the person's basic personality disturbance.

If a psychotic person is not so severely disturbed that he needs hospitalization, much profit can be gained from intensive psychotherapy. It is important to realize, however, that counseling with a psychotic individual is vastly different from working with neurotic persons. In most types of personality maladjustment, the therapist calls the subject's attention to many unconscious conflicts. He deals with threatening impulses and the subject's inappropriate defenses. By discussing freely these areas the person is able to see his ineffective adjustment and to make a more appropriate emotional response. A psychotic person, however, is unable to distinguish between reality because he found conflicts and frustrations too disturbing. If the counselor focuses upon these conflicts, he will compound the psychotic's poor adjustment and force him to withdraw even further from reality.

With this in mind, psychotherapy with the psychotic person should lie only in the hands of the exceptionally well-trained. Immediate referral to qualified personnel should always be made by the person who has not had extensive training in psychotherapy.

Since the psychotic is afraid of life, he will find it difficult to place his confidence in the therapist. For this reason the counselor must be very sensitive to his responses to the client. The therapist cannot give any indication of rejection or dissatisfaction with the client without hindering the therapeutic relationship. Even when the psychotic person tells of bizarre fantasies or ideas of persecution, the therapist should not disagree with these reactions. The psychotic is suffering from a shattered ego. He has no faith in his own abilities. If the counselor disagrees with him, this only weakens his already inadequate defensive structure. If the counselor questions the validity of the psychotic's statements, he is likely to lose the confidence of the client. It may take many months of this total acceptance of bizarre thought processes before the client develops this confidence in his therapist. Only then can the counselor begin to offer alternative interpretations to the patient's distortions.

In working with psychotic persons the therapist may have to be much more active than with other clients. For example, the counselor may have to help him make decisions which affect daily living. The normal person is able to reach his own conclusions about various vocational considerations and family conflicts, but the psychotic may not have adequate reasoning ability to make these seemingly simple decisions. Because of this the counselor may need to offer specific suggestions.

After a number of months of supportive therapy, the counselor may begin to help the patient correct his distortions of reality. At first this may be done by offering alternative solutions to the patient's statements. For example, a client may state, "That man pulled right in front of me on the highway and tried to slow me down." If this comment had been made during the first few months of therapy, the counselor may have accepted it with a remark such as, "That's too bad; the highways are sometimes very frustrating." In later therapy, however, the counselor may attempt to correct the client's distortion of reality by reacting with a statement such as, "I wonder if he pulled in front of you because his lane was blocked and he was in a hurry?" This counselor reaction is an effort to substitute a realistic interpretation of the event for the psychotic's distorted idea of self-reference or persecution. The therapist can gradually begin to make use of substitute interpretations, such as the above, in order to lead the client to an acceptance of reality. This process may take many months. Hundreds of daily experiences must usually be re-evaluated in order to correct the psychotic's distortions of reality.

Spiritual factors are of utmost importance in dealing with psychotic individuals Because of the severity of the emotional disturbance, however, many psychotics are unable to understand the claims of Christ until they have had a long process of therapy. Since they are unable to distinguish reality from fantasy, they may not be able to reason out and accept the Lord's offer of forgiveness and salvation.

As the patient begins to progress the therapist can be sensitive to the timing of spiritual concepts. The acceptance of Christ as Savior can be a tremendous step for the psychotic individual. One psychotic lady, for example, related her experience of salvation. She stated that since early childhood she had been living in a world of fantasy. During her twenties, however, she heard the Gospel and accpeted Christ as her Savior. She said that although this did not resolve her emotional disturbance, it did give her the strength to begin to face life's frustrations without a continual retreat into fantasy.

A genuine conversation experience and subsequent spiritual growth are basic factors in the process of readjustment of the psychotic individual. This person needs to gradually understand the love and acceptance of God. As he comes to recognize this love, the person can begin to accept life as less threatening and frustrating. He sees that the Lord is interested in him and that he does not have to go through life an alien from his family and friends.[2]

This program of treatment for the person suffering from a psychotic condition may require many months or even several years. If a total therapy program of physical, emotional and spiritual treatment is followed, extremely rewarding changes can be made. A life headed for severe emotional disturbance can be salvaged and turned to an acceptable level of adjustment.

[2] For a discussion of the relationship of spiritual insight to emotional disturbances, see the section on Treatment under DEPRESSION in this volume.

52. Pyromania

Description
Some individuals have a chronic impulse to set fires and watch them burn. Those who have this compulsion and who obtain pleasure from such activity often have serious underlying personality maladjustments. Such a pyromaniac is to be distinguished from an arsonist who burns his own property in order to receive illegal financial gain.

Etiology
Fire setting behavior is symptomatic of serious personality disturbances. Many children and adults who have been responsible for setting a number of fires have been found to be *hostile and rebellious*. They sometimes have daydreams associated with fires. In such instances they imagine a parent, teacher, competitor, or some other person is consumed in the blaze. Through watching a fire and entertaining such fantasies, the person is able to indirectly express his strong feelings of hostility or jealousy.

A second major cause of pyromania is *the need of exaggerated stimuli or excitement*. Some people have difficulty achieving gratification from daily experiences and in order to gain a degree of emotional excitation they engage in bizarre behavior such as fire setting. This, too, is symptomatic of serious personality disorders.

Another mechanism underlying this problem is the *search for attention*. When a person feels deprived of attention, respect or affection, he may turn to such activities in an attempt to meet this need. Although he may receive severe punishment, he would rather have this unpleasant attention than to go completely unnoticed and uncared for. Naturally, these basic needs may not be understood by the person and may be operating on an unconscious level.

In some cases of pyromania, the subject's personality disturbance is related to *sexual maladjustment*. For example, teenage boys and men have been found to have received sexual excitation and have experienced orgasms by setting a fire and entering into the highly emotional activity which accompanies the intense burning. In these cases the adolescents and adults generally have poor heterosexual relationships and may feel insecure and inadequate in their masculine roles.

Many instances of compulsive fire setting are related to *broader patterns of antisocial activities.* [1] These individuals frequently exhibit undesirable behavior such as theft, truancy, and other forms of aggressive, hostile reactions.

Illustration

Identification: White male, age 13

Presenting Problem: This boy was apprehended by the police when it was discovered that he had been responsible for setting several fires in neighborhoods near his home.

Personal and Family History: The subject is the oldest of three children. His father is a professional person who is unable to spend much time with the subject due to heavy office responsibilities. Although the boy is generally quiet and fearful, in recent years there have been instances of lying and severe temper tantrums. This boy's fire setting activity began shortly after he learned his father was to be transferred to a new job which would necessitate his being away from the family for longer periods of time.

During therapy the dynamics behind this boy's activities became clear. He was a generally insecure child because the parents failed to spend adequate time with him and meet his emotional needs of love, affection and security. Being an insecure person, he also had difficulty establishing friendships with others in the neighborhood. Over the years the subject built up strong hostile feelings toward his parents because of their passive and sometimes active rejection of him. The father's anticipated transfer precipitated the fire setting and was the boy's attempt to gain needed attention and to express hostile feelings toward the father for rejecting him.

[1]See DELIQUENCY and SOCIOPATHIC PERSONALITY in this volume.

Treatment

Therapy with the compulsive fire setter must be directed toward an understanding of the basic causes. It does little or no good merely to scold or threaten the person. What is needed is therapy which will resolve the underlying causes. The counselor needs to determine what the subject is trying to say and accomplish by his behavior. Is it an expression of hostility? A need for attention? Or is it associated with a general pattern of antisocial behavior?

Spiritual factors may also be important, especially when the difficulty is related to hostile, rebellious feelings. When the subject comes to know Christ as his Savior, his feelings of rebelliousness and hostility can be mellowed by the love and acceptance of the Lord. As he grows spiritually, he will develop new attitudes both toward himself and his fellow men.

The role of parents and teachers is of utmost importance. As they begin to understand the emotional needs of children they can change the home and school environment. This will gradually reduce the factors which have precipitated the pyromanic activities.

53. Schizophrenia

Description

One of the most severe psychological disorders is schizophrenia. This illness is responsible for approximately twenty-four per cent of all first admissions to public mental hospitals in the United States. In general, schizophrenic individuals are characterized by a loss of interest in their environment, withdrawal and varying degrees of thought disorders. Among the symptoms most frequently observed are:

- Seclusiveness and withdrawal from society
- Irritability, ranging from mild to extreme forms when seclusion is disturbed
- Daydreaming, or preoccupation with thoughts and fantasies definitely in excess of the normal range
- Delusional thinking characterized by loosely-organized ideas, self-pity and feelings of persecution
- Bizarre behavior which consists of incongruous actions and activities such as repeated, purposeless motions, unintelligible language and irrelevant expressions of emotion
- Diminution of interests or failure to be attracted to objects and activities of interest to others of like age and culture
- Neglect of conduct and personal care such as neatness and dress
- Regressive personal interest or the voluntary selection of amusements and occupations which customarily attract those of a younger age level
- Over-sensitivity to criticism and comments by others

The disorder of schizophrenia is difficult to delineate. Individuals exhibiting some symptoms of schizophrenic behavior may range from a mild exaggeration of normal behavioral patterns to serious maladjustments requiring hospitalization. Less severe personality disturbances are sometimes designated as schizoid personality types. These individuals are usually characterized by a withdrawal from social relationships, extreme sensitivity and diminished interest in their environment.

Schizophrenic reactions are usually divided into four categories:

Simple: The basic symptoms of simple schizophrenic show themselves in narrowing interest patterns and social withdrawal. The following characteristics are often detected:

- Apathy (listlessness, tiredness)
- Carelessness about personal appearance
- Neglect of hygenic practices
- Inability to carry thought through to its conclusion
- Meaningless or flighty speech
- General loss of interest in the affairs of life

Cases classified under this category show essentially defects of interest with gradual development of an apathetic state. They are without other strikingly peculiar behavior and without delusions and hallucinations.

Hebephrenic: Hebephrenic reactions generally appear at an earlier age than other types. These symptoms are also among the most severe. The patient typically has a history of queerness, overconcern with trivial matters, and a preoccupation with distorted religious and philosophical issues. In addition to showing symptoms similar to those of the simple type, the hebephrenic may exhibit the following patterns of behavior:

- Tendency to assume certain expressions and mannerisms
- Inappropriate emotional responses (for example, laughs while speaking of death)
- Delusions
- Depression
- Often feels he is under the control of an outside (supernatural) force
- Tendency toward youthful sexual reactions

Catatonic: The most dramatic symptoms of schizophrenia are found in the catatonic patient. It is this type that an almost complete withdrawal from outside relationships is seen. The catatonic schizophrenic may remain in one position for hours or even days, to the complete exclusion of activities going on about him. Among the more prevalent symptoms of the catatonic schizophrenic are:

- Muscular rigidity, resistance to movement, negativism

- Tendency to pose, make statues
- Tendency to mock others, such as repeating words and sounds
- Alternate stupor and active periods
- Noisiness and aggressiveness during active periods (may make unprovoked attacks, be destructive)
- Suicidal tendencies possible in his active state
- Untidiness (sometimes collects and saves bodily waste)

Paranoid: Persons classified as paranoid schizophrenics may have some of the symptoms described in the other types of schizophrenia, but they generally display emotional disturbance and greater confusion in interpreting their thoughts and environment. Patients of the paranoid type often suffer from:

- Delusions of persecution (often quite logical)
- Delusions of grandeur (believes himself very talented, an important discoverer, the chosen one of God, or even God himself)
- Hallucinations often supporting his delusions
- Tendency toward self-decoration and display
- Assaultive tendencies under the stress of delusions

Etiology

Investigators have as yet been unable to clearly determine the etiological factors in schizophrenia. Some researchers place much importance on *physiological factors* while others believe this disorder results largely from *emotional disturbances*. Among the biological factors studied in the etiology of schizophrenia are *heredity, body build, and endocrine and chemical imbalance*. Evidence is insufficient, however, to show the actual importance of these elements.

While specific psychological causes have not been determined, most investigators recognize the importance of psychological factors in the etiology of schizophrenia. *Inadequate response to frustration and conflict in childhood and adolescence* appear to play a major role in the development of schizophrenia. *The individual learns to rely too heavily on defense mechanisms*, often establishing this pattern at a very early age. As the individual enters adolescence he is often overly serious and does not make many friends. The increased demands and frustrations of adolescence may bring an even greater retreat within himself, thus leading to overt schizophrenic reactions.

Closely aligned with the process of withdrawal is the problem of *poor family relationships.* The failure of the schizophrenic to develop adequate social rapport and the development of a low frustration tolerance is largely the result of his home environment. The prime causative factor in family relationships is not social prominence or position, but rather *a pattern of rejection coupled with a dominating, perfectionistic parent.* This type of parent-child relationship may produce the schizophrenic who as a child was rigid, sensitive, unrealistic in his expectations and lacking in ability to socialize.

Related to parental domination and overprotection is *the lack of reality checks.* The adult schizophrenic has usually exhibited a well-developed fantasy life as a child. In response to rejection and an inability to cope with new situations, the child has turned to fantasy to meet his needs for achievement and satisfaction. As an adult, he leans more and more heavily on this defense and gradually moves from a world of reality to one of fantasy.[1]

Occasionally a woman becomes severely disturbed shortly after the birth of a child and she may be diagnosed as schizophrenic. This condition is known as postpartum disturbance.[2] In most cases the person has had a history of poor physical and mental health. With the birth of the child she is unable to cope with life and must seek professional psychiatric care. Some specialists place emphasis on the physical factors as causative while others believe that emotional factors are predominant. Still others attribute the condition to a combination of physical and emotional factors.

Illustration

Identification: White female, age 37
Presenting Problem: The patient was referred for psychiatric

---

[1]For a comprehensive review of the problem of schizophrenia, see Bellak, Leopold, M.D. and Benedict, Paul K. M.D. (Eds.): *Schizophrenia: A Review of the Syndrome,* Harper, New York, 1961.
[2]See the discussion of POSTPARTUM PSYCHOSES in this volume.

treatment by her physician who had seen her frequently for several years. She had complained repeatedly about her ill health and the poor treatment she received from her husband, two sisters and her in-laws. First attempts by her physician to refer her to a psychiatrist failed. Finally, however, since her health interfered with her housework, she consented to seek treatment.

During her first visit to the psychiatrist she talked freely about her poor health and unfortunate treatment by family members. She discussed the fact that "everyone seemed to get on her nerves." During one period of severe disturbance the subject was hospitalized for three weeks.

Personal and Family History: The patient was raised in a family with a younger and an older sister. The family struggled financially to make ends meet and there was little happiness in the home. The mother and older sister were both dominant and made unrealistic demands on the subject. As a child she had few close friends and often turned to daydreaming to seek a more pleasant world. She found it impossible to cope with the frustrations and conflicts at home and school. As a result she often withdrew from situations which she felt were too demanding.

She found very little relief from this type of life until she was married at the age of seventeen. But then she found she was confronted with a husband who was perfectionistic and dominating. He did not understand her reactions and often laughed at her, or tried to force her to face situations.

Within three years after her marriage she had two children. In time, she had two other children, but she seemed unable to meet the demands placed upon her.

The psychiatrist discussed the problem with the husband but found that he had little or no understanding of his wife's condition.

Treatment

Not only is this disorder extremely severe and disabling, but it is also one of the most difficult disturbances to treat.[3] Perhaps

[3]For a more thorough discussion of treatment of this condition, see PSYCHOTIC DISORDERS in this volume.

in schizophrenia more than any other disorder, methods of treatment are extremely diversified and inconclusive. Many types of therapy have been employed but none have proved widely successful with severe cases.

Experienced psychotherapists report that some patients respond favorably to medication combined with supportive counseling. Considerable relief is achieved if the patient is able to relate closely to the therapist and consequently feels free to reveal innermost feelings.

Since the schizophrenic's major disturbance lies in withdrawal from reality, the counselor's principal task is to lead the client to the root of the reasons for this escape from reality and attempt to overcome the casual factors. The most important initial step is to gain the complete trust of the client. This may be a difficult task since the schizophrenic is usually unable to trust in and depend on another human being. The schizophrenic feels isolated in a world of people. Consequently, he withdraws into himself, feeling lonely and afraid. He cannot depend on anyone for a sense of human relatedness. If the counselor is loving and accepting, however, the client sees that he can trust his counselor and place confidence in him, he can then begin to respond more normally to others.

An examination of the reasons for his aberrant behavior is also necessary. Seeing the world as a hostile, unpleasant place to live, the schizophrenic has usually retreated to a world of fantasy. He needs to gain an understanding of the factors which have brought about his flight from reality.

An important step in the reorientation of the schizophrenic is a deep understanding of the security found in Christ. As he begins to see the relationship of situational crises of this world to the believer's ultimate security in the Lord, the schizophrenic can reevaluate his withdrawal from society. When God's unconditional love begins to penetrate his thinking, the patient suffering from schizophrenia can develop a new image, both of himself and of others. This will eventually lead to more satisfying relationships in his daily life.

54. Senility

Description

As a person enters the later stages of his life span, there is regression of the functioning of his bodily processes. Along with the physiological changes such as still joints, wrinkled skin and decreased visual performance come changes which affect the individual's mental and emotional functioning.[1]

Among the most common symptoms associated with senility are:

- Loss of memory
- Narrowing of interests and ambitions
- Difficulty in adjusting to new situations
- Increase in effort necessary to perform familiar tasks
- Impairment of ability to do abstract thinking
- Unreliable judgment
- Lessening of social interest and increasing egoistic desires
- Irritability, low frustration tolerance
- Carelessness in personal habits; uncleanliness
- Reminiscing of events which happened many years ago
- Delusions and hallucinations

Disorders associated with senile brain disease are grouped into five categories.

Simple Deterioration: This disturbance is characterized by an exaggeration of symptoms normally found with old age. Behavior is marked by memory loss, restlessness, lack of ambition, narrowing of interests and poor judgment. Difficulty in concentrating and irritability are also common.

Paranoid Type: This disorder is characterized by the gradual formation of delusions, usually of a persecutory nature. Beliefs that one's friends are turning against him, that someone is trying to harm him, or steal his property are frequent. Although this disorder may also include some loss of memory, it is usually not as pronounced as in other senile disorders.

---

[1]For a discussion of basic considerations of the aged see the author's book, *The Mature Years*. This deals with the adjustment problems of the average aged person rather than the truly senile.

Presbyophrenic Type: This type is characterized by marked impairment of memory, fabrication, disorientation and a jovial mood. This person may fabricate stories to fill his memory gaps. He is usually active and restless and may talk freely. He appears to be quite alert, but is often engaged in aimless activities.

Delirious and Confused Type: This category is characterized by poor mental functioning, restlessness and incoherence. The person may not recognize friends and acquaintances and may be subject to frequent delusions and hallucinations.

Depressed and Agitated Type: The person suffering from depression associated with senile brain disease is characterized by fears of serious illness, of poverty and of general uselessness. He may become self-accusatory and develop the idea that he can do nothing right.

Etiology

Mental disorders resulting from brain deterioration ordinarily develop very gradually. The person typically experiences a slow decline in mental efficiency. Memory span becomes shorter and abnormal personality characteristics may appear.

The type of mental disorder which an aged person develops is influenced by his *lifelong personality characteristics and the nature and extent of brain tissue deterioration.* A person who has had some personality difficulties throughout life but has been able to overcome them by mental alertness may succumb to these disorders when his intellectual functioning begins to decrease. The suspicious individual may begin to exhibit paranoid behavior as his mental functioning declines. A basically unhappy and pessimistic person may become severely depressed in his old age.

Among the physical disturbances contributing to senile brain disorders are *faulty blood circulation, deterioration of brain cells, diminished oxygen consumption and avitaminosis. Hardening of the arteries of the brain leads to faulty circulation and inadequate cerebral nutrition.* The lack of oxygen accompanying the poor circulation furthers degeneration of the brain cells.

In some cases of senile psychoses, *nutritional deficiencies* appear to play an important role. Administration of large quantities of vitamins have proven to be of value in treating some of these disorders.

Stress situations encountered in later life may contribute to the development of senile psychoses. The sudden realization that a person is approaching the end of his life, that he is dependent on others for his living, and that he may soon become completely bedridden often produces severe emotional disturbances in individuals who have not been able to adjust to this stage of their life span.

Illustration

Identification: White male, age 76

Presenting Problem: The subject's son and daughter-in-law consulted their family physician because they were concerned about their father's deterioration and its effect upon their household, as he was living with them.

Personal and Family History: The subject was from a large rural family. He apparently had a satisfying childhood. There was no history of mental disorder in the family.

The patient was married at 25 and became the father of three children. He was active in his local church and taught an adult Sunday school class for many years. At 65 he retired and by 70 he began to show considerable mental deterioration. This condition increased after his wife died. The son reported that his father's memory had become very poor and that his thought processes were disordered. He misplaced items of clothing and was unable to recall where he had put them. In recent months he had become easily irritated and was constantly criticizing the other family members and scolding the children for their lack of attention and concern for his welfare. He also exhibited typical physical deterioration, including lack of energy, stiffness of joints and visual loss.

Treatment

Extensive therapy for senile psychoses is generally impractical and not very successful. Older persons are usually set in their ways and their personality structure is quite rigid and not susceptible to much change. Counseling may prove beneficial, but this should usually be aimed at removing the most serious symptoms rather than attempting a deep personality reorganization.

One of the major concerns of treating senile disorders is the question of hospitalization. Many aged people exhibiting loss of memory, reasoning ability, and overall degeneration can be cared for at home. When an individual becomes extremely confused and difficult, it is probably best to consider placing him in an institution equipped to handle such cases.

Medical care is an indispensable part of caring for the aged. It is now possible to treat conditions of high blood pressure and hardening of the arteries which aggravate the personality disturbances of advanced age. Medications are available which may be helpful by increasing the flow of blood to the brain. Proper diet and medical treatment to remove any toxic conditions are also necessary.

Attempts should be made to provide the aged person with pleasant surroundings. Companionship with older people and hobbies to occupy his time often assist the senile individual to adapt to his disorder.

Preparation for old age is effective in the prevention of these disorders. The best preparation is a healthy, happy, useful life in which Christ has control. When a person knows Christ as his personal Savior and has, through the years, lived in close fellowship with God, he continues to rely upon the Lord in his old age. Even though an individual may experience some amount of brain degeneration, if he is a well-adjusted person and is willing to accept his limitations and role as an older person, he is in a much better position to avoid the more severe aspects of senile psychoses.

Another important consideration is the effect of the aged person's maladjustment upon his relatives. Sons and daughters of these people can profit by counseling sessions to consider their own attitudes and to make plans for their aging parents.

55. Sexual Deviation

Description
The person engaged in professional counseling sees many clients who present a variety of sexual maladjustments.[1] As children, adolescents and adults bring their problems to light, it is noted that a great number of maladjustments are of a sexual nature. But as the counselor reflects on the nature of sex, he understands why so many problems do have sexual connotations. Following are some of the reasons why sexual maladjustments may arise.[2]

- Many sex problems grow out of the fact that sex is a persistent, dynamic force in life.
- Some sex problems arise becuause sexual adjustments are a reflection of, and have an influence on, various aspects of one's total personality.
- Since sex acts often result in human reproduction, many serious problems may follow.
- Sex problems and adjustments often stem from the great variation in sex drives.
- Many sex problems come from lack of wholesome sex education.
- Faulty childhood impressions and unwise handling by parents have profound effects, sometimes causing sex problems later in life.
- Organic abnormalities may be significant in sex problems, predisposing one toward maladjustments.
- Sex problems are sometimes created and/or aggravated by a secular society which places unusual emphasis on sex.
- Spiritual factors (lack of spiritual devotion) are important in cases of sexual maladjustment.

The sexual deviations considered in this section include: voyeurism, sadism, masochism, tranvestism, fetishism, pedophilia,

---

[1] See also: EXHIBITIONISM, IMPOTENCE AND FRIGIDITY, HOMOSEXUALITY, INCEST, MASTURBATION, UNFAITHFULNESS, and UNWED MOTHERS in this volume.

[2] For a more complete discussion of these points, see the author's book, *The Psychology of Counseling.*

rape and bestiality. In many cases the underlying dynamics of the maladjustment are similar. Only minor differences in circumstances may cause individuals to express their maladjustment in different ways.

Voyeurism

This is a condition in which an individual gains sexual stimulation from watching members of the opposite sex undress or in a state of nudity. Voyeurism is synonymous with scopophilia and inspectionism, and the lay term, "Peeping Tom." Voyeuristic impulses are seen in minor forms in those individuals who view and read pornographic literature and who frequent burlesque theaters. In more severe cases the indivudals may be arrested for peeking through bedroom windows in an effort to view an unclad woman. In addition to viewing naked women, some indivuduals gain sexual gratification by observing a couple engaged in sexual intercourse.

Voyeurism occurs most frequently among young males, but it is also found among married men of older ages. In these cases the individual usually exhibits an inadequate sexual adjustment in marriage.

One of the basic dynamics underlying this behavior is a *serious feeling of inadequacy in the sexual role.* Sometimes a person has very poor relationships with the opposite sex. Fearing actual sexual contact, he turns to viewing the opposite sex for gratification. This enables him to avoid sexual involvement and the associated fears.

Another common factor underlying "peeping" behavior is a *lack of wholesome sex knowledge and attitudes.* When a child is not supplied with adequate sex education he grows up with curiosities and misconceptions concerning sexual functioning. Feeling that sexual matters are taboo, he must sneak about unnoticed in an attempt to satisfy his craving for sexual knowledge and stimulation.

Sadism

The term sadism is broadly used to denote the receiving of pleasure from inflicting pain upon others. In more limited usage, however, it applies only to a sexual maladjustment in which a person receives sexual gratification from inflicting pain upon another person.

Sadism is found most frequently among men. This behavior may range from minor infliction of pain upon a sex partner, by pinching or slapping, to severe bodily harm and sometimes murder.

Some cases of sadistic behavior result largely from *generalized feelings of hostility*. The insecure individual who is angry and retaliatory may gain gratification by expressing his hostility in relation to sexual activity. By inflicting pain upon a sexual partner the sadist may gain a feeling of satisfaction that he has proved himself the superior or has repaid society for its misdeeds to him.

Other instances of sadism are related to *strong hostility toward parents of the opposite sex*. Some men, for example, who have strong feelings of resentment and hositility toward their mothers, may attempt to ventilate their hostility to women by inflicting pain during sexual intercourse.

Men who feel inadequate and insecure in the masculine role may turn to sadistic behavior in order to demonstrate their masculinity. By injuring a sex partner they gain real feelings of power and think that they have demonstrated their masculine strength.

Other individuals turn to sadistic behavior because of *poor sex education and the associated unwholesome attitudes*. When a child is taught that sex is "dirty" and not to be discussed, he may feel that all sexual activity is sinful. Feeling this way, he associates punishment with sexual activity. Thus he proceeds to inflict pain upon his sexual partner as an expression of his feelings of the evil of sex.

One question which should be considered in working with a person with strong sadistic impulses is the following: "Is this behavior a part of a total picture of marked personality maladjustment?" Sadistic behavior may be a reflection of a severe psychotic process or a serious sociopathic personality pattern. In these cases the total personality maladjustment must be treated.

Masochism

Another sexual deviation with dynamics similar to sadism is masochism. When speaking of sexual maladjustments, this term indicates a condition in which a person receives sexual gratification by suffering physical pain. This phenomenon is found more frequently among women, and a masochistic woman often marries a sadistic man. In this arrangement, they both are able to meet their deviate sexual needs.

One of the most common dynamics underlying masochistic behavior is the *felt need for punishment.* A person who has grown up with the idea that sex is sinful and degrading may feel a conscious or unconscious need for punishment. By submitting to serious physical pain, a woman may attempt to "atone for her sinfulness." Such behavior is, of course, based on seriously distorted sexual attitudes.

Other individuals may desire the infliction of pain in order to *increase sexual stimulation.* The emotional excitement associated with pain sometimes permits a disturbed person to receive more stimulation and sexual gratification during intercourse.

Fetishism

In fetishism an individual gains sexual stimulation through contact with various articles of clothing. The fetishist substitutes garments such as hose, handkerchiefs, undergarments, and shoes for actual physical contact with a person of the opposite sex. Some individuals also have a fetish for certain parts of the body, such as the hair, breasts or legs. Individuals may receive sexual gratification from smelling, feeling, or kissing and licking these.

Since the fetishist finds sexual gratification through various inanimate objects, he may turn to stealing in order to get the desired sexual object. Some cases of kleptomania,[3] for example, have been largely concerned with the theft of women's underclothes. In other instances, men with a fetish for women's hair have been known to cut locks from a number of women. Some

[3]See the discussion of KLEPTOMANIA in this volume.

develop a large collection of hair and receive sexual stimulation from contact with this.

The dynamic underlying fetishism is the *transference of a sexual drive from its natural object to something such as an article of clothing which symbolically represents the original sexual object*. The fetish serves as a substitute for the desired sexual object which is unavailable or overly threatening and fear producing.

The fetishist is nearly always a person with strong feelings of inadequacy in relation to members of the opposite sex. He is insecure in his sexual role and does not become involved sexually because of fear of rejection or humiliation.

Another factor in fetishism is the development of *inadequate sexual attitudes because of poor sexual education in childhood*. The fetishist is a person who has confused attitudes toward sex and does not understand its proper perspective in life. These unwholesome attitudes cause the person to avoid actual sexual involvement and turn to the privacy of sexual stimulation with inanimate objects.

In addition to general sexual maladjustment, fetishism may grow out of *earlier situations in which sexual gratification was associated with some article of clothing*. Having received sexual excitement from one experience and being fearful of actual sexual involvement with the opposite sex, the individual may develop a consistent pattern of sexual gratification through inanimate objects. This satisfies the person's sexual needs and protects his feelings of adequacy by avoiding the threatening feelings associated with actual sexual intercourse.

Transvestism

This is a sexual aberation in which an individual dresses in clothing of the opposite sex. Some individuals wear only undergarments of the opposite sex, while others may dress entirely in such apparel. This behavior is indicative of a definite inability to accept one's sexual role. The dynamics are a combination of those found in fetishism and homosexuality.[4] A large

---

[4]For a discussion of the basic dynamics of this disorder, see HOMOSEXUALITY and FETISHISM in this volume.

portion of transvestites regularly engage in overt homosexual experiences. The remainder show serious sex role confusion and latent homosexuality.

Pedophilia

This is a sexual maladjustment in which a person attempts to gain sexual gratification by engaging in sexual activities with children. The pedophiliac may indulge in either heterosexual or homosexual experiences. In some instances the child or young adolescent may be a willing partner to an adult's sexual advances, while in others an adult may force the child to submit to him.

The pedophiliac is a person who has *failed to develop adequate adult heterosexuality.* Being *insecure in his sex role,* a man may be threatened by the possibility of sexual contact with adult women. He feels sexually inadequate or inferior and is *fearful of exhibiting his sexual inadequacy* if he attempts adult heterosexual relationships. In addition to inadequate sexual adjustment, these individuals often show a broader inadequacy by their *poor social relationships* generally. They do not interact freely with adults because they feel insecure and inadequate.

Fearing adult sexual involvement, the pedophiliac directs his sexual drives toward children. Here he finds a sexual outlet without the fear of being proven inadequate or inferior in adult sexual relationships. In some cases of pedophilia the person also has *strong homosexual tendencies.*

Bestiality

Bestiality is a sexual deviation characterized by sexual contact with animals. It is also known by the term zoophilia. This type of abnormal behavior is found most frequently among the mentally retarded and those living in rural areas.

The basic dynamic is similar to pedophilia. The person feels *inadequate and insecure in his sexual adjustment and is not comfortable in human relationships.* Fearing contact with other persons, he turns to less threatening sexual objects such as dogs, goats, and cows. Adolescent boys living on farms and ranches may experiment sexually with animals for a short time but later establish normal heterosexual patterns with the opposite sex.

Rape
Forcible sexual intercourse against the will of another person is known as rape. Intercourse with a minor, even with her permission, is known as statutory rape. In some cases of rape, the offender will also inflict serious physical harm or death in order to prevent the victim from later identifying him. A large portion of rapists are men in their twenties, many of whom are married and have families.

One of the basic factors underlying forcible sexual intercourse is a *strong hostile attitude toward the opposite sex.* The man with unresolved anger and resentment toward his mother may vent this hostility by raping an unsuspecting victim.

Frustrated sexual drives are often an important aspect of understanding the rapist. Although this alone is not sufficient to cause such behavior, the inability to obtain normal gratification is a contributing factor to this maladjustment.

Feelings of sexual inadequacy are found to underlie the behavior of a rapist. Through his actions the rapist is endeavoring to prove to himself and others that he is an adequate male capable of expressing himself sexually.

In some cases of rape the offender is found to have a *serious sociopathic personality makeup.* In these instances rape may be only one aspect of a broader picture of maladjustment and antisocial action.[5]

Treatment
In counseling with individuals suffering from sexual maladjustments, it is important to realize that therapy for these disorders is not grossly different from that with any other personality disturbance. In each case, it is the counselor's task through diagnosis to determine the cause of the current adjustment difficulties and to help the person resolve the conflicts. If the sexual maladjustment is thought of in terms of a personality

[5]See the discussion of SOCIOPATHIC PERSONALITY in this volume.

disorder, the problem will be viewed in correct perspective and treatment will be facilitated.

Since sexual maladjustments are thought of as especially sinful and degrading, many individuals with these disturbances also suffer from serious feelings of guilt and rejection. Newspaper articles condemning sexual offenders and messages on the evils of such actions have reinforced the person's feelings of sinfulness, isolation and rejection. Many times a person hesitates to bring sexual maladjustments to a minister or another counselor for fear of condemnation. With this in mind, it is important that the counselor be accepting of the individual suffering from these adjustment difficulties. When the counselor takes a condemning attitude toward such a person, he loses rapport and greatly lessens the possiblility of helping the counselee. In refusing to condemn the person for his sexual behavior, the counselor is not condoning the actions as permissible. Instead, he is in essence telling the client that he understands the difficulty, that he does not criticize him for it, and that he is willing to work together toward a solution, recognizing the physical, psychological and spiritual aspects of the problem.

As the counselor accepts the person and encourages him to talk about his problem, the client begins to freely discuss his feelings. In doing so, he gains insight into his behavior and the reasons for his actions. The very process of talking about his maladjustment gives the person some relief from his feelings of anxiety and constitutes an important step toward recovery.

In most cases of sexual maladjustment the client is suffering from a large measure of guilt. In these instances it is important that this be dealt with thoroughly. If the person is unsaved he needs to come to know Christ as his personal Savior and to experience the true forgiveness of sins through the shed blood of Christ. If the person is a Christian he needs to take his sins to the Lord in true repentance. "If we confess our sins, he is faithful and just to forgive us our sins, and to cleanse us from all unrighteousness" (I John 1:9).

Even though the Lord's forgiveness is immediate and total, the counselor will often find that feelings of sinfulness will persist in the client. This is because the patterns of behavior are

298 Encyclopedia of Psychological Problems

longstanding and the person's attitudes of guilt and sinfulness have been formed over a period of many years. Asking the Lord's forgiveness may not immediately remove the client's feelings of guilt. Although the counselor realizes that in God's sight these sins are forgiven, weeks or even months may be required before the individual is totally freed from the binding influences of the feelings of guilt and shame.

With the individual's ventilation of his problems and his attitudes toward them, the counselor must then begin to lead the client into an understanding of the influences in his background which have produced his present behavior. Factors such as inadequate sexual education, poor parent-child relationships and overidentification with one parent need to be considered. Insight into these causes is generally gained gradually, sometimes with weekly counseling sessions over a period of months. A person with a sexual maladjustment, for instance, needs many sessions to thoroughly evaluate all of the factors related to both his sexual adjustment and his overall personality development. The voyeur's problem is not solved merely by being told that the basic reason for his compulsion to view undressed women is a result of feelings of inadequacy in the masculine role.

Another consideration of utmost importance is the development of new and wholesome attitudes toward sex. A person can have excellent insight into the causes for his abnormal sexual behavior and still continue in it. Understanding is not enough. The person must replace his old attitudes and actions with new feelings. It is here that a process of sexual reeducation is basic. Counselors never cease to be amazed at the naive and unwholesome attitudes toward sex held by some maladjusted individuals. One teen-age boy, for example, was apprehended for exhibitionism. During therapy the counselor led the discussion to a consideration of the boy's sexual attitude and it was learned that this boy did not understand the basic facts of human reproduction. He believed that conception took place if a couple engaged in prolonged kissing. Erroneous attitudes are frequently held by those who have serious sexual maladjustments. In these cases the counselor usually needs to spend several hours with the person in a very basic program of sexual reeducation. Charts indicating sexual functioning of men and women are helpful, as well as a discussion of the Biblical perspective of sex.[6] The person with a serious sexual maladjustment rarely had a wholesome Biblical concept of sex. This person needs to see God's purpose of fulfillment in marriage through sexual intercourse and in the creation of new life. The wholesomeness of sex within marriage and the sacred institution of marriage by the Lord need to be discussed. As these things are brought to light the individual can gradually replace his previously warped attitudes toward sex with wholesome and correct feelings. This is of utmost importance in order to achieve any lasting benefit through counseling.

A final consideration in counseling is the necessity of working with both husband and wife when either of them has a sexual problem. In these instances the most thorough improvement is made when the counselor is able to consider the attitudes and actions of both marriage partners. Often it is found that a portion of the difficulty has resulted from an adjustment problem or a lack of understanding by the apparently well-adjusted partner.

[6]For a Christian view of sex and a full discussion of male and female sexual functioning, see the author's book *Life and Love.*

56. Sleep Disturbances

Description

Disturbances of sleep are among the most common problems of children.[1] One child may be bothered by wakefulness, another by restlessness, another by dreams and still another by excessive drowsiness during the daytime.

Authorities on child behavior have attempted to establish norms for the amount of sleep a child requires. While there is some value in this, parents should realize that there are variations in the amount of sleep needed by individuals. By attempting to force a child to comply with absolute sleep standards, parents may bring on emotional problems.

The problem of *wakefulness* is common to many children. They often lie in bed for some time before finally falling asleep. They may ask for a drink of water, go to the bathroom, or decide that they want more or less covering. Other children awaken during the night and find it difficult to return to sleep.

All children make many *movements during sleep*, but some are excessively restless. They toss and turn in their beds, flail their arms and legs, move their heads from side to side and flop from one end of the bed to the other.

It is normal for children to dream occasionally. However, dreams can sometimes become upsetting and frightful. A *nightmare* is a frightening dream which wakes the child from his sleep. The child often exhibits terror and fear as a result of the dream. When he awakens, he recognizes his surroundings and can usually be calmed by his parents.

A *night terror* is more severe than a nightmare. It differs in that the child may manifest fear, screaming and bodily activity. The child also experiences hallucinations. If awakened, he may not recognize those about him. When fully awake, however, he has no recollection of screaming and is unable to recall either the episode or the content of the dream.

---

[1]Many sleep disturbances of childhood are carried over into adulthood. The dynamics of these sleep disturbances may be similar.

Some children seem to have an intensified *need for sleep*. They may fall asleep in a chair during the daytime, as well as demand excessive hours of sleep during the night. They may want to go to bed early and sleep late in the mornings.

Etiology

In many cases the cause of wakefulness can be traced to *inadequate training or a lack of routine.* Parents may fail to establish a regular bedtime routine, or may be inconsistent by allowing a child to stay up late part of the time while forcing him to retire early other nights.

The child who is *deprived of love* may also exhibit problems of sleep. If he does not receive sufficient attention during the day, he may resort to attention-getting devices when put to bed. When a child is worried about how his parents feel toward him, he may lie awake at night occupying himself with thoughts of unjust discipline and rejection.

Another factor which can cause sleep disturbance is *excitement or overactivity just before bedtime.* Children are often unable to reverse their attention from an activity of stimulation such as watching television or rough play, to the need of sleep.

Unfavorable sleeping conditions are sometimes responsible for a child's wakefulness. Excessive noise, light and excitement in adjacent rooms make it difficult for a child to sleep.

Some children are afraid of the dark and dread being left alone. The silence of the room may prove frightening. An unexpected rattle of the window pane or a creaky floor will cause some children to stay awake. The insecure child may even fear that his parents will leave him while he is sleeping.

Many things may bother a child and cause him to be emotionally upset to the point that he cannot sleep. *Happenings in school, relationships with playmates, fear of punishment, quarreling of parents*—these and many other factors may occupy a child's mind so that he cannot sleep easily.

Some younger children are unable to sleep well at night if they are *forced to take a nap during the afternoon.* But with no daytime nap (especially in the late afternoon), they are able to fall asleep easily at night. Inability to sleep at night may also be attributed to *insufficient exercise during the day*. Certain children are very active and need much exercise. If they do not have it, they may be restless and stay awake for long periods in the evening.

Restlessness may be the result of a *physical condition*. Children who are not well may find it difficult to sleep soundly. Hyperactive children are especially prone to be restless during sleep.

A certain amount of dreaming is to be expected in childhood, but when a child experiences nightmares and night terrors, a corresponding *personality disturbance* usually exists. One who has such sleep disturbances is usually emotionally upset, anxious and fearful. Unsatisfactory parental relationships and emotional tensions in the home are frequently the cause of these manifestations.

The drowsy child may be suffering from a hidden *physical ailment*. On the other hand, he may not be sleeping soundly at night, thus requiring additional sleep during the day. Drowsiness may also be a means of passing time or even *escaping unpleasant experiences* which one encounters when he is awake. The unhappy child may turn to excessive sleeping to avoid feelings of unhappiness.

Illustration
Identification: White male, age 10
Presenting Problem: The subject was referred to a counseling clinic by the family physician. The parents complained that the boy was having severe nightmares several times a week. The physician had prescribed medication which brought some relief but the child persisted in having nightmares. Consequently, the medical doctor referred the boy and his parents to a local clinic for psychological study.
Personal and Family History: The subject is of medium build and has had the usual childhood diseases. The parents stated that he had always been rather "frail and sickly."

He is now in the fifth grade, making average grades. On several occasions during the boy's five years in school, his teachers have told the parents that they felt he was capable of doing better but that he was nervous and had a short attention span. Now, in the fifth grade, the subject seems to be in better health and is showing fewer signs of nervousness in the classroom and at home.

The family lives in a modest home in a small community. The father is a salesman and is away from home much of the time. The mother is a homemaker. The subject has one older and one younger brother.

The psychological tests indicated that the boy had rather severe fears. Interviews revealed that some of these were associated with the death of the boy's grandfather who lived with the family and who died approximately two years before.

It was also learned that the boy had a fear of falling and that he had actually fallen from a tree when he was four years of age and again from a car at the age of seven.

Through a series of counseling sessions the boy was able to talk freely about his fears and their causes. The counselor also made suggestions to the parents. After two months of therapy and improvement in home conditions, the nightmares became much less severe and less frequent.

Treatment

In many instances sleep disturbances are resolved when parents establish a daily schedule of sleep for the child. It also helps to prepare him mentally by telling him when bedtime is coming. A child who finds it difficult to go to sleep needs to be handled kindly rather than harshly. Yet parents must be sufficiently firm that a child understands he is expected to go to sleep and his various maneuvers will not be rewarded by permission to get up and resume his play.

Exciting stimuli should be avoided near bedtime. Pleasant, quiet activities and a story from the Bible tend to produce an atmosphere conducive to sleep. After the child has gone to bed, parents can point out the beauty of the stars, the quiet peace of the darkness, and the fact that it feels so good just to relax. It is especially important that parents pray with their child at bedtime. Through a regularly scheduled time of prayer a child cannot only submit himself to the care of God; he will also understand that his parents love him and are concerned about his welfare. Such pleasant experiences will blend the approaching night into an enjoyable and acceptable portion of the child's daily routine. After the child is in bed parents should see to it that he is not disturbed by excessive light or by noise from other members of the family.

If a child's sleep disturbances appear to stem from emotional stresses, parents should attempt to find the causes. They can help a child resolve his frustrations by encouraging him to quietly talk about his feelings. When he is able to discuss the things which are occupying his mind he will usually find sufficient release to fall asleep. A child may hear various things during the day which he does not fully understand. If so, he may stay awake at night trying to comprehend them. By providing explanations, parents can help a child resolve his perplexities and consequently sleep soundly.

Most children fear the dark, at least to some extent. Parents can help a child by keeping a small night light on in his room. He may also need to be reassured that mother or father is nearby and will come into his room occasionally to see how well he is sleeping. This reassurance usually puts a child at ease and enables him to go to sleep. It is important that parents assure a child that he is loved and is an important member of the family.

If a child's sleep disturbances are severe, professional help should be sought. Medical doctors frequently prescribe mild sedatives for children who are hyperactive and unable to sleep. After parents have enabled a child to establish regular sleep patterns through the aid of medication, it is not uncommon for the child to continue to sleep well even though medication is discontinued.

The emotional factors underlying the person's difficulties must be resolved. If a child is insecure and fearful because of feelings of rejection or continual tension in the home, the sources of these feelings must be eliminated. Parents often need several counseling sessions to see the importance of a quiet and stable home environment upon the sleep patterns of the child. As the parents begin to resolve their own personal and marital difficulties, they will in turn be able to provide a more satisfying home environment for their children.

57. Sociopathic Personality

Description

The terms sociopathic personality and psychopathic personality apply to individuals whose behavior is chronically antisocial. The sociopath is at odds with society and his behavior is often of a criminal nature, including petty offenses, theft and sexual deviance. He may verbally conform to social standards, but inwardly he has no concern for his amoral and unreliable behavior. These people do not respond to punishment and they have inadequate superego (conscience) development.

Sociopathic personality disturbances are generally classified into four major categories:

Antisocial reaction: Individuals in this diagnostic category exhibit persistent patterns of unlawful behavior and irresponsible acts. Such people seek immediate gratification of their impulses and do not profit from punishment and correction. In addition to these patterns of behavior, antisocial individuals fail to develop close emotional relationships. They are unable to give and to receive affection and are not capable of forming group or individual loyalties without help. These people may come from homes of any socioeconomic level, high or low.

Dyssocial reaction: Many people exhibiting sociopathic behavior have developed their patterns of reacting because of living in an inadequate moral environment. They may commit many unlawful acts because this behavior is accepted in their subculture. Unlike the antisocial reaction, individuals in this category may be able to form deep loyalties and to express feelings of love and affection. Such people frequently do not have the serious personality disturbances of those diagnosed as antisocial reactions. Instead they are maladjusted largely in terms of their society. If they have been reared in an acceptable moral environment, they would have been considered well-adjusted.

Sexual deviation: Some people suffering from sexual maladjustments do not evidence other serious personality disturbances such as psychotic conditions. Maladjustments of this type are classified as sexual deviation. When the sexual maladjustment is a result of other severe personality disturbances the person is classified according to primary maladjustment rather than the sexual deviation which results from the basic disturbance. Sexual deviations are discussed separately in this volume.

Etiology
Sociopaths develop deviant behavior from early interactions with their parents. Parental neglect, cruelty and inconsistency provide the child with an atmosphere which is conducive to the development of antisocial behavior.

When parents fail to provide security and an example of appropriate behavior, they deprive their child of an adequate sense of direction. Because of this early rejection, the child is not concerned with others and lets his impulses direct his behavior. His actions are characterized by emotional immaturity and impulsive acts.

Among the factors frequently found in the childhood of many sociopaths are:

Lack of parental authority based upon love and affection. Parental authority which emanates from hearts of love and concern is interpreted by a child as security. He knows that he is loved and that he has limits which offer him added protection. But when a child sees parents as authority figures without love and affection, he senses the unfairness and secretly wants to retaliate.

High frequency of illegitimacy. A child who is born in an atmosphere of illegitimacy is often the object of guilt, shame and even hatred. Even a small child soon senses the dynamics involved and he may easily come to dislike himself and others as well.

Loss of parents or desertion. A child can sustain the loss of a parent, or even both parents, if this is adequately interpreted to him and if he has others in his immediate environment who help him to feel right about himself and the world. But the loss of parents frequently brings feelings of hostility and resentment to a child and he carries these attitudes into adulthood.

Parental discord. Disharmony in the home often takes its

toll from a child who becomes the center of feelings of hate and jealousy. Such attitudes become a part of his developing personality which turn against society as he attains adult maturity.

Emotional Deprivation. Each child has basic emotional needs. If these are not met in childhood, they are searched for throughout life, often taking the form of antisocial behavior in adulthood.

Lack of standards of appropriate behavior. Children typically follow the example set by their parents. If these examples are poor ones, the child will still grow up following these as the norm.

Parental overindulgence. Some parents feel emotionally deprived themselves so they turn to a child in an effort to meet their own needs. They do not allow the child to develop on his own. They supply his every need, and limit his personality development. As the child grows older he may become resentful of this parental behavior and begin to act out his hostilities.

Neurological impairments. Research studies indicate that a large percentage of sociopathic personalities are suffering from injuries to the brain. Both the physical and emotional complications of these neurological handicaps are often important causal factors in antisocial behavior.[1]

Lack of spiritual conversion and maturity. Human beings are spiritual beings with spiritual needs. When a person has not accepted Christ as his personal Savior he is continually controlled by the old sin nature "Ye are of your father the devil, and the lusts of your father ye will do. He was a murderer from the beginning, and abode not in the truth, because there is no truth in him. When he speaketh a lie, he speaketh of his own: for he is a liar, and the father of it (John 8:44). Without the indwelling of the Holy Spirit a person is left open to domination by his sinful nature. Many cases of sociopathic behavior have as their basis a lack of spiritual conversion and subsequent growth.

---

[1]For a discussion of this topic see BRAIN DAMAGE in this volume.

Illustration
Identification: White male, age 27
Presenting Problem: The patient was referred for psychological help as a requirement for his parole. He was apprehended by the police for burglary.
Personal and Family History: The subject is one of four children born into a lower middle-class home. His father was an alcoholic and the mother had to work part time in order to support the children. There was constant arguing among the parents and little happiness in the home. The parents did not establish standards of discipline and appropriate behavior.

During childhood this man had few friends. He spent little time with age-mates. While still in elementary school he was apprehended for petty theft, and was often truant. During adolescence he began drinking excessively. He dropped out of high school and took a job in an automobile garage. Eventually, he was discharged for stealing equipment from the company. He justified his actions by stating that his salary was too low and that the garage owner would never miss the items.

The patient was then apprehended for burglarizing a grocery market. He has received parole with the understanding he would seek psychological assistance.

Treatment
The sociopath's behavior is ego syntonic; that is, it is pleasurable and acceptable to him. As a result, it is difficult to alter his behavioral patterns.

It is important that the counselor establish a warm, understanding relationship with the antisocial individual. The counselor may well be the first person who has shown a genuine interest in him. Because the sociopath is distrustful of others, it frequently takes many sessions before he is willing to confide in the counselor.

As the individual begins to gain confidence in his therapist, the client feels free to explore his own feelings and the dynamics of his life and personality. When he comes to a better self-understanding and is able to release his pent-up emotions during the interviews, the person will learn to accept the standards and requirements of society, recognizing his responsibility to others. Among the most important dynamics to be explored are the subject's strong feelings of hositlity and resentment. The sociopath needs to realize that he is taking out on society his own feelings of anger and hostility. He must come to an understanding of the basic causes of these hostile attitudes and to a resolution of these feelings.[2]

The sociopath will sometimes respond to spiritual help. He needs to experience God's love and concern for him. He also needs to learn of God's plan for his life and His power to motivate and control his daily living. However, little good is accomplished by preaching to him and pointing out his shortcomings. Seldom does the sociopath respond to commands or restrictions. He must first learn to trust in another person, such as his counselor, and through this experience begin to comprehend the love and dependability offered by God. With spiritual conversion there is sometimes a dramatic personality change. More often, however, the old patterns of childhood are erased slowly as the person grows spirituality. After the sociopath has committed his life to Christ, the counselor should help him, session after session, to thoroughly understand his partnership with God and the great resources available for dynamic Christian living.[3]

[2]For a discussion of this difficulty, see HOSTILITY in this volume.

[3]For a discussion of therapy with maladjustments having dynamics similar to SOCIOPATHIC PERSONALITIES, see ALCOHOLISM, ADDICTION, DELINQUENCY and UNFAITHFULNESS IN MARRIAGE in this volume.

58. Speech Disturbances

Description

Many facets of one's personality are revealed through his patterns of speech. A person's speech gives clues to his sociological background and his educational experience. Speech also reveals much about one's physical and emotional health, especially when normal patterns of speech are disturbed.

The widespread incidence of speech defects has brought an increasing awareness of this problem and many attempts to assist those suffering from such disturbances. Recent estimates of the number of individuals in the United States suffering from some form of speech defect run as high as eight million persons.[1]

Among the most of these speech disturbances are the following: Aphasia (discussed separately in this volume), articulatory defects, cluttering, delayed speech and stuttering.

Articulatory Defects (Dyslalia)

Included in the category of defects in articulation are (1) substitution of one sound for another, such as "th" for "s" (thay for say), "w" for "r" (wun for run), "t" for "k" (tite for kite), "d" for "g" (wadon for wagon); (2) omission of a sound in words, such as "pay" for "play," "dink" for "drink," "ee" for "see," "pease" for "please"; (3) additions such as "gulad" for "glad" and "pulease" for "please"; and (4) distortions or a consistently faulty formation of sounds due to poor speech habits. For example, in a careless or inaccurate "s" sound the breath may escape over the side or sides of the tongue to produce a lateral lisp; or an unnecessary speech sound may be added or inserted, as in "stee" for "see."

Articulatory disorders are the most frequent type of speech difficulty. Not only are they common among children, but many boys and girls carry these defects into their adult life. In a survey of 33,339 students entering the University of Michigan,

[1] For a detailed discussion of speech problems and therapy, see: Van Riper, Charles: *Speech Correction*, Prentice-Hall, Inc., Englewood Cliffs, 1963.

it was found that 3.85 per cent of them had speech defects and that approximately one-half of these were articulatory in nature.[2]

Etiology

These defects may result either from organic or functional sources. Among the structural disorders which often give rise to articulatory defects are *abnormalities of the teeth and jaws, harelip, abnormal tongue size and cleft palate.* Approximately one child in 700 suffers from some form of cleft palate. Hearing defects may also be important factors in the development of articulatory disorders.

Due to the emotional trauma associated with the birth of a physically defective child, some parents make serious errors in child rearing. For example, parents of a child born with cleft palate may become extremely over-protective and indulgent, or they may be rejecting and cold. Both of these extremes further complicate the child's development of proper speech patterns as well as his emotional adjustment.

Another factor in articulatory disorders is the *intelligence* of the individual. There is much higher occurrence of such problems among the mentally retarded than among those of normal intelligence.

Some children develop speech disturbances because of a *poor speech environment.* A child learns to articulate sounds by imitating others. If the parents' speech is careless, it is natural for the child to develop defective speech.

A child will sometimes continue to use *immature speech which gained him attention in early childhood.* Speech which was considered cute by parents may be used by the lonely child to continue to gain their attention.

As with other speech defects, dyslalia may also be the result of *emotional disturbances.* Unhappy home situations, excessive pressure, tensions and faulty discipline may all contribute to this type of disturbance. Individuals suffering from speech disturbances have frequently been subject to undue tension and

[2]Morley, D. E.: "A Ten-year Survey of Speech Disorders Among University Students," *Journal of Speech and Hearing Disorders,* vol. 17, pp. 25-30, 1952.

anxiety in the home. This has made the person insecure and nervous and has hindered the development of proper speech habits.[3]

Treatment

Although the majority of articulatory defects are not of organic basis, it is wise to begin diagnosis by having a thorough physical examination. This will either rule out an organic cause for the defect or identify structural abnormalities which may be influencing the child's articulation difficulties. In some cases surgical correction of physical deformities can correct the organic basis of the disturbance and prepare the child for special speech training which will enable him to develop normal speech patterns.

After physical defects are either ruled out or corrected, the emotional basis of the disturbance must be considered. If there are emotional factors in the home which are hindering the child's development, steps to relieve this situation should be taken.[3]

A process of reeduction should be undertaken after physical and emotional factors are carefully evaluated and treated. The child may first be taught to produce a single sound. After he has mastered this, he can learn to combine a number of sounds into words and eventually into sentences and normal conversation. Most communities have trained speech therapists which specialize in this type of corrective instruction.

Cluttering

Cluttering is a disorder affecting the rhythm of speech. It is characterized by rapid speech which is often confused and jumbled. One clutterer may exhibit unusually rapid speech, while another will not only speak rapidly but will so jumble his speech that it is almost impossible to comprehend. The clutterer sometimes begins a sentence in several ways before finally completing it. He may omit some words and interchange others. Hence,

[3]For a discussion of therapeutic techniques with problems which often have similar causes, see ANXIETY REACTION, ENURESIS and INSECURITY in this volume.

he is difficult to understand, and it appears that his ideas are confused.

In addition to difficulty in speech, the clutterer may show awkwardness in motor tasks. Attempts to perform any complex motor movements may be characterized by clumsiness. He is often hurried, erratic and poorly organized. He may be impulsive, overactive, easily distracted, forgetful and unstable. In early childhood the clutterer may have exhibited other language dysfunctions such as delayed speech and reading disability.

Etiology

Cluttering is generally believed to be a *constitutional anomaly of the language functions.* Case studies of clutters frequently point to histories of cluttering in parents, grandparents and other family members. This is often true even when the afflicted members of the family have never met and have not had the opportunity to imitate each other. Thus, the problem is regarded as organic and hereditary in nature. If a clutterer is exposed for a long period of time to an unfavorable home or school environment, he may develop additional speech problems.

Treatment

In contrast to the stutterer whose speech may become worse when his attention is called to it, the clutterer can usually improve his speech if he concentrates on it. Unlike the stutterer, the clutterer has his greatest difficulties of speech when he is in a familiar situation and is not concerned with his problem.

Although cluttered speech is believed to be due to organic factors, there is no satisfactory medical treatment for this disturbance. Treatment for the clutterer consists largely of developing self-control and precision in his speech. He must learn to concentrate on his difficulty and to pronounce each word separately and distinctly. One effective means of doing this is for the clutterer to clearly enunciate each word as he is writing. This necessitates slow speech and enables the person to focus his attention on the problem.

Delayed Speech

Some children do not develop speech patterns in accordance with their age level. This retardation in speech, or the continued use of infantile speech patterns, is known as delayed speech. Not all cases of delayed speech are indicative of severe problems. Slow development of speech until three or four years of age is sometimes suddenly overcome and the child quickly catches up with playmates who began communicating at an earlier age.

Etiology

Among the most frequent causes of delayed speech are: *hearing losses, mental retardation, forced change-of-handedness, brain injury, endocrine dysfunction, lack of motivation* (parents supplying all needs, so that the child does not need to learn to speak), *two-language homes, aphasia and emotional conflicts.*

Mental retardation is often the cause of delayed speech. Abt, Adler and Bartelme,[4] in a study of 1,000 children, found correlations of $-.41$ and $-.39$ between speech onset and intelligence in boys and girls respectively. In other words, the lower the intelligence the more likelihood there was of late speech development. In some instances, however, delayed speech is responsible for apparent low intelligence and marked changes in intelligence test performance may be seen if the speech difficulty is overcome.

In order to develop proper speech the child must have adequate hearing processes. An infant who is born with a serious hearing defect often needs special training if he is to develop normal speech patterns.

Treatment

A thorough physical examination is one of the first steps in the treatment of a child with delayed speech. An audiologist should be consulted to determine if the speech difficulty is a result of

[4]Abt, I., Adler, H. M. and Bartelme, Phyllis: "The Relationship Between the Onset of Speech and Intelligence," *Journal of the American Medical Association*, vol. 93, pp. 1351-1356, 1929.

inadequate hearing processes. If a defect is found, medical treatment for the hearing defect can be combined with parental efforts to assist the child to develop speech.

A diagnosis of brain damage or mental retardation is of value in planning treatment for delayed speech and for more realistically setting goals of achievement for the child. Speech therapy is helpful in some cases of mental retardation, but the results are usually limited by the degree of mental deficiency.

If the speech difficulty appears to be the result of an emotional conflict, the parents should seek help in gaining a deeper understanding of their influence on the child and the importance of providing a relaxed home atmosphere which is free from emotional stresses and tensions. This is true of the parents who have forced the young child from his normal pattern of left-handed functioning to the more acceptable right-handedness. In some cases the parents are so determined to make their child right-handed that their constant concern over his handedness may become a source of serious emotional conflict.

In all of the above instances the family should create a need for verbal communication. They should provide an environment which is stimulating to the development of speech and in which the child receives enjoyment and satisfaction from his verbal behavior.

Stuttering

Stuttering is characterized by a disturbance in the rhythm of speech. This may include either blocking (inability to articulate certain sounds) or repetition of a sound. The audible speech defect is often accompanied by visible signs in the individual's facial expressions and body tension. These tensions appear to be a reaction to frustration. Approximately one per cent of the population of the United States is affected by this speech disorder during childhood.

There is a large variation of symptoms among stutters. Some are characterized by hesitations or pauses, others by complete stoppages, and still others by repetition of certain sounds or phrases. Some have a combination of more than one of these. There is also great variation between individuals in respect to the occurrence of symptoms. Some people are affected only in a new and unfamiliar setting such as a new school. Others may have speech difficulty in the presence of certain individuals while exhibiting no similar problems among others. Nearly all people find it more difficult to speak when they are excessively tired or ill. Similarly, some children and adults have very little trouble with stuttering unless they are seriously fatigued or not feeling well. Repetition of words and syllables occurs in most children but should not be interpreted as stuttering. It is normal for a young child to make a number of repetitions while he is developing his speech abilities.

Stuttering is generally divided into two stages, primary and secondary.

"The primary state is characterized by repetition, prolongations and hesitations without awareness or anxiety and without reactions of struggle or avoidance."[5]

The secondary stage is characterized by attempts to avoid the occurrence of the stuttering, which may complicate the problem. During the primary stage, at the beginning of stuttering, the child will not feel sensitive about the problem. He may think others have the same difficulty and will pay little attention to it. As others begin to call attention to his problem, the individual often becomes sensitive and fearful of any attempts at speaking. He wants to participate in the conversation, but is afraid of exhibiting his speech difficulty. This, of course, may lead to more serious emotional conflict.

Most specialists in the field of speech disorders agree that stuttering is primarily psychological in origin. Although investigators have been unable to find a universal personality pattern common to stutters, there are a number of dynamics which these individuals hold in common.

Feelings of insecurity. The stutterer is generally an insecure individual. He lacks self-confidence and as a result is fearful of expressing himself verbally.[6]

---

[5]Levin, Nathaniel M.: *Voice and Speech Disorders: Medical Aspects*, Charles C. Thomas, Springfield, 1962.

[6]See the discussion of INSECURITY in this volume.

Worry and anxiety. Another personality characteristic common to stutters is a high degree of anxiety and tension. Because the person lacks confidence in himself, he is susceptible to tension and frustration and continually anticipates situations in which he will be shown inadequate.

Feelings of inferiority. Individuals suffering from stuttering frequently feel that they do not measure up. They feel inadequate and inferior. Because of this they are anxious in the presence of others whom they view as more competent and successful.[7]

High parental expectations. Extremely high parental standards are a common cause of feelings of insecurity and inferiority. When parents set unrealistic goals for their children they are predisposing the child to failure and feelings of unworthiness. As the child internalizes these attitudes he becomes worried and tense and is more likely to develop a disturbed speech pattern.

Traumatic experiences. In some insecure individuals a sudden frightening or emotionally upsetting event may precipitate stuttering. These events include such experiences as accidents, illnesses, parental separation, moving to a new neighborhood and entering an unfamiliar school.

Poor physical health. An important factor in many cases of stuttering is the physical health of the individual. It is frequently observed that stuttering is most noticeable when a person is suffering from ill health and is in a weakened condition. Although poor health alone does not cause stuttering, it is an important contributing factor in many instances.

Any combination of the above dynamics or any family experiences which lead to these feelings can be major etiological factors of stuttering as well as other types of speech disturbances.[8]

---

[7]See the discussion of INFERIORITY in this volume.

[8]For further information on this topic, see Fletcher, John Madison: *The Problem of Stuttering.* Longmans, Green Company, 1928.

Barbara, Dominick A. (Ed): *Psychological and Psychiatric Aspects of Speech and Hearing,* Charles C. Thomas, Springfield, 1960.

Treatment

In counseling with individuals suffering from disturbed speech patterns it is necessary to evaluate the basic emotional dynamics underlying the difficulty. When this is done it will soon be found that the stuttering is merely a symptom of a deeper personality conflict. The principles of therapy with individuals who stutter are essentially the same as those described for problems with similar etiological patterns discussed in this volume.

In treating a person who has suffered from stuttering for some time, the parents or other close associates should be shown the need to understand the person's emotional difficulties. The stutterer needs the opportunity to participate actively in groups and to carry on a normal life. Those who are near to the stutterer can be of great assistance by providing an accepting and non-critical environment. One of the most important factors in stuttering is the relationship of the speaker to the listener. If the family and friends learn to be kind and sympathetic listeners, the stutterer will be more at ease and able to communicate more freely.

In children, the environment established by the parents is of special importance. Parents should have a good understanding of their child, his temperament and his needs. They must instill in the stutterer feelings of confidence and security. Situations which produce anxiety and tension should be alleviated. By taking time with the child and kindly and patiently explaining things to him, the confidence needed to overcome speech difficulties will gradually be gained. A Christ-centered home where there are good relationships between parents and children will add to the security and tranquility of the stutterer.

Parents need to be realistic in their expectations. The stuttering child is a child in tension. By seeing that overemphasis is not placed upon achievement and perfectionism, the parents can help to reduce the stutter's tension and anxiety.

A therapeutic technique sometimes helpful with children is the use of puppets. Although a child may stutter severely when speaking directly to another person, he is often able to speak fluently when he takes part in an imaginary conversation between a puppet he holds and the one his parent or therapist controls. By talking through the puppet the person gains distance from his own emotional involvement and is freed from his tension and anxiety. When a person sees that he can speak freely through a puppet, he can gain increased confidence in his ability and begin to make significant progress.

By initiating a total program of therapy directed toward an improved environment and increased feelings of self-confidence and security, the stutterer will gradually be able to overcome his difficulties.

59. Stealing

Description

The problem of *stealing* is often confused with *kleptomania*. Although both are concerned with taking items that do not belong to one, they usually differ from each other in their frequency and in the causes which prompt such behavior. In this section the two are treated separately in order to better understand the nature of the psychodynamics involved in each.

Stealing

Persons of all ages engage in stealing. However, theft is more common among children and adolescents. Some children who have stolen considerably throughout childhood have adopted new patterns of behavior as they became adults and no longer take things which do not belong to them. Others, however, have continued to steal throughout their lifetime.

Etiology

The most common causes of stealing include the following:

Meeting the necessities of life. In some cases children and adults do not have sufficient food or clothing to meet their basic needs. In such cases they steal articles of clothing or food in order to keep from suffering. This is especially true in low economic cultures. Having become clever in taking things unnoticed, they often take additional items, some of which they do not actually need.

Lacking moral standards. When a baby comes into the world he does not distinguish what is his and what is another's. But as he grows and develops, his parents and teachers help him to become aware of his own belongings as contrasted to those of others. Under normal conditions a child gradually understands ownership and becomes content to work for things which he does not have or to feel content without them. There are children, though, who have not been taught that stealing is wrong. In some cases, they see a continual pattern of stealing at home. Since their parents are engaged in stealing, they feel little or no guilt about this behavior.

Lack of spirituality. Closely related to poor moral standards is the consideration of the person's relationship to the Lord. When one is walking in close fellowship with Christ he is satisfied with what the Lord has given him and he does not feel a need to gain property for himself by stealing from others.

Gaining status and friends. A person may steal in order to gain status or to surround himself with friends. By having extra money for certain articles, he may feel he has bettered himself and that others will admire him more. An adolescent girl, for example, may steal a new coat, hoping to impress her acquaintances. A child may steal money, candy, soft drinks or toys and give them to other children, hoping to gain their friendship.

Giving vent to hostility. An individual may steal in an effort to "get even" with the person from whom he stole or to give vent to hatred which he holds toward a completely different person or to society.[1] He need not steal from the so-called offender in order to get relief from his strong feelings of hostility. If a child, for example, feels that he has been mistreated by his parents, he may feel justified in stealing an article from a store. This added possession and the pleasure it brings is a fair compensation, he feels, for injustice inflicted by his parents. Hardened criminals are sometimes driven to steal because of injustices which they feel have been shown to them. Such feelings may be on an unconscious or a conscious level.

Participating in gang activities. Studies of teen-age gangs show that some members steal because they are under pressure by their leaders to do so. Others steal because of the prestige they feel they get in the gang. Still others feel that group stealing is not personal and, therefore, not immoral if it is done for or with gang members. Although such a person may not steal "on his own," he does not feel personally responsible if he steals in connection with an organized group.

Kleptomania

The person suffering from kelptomania has a strong, almost uncontrollable, urge to steal. Kleptomania differs from most cases of stealing in that it is impulsive and seemingly without

[1]For a discussion of this problem, see HOSTILITY in this volume.

cause. Parents and relatives may understand why a certain person is stealing, but they are left bewildered in the case of a financially secure person being caught for habitual shoplifting. When such a person is apprehended, she is usually embarrassed and at a loss to explain her actions.

One woman, for example, came to her pastor and confessed that over a period of time she had stolen many articles from different department stores. "I feel so guilty," she said. When the pastor asked her why she had stolen, she said that she had no idea, except that a strange feeling came over her and she felt compelled to shoplift. Although she had been able to steal articles, she could not return them unnoticed. She then told the pastor that she had stolen three trunks full of merchandise and that they were all hidden in her basement. Her husband, an outstanding businessman, knew nothing of her compulsion to steal.

Etiology

Following are some of the psychodynamics of kleptomania:

Need for punishment. This is a significant factor in compulsive stealing. Most kleptomaniacs are apprehended shortly after they have stolen. In fact, many seem to be relieved when they are caught. Their behavior leads the counselor to believe that the person sensed a need for punishment. Unresolved guilt feelings from childhood and adolescence may be at the basis of such actions.[2]

Reaction against authority. Kleptomania may be understood in some cases as reaction against authority figures whom they knew early in life. Store managers, policemen and others are the immediate targets, but they may only represent parents, teachers or other significant figures in the past.

Expression of generalized hostility. Psychodiagnostic testing often reveals an unusual amount of generalized hostility in the kleptomaniac. This need not be directed toward a specific person; rather, it may be an accumulation of hatred which has built up over the years.

---

[2]For a further discussion of this problem, see GUILT in this volume.

Defiance of convention. Kleptomaniacs are sometimes acting out their defiance of early home or school training. When a person has been raised in a strict environment without love, and when his environment has imposed moral and ethical standards which he has not internalized personally, he may act out his hostilities in adulthood. This is true in some instances of kleptomania.

Need for erotic excitement. The study of those engaged in kleptomania discloses that in some cases there is a sexual element present.[3] Such persons occasionally reveal a certain sexual excitement and satisfaction associated with stealing. Since they are insecure in their own attitudes toward heterosexual relations, they turn to a substitute activity. One young woman, for example, told her counselor that during the time when she was stealing an object and taking it out of the store to her home, she experienced unusual sexual feelings. Unconscious fantasies of sexual activities are stimulated in some cases of kleptomania.

Treatment

In cases of stealing, treatment is aimed at uncovering the basic causes, then working through in therapy until the problem is resolved.[4] The subject first needs to ventilate his feelings and freely discuss his actions. As this is done, the counselor can help the individual to gain an understanding of the causes of his behavior. The person needs to see whether his stealing represents an attempt to gain friends, whether it is an expression of hostility, or if it is caused by some other underlying dynamic. If the kleptomaniac's stealing is a defiance of convention or a felt need for erotic excitement, he needs to come to grips with the true causes of his feelings.

As the client begins to gain an understanding of the reasons for his behavior, he should be led to a personal knowledge of Christ. After he has been born again,[5] he should seek complete forgiveness for his sins of theft. "Let the wicked forsake his

---

[3]For a discussion of related disturbances, see SEXUAL DEVIATION in this volume.
[4]For more information on therapy with these individuals, see DELINQUENCY and SOCIOPATHIC PERSONALITY in this volume.
[5]For a Biblical discussion of the new birth, read the third chapter of John.

way, and the unrighteous man his thoughts; and let him return unto the Lord, and he will have mercy upon him; and to our God, for he will abundantly pardon" (Isaiah 55:7).

After the client turns to God for forgiveness, he should continue to grow spiritually. He needs to develop new friends and to change his life actions so that his old patterns of behavior are replaced with new and acceptable ones. As a person stays close to the Lord, he will find increased strength to overcome past habits and to develop a new way of life which is centered upon the Word of God.

60. Suicide

Description

The problem of suicide and sucidal attempts frequently faces the professional counselor. The range of severity of this difficulty varies from the threat to take one's life in order to gain attention to the "successful" suicidal attempt. Whether a person merely threatens to take his life or actually carries it out, it is an indication of emotional disturbance.

It is often said that the person who threatens to take his life will not actually carry this out. But such is not the case. It has been noted that approximately 75% of persons who do commit suicide gave definite warnings to their intent.[1] Some who speak of suicide do not actually attempt to end their lives, but their threats should not be ignored. The reality of the emotional disturbance does not depend on whether or not the person actually attempts to take his life. Regardless of his words, he still needs help.[2]

Etiology

Some individuals threaten to take their lives *in order to gain sympathy and attention.* When this happens it is a sign that the person is dissatisfied with life and is experiencing feelings of rejection and unworthiness. He may attempt to shock friends or relatives by threatening to "end it all."

In other instances the possibility of an actual suicidal attempt is more real. In these cases the individual is suffering from severe emotional disturbance and is in need of immediate treatment.

The basic factors underlying suicidal thoughts center upon *feelings of depression and dissatisfaction with life.* The person who considers taking his life is an unhappy individual who sees no purpose or meaning in living. He feels that that the only

[1]"Patterns of Disease," Parke, Davis and Company, May, 1963.
[2]For information on suicide see: Shneidman, E. S., et al: "Some Facts About Suicide," Publis Health Service, Printing Office, 1961.

way to escape his continual feeling of worry, despair and depression is to end his life.[3]

The depressed person is a guilt-ridden individual who feels he deserves punishment for his misdeeds. Sometimes he attempts to take his life, not only to escape an unpleasant situation but also to inflict and sustain the punishment he believes is merited.

Spiritual factors and one's philosophy of life are important in many suicidal attempts. The person who does not know Christ as his Savior does not have a proper perspective on life. The unsaved person does not understand the meaning of life and the purpose of human existence. As one unsaved person has stated, "Life is the process which produces corpses." With such an attitude, it is little wonder that many people see no reason to continue living. When a person has emotional difficulties he is especially prone to dwell on the negative and to find only futility and failure in human existence. There are many instances when a person in despair and dejection has turned from purposeless living and suicidal thoughts to the reality of living found through the acceptance of Jesus Christ as Savior. ". . . I am come that they might have life, and that they might have it more abundantly" (John 10:10).

Christians, however, are not exempt from suicidal thoughts. Their emotional scars from childhood may be severe and unresolved. Consequently, they may question whether life is worth living. Naturally, such individuals are in need of therapy.

Treatment

Counseling with the depressed person is generally a long-term process. If the suicidal threat is an attempt to gain sympathy and attention, the counselor must explore with the counselee the factors which have led to his feelings of rejection and unworthiness. When such a person says, "I am going to end it all," he is in essence saying that he feels himself to be a failure and he thinks no one is interested in him. He is sending out

[3]For a more complete treatment of the dynamics involved in many suicidal cases see the discussion of DEPRESSION in this volume.

signals to the counselor telling that he is in need of affection and attention.

When one of the dynamics involved in a suicidal threat is this search for attention, the counselor must be very careful not to quickly point out to the person that his threat of suicide is his way of seeking sympathy. Although this is a dynamic, it is often only after many counseling sessions that the client is ready for such interpretation. If he is told during the first few sessions that he is seeking attention by threatening to take his life, it is probable that he will feel even more depressed. This interpretation only tears down the person's defenses and makes him more aware of his feelings of rejection.

Instead of this rapid interpretation, the counselor must help the person to discuss his feelings of rejection and to gain insight into the causes of these attitudes. An important consideration is that the person come to recognize the fact of the Lord's love and concern for him. Although the person feels rejected by his loved ones, he can come to see the grace and love of God and to find his sense of security and well-being through his position in Christ. Scriptures such as Psalm 27:10, for example, demonstrate the care of God for His children. "When my father and my mother forsake me, then the Lord will take me up."

When a person's suicidal thoughts are very real the problem of depression is usually acute and may require temporary medical attention and hospitalization. In these cases an antidepressant medication may minimize immediate feelings of depression. After this a long-term therapy program should be initiated. Even though severe thoughts of depression and sucide may be alleviated by medication, the basic emotional disturbance can only be corrected with gradual insights and personality reorganization.

In addition to considerations common to counseling with depressives,[4] special factors need to be included when dealing with a potential suicide. Along with the medical treatment already discussed, the person's total environment should be considered. For example, the depressed person should not be left

---

[4]See the section on Treatment in the chapter on DEPRESSION in this volume.

alone for long periods to contemplate his feelings of dejection and despair. In meeting this need, it is often necessary to bring other family members into the therapy situation in order to evaluate the assistance they can bring to the disturbed person. Any circumstances which could result in increased frustrations and feelings of failure should be closely considered by the counselor, as he may want to suggest some specific changes in the person's activities to avoid unnecessary conflict and bewilderment.

With seriously depressed individuals, it may be necessary to have several counseling sessions each week. Whereas in dealing with most personality problems one or two sessions a week are usually desirable, the depressed person may need much more than this during the first few weeks of his counseling. When a person is so acutely distressed as to contemplate taking his life, he may need daily opportunity to express his feelings and to gain insights into his behavior. After some progress is made, the frequency of the counseling sessions can gradually be reduced.

Good understanding of the Word of God is also basic to improving the individual's attitudes and emotional reactions. Being depressed, the potential suicide frequently sees life as evil, threatening and purposeless. He may feel that the world is in such a bad condition that there is no use fighting any longer. In these instances a Biblical perspective of the evil of the last days, but God's continued abidance with the believer, should be discussed with the client. As he begins to gain an outlook of God's dealings with man through the ages, and God's purpose and plan for the present and future, life takes on new meaning and purpose. This Biblical knowledge is an important consideration which should be combined with the person's insights in a total therapy program.

61. Syphilis

Description and Etiology

Syphilis is an infectious venereal disease caused by a micro-organism called Treponema pallidum. This spirochete gains entrance into the body through minute abrasions in the skin or directly through the mucous membrane. Syphilis is generally transmitted from person to person during sexual intercourse, but can be transmitted through other contacts with syphilitic sores. It may also be passed from mother to child during pregnancy. This latter instance is referred to as congenital syphilis. Almost every tissue of the body can be affected by this disease. For this reason syphilis has been referred to as "the great mimicker." The development of syphilis in the human body follows four well-defined stages:

1. As soon as the syphilitic spirochetes enter the body they begin to multiply rapidly. From three to six weeks after the initial infection, a small sore known as a chancre appears at the place of the first infection. This chancre or primary lesion is usually in the form of an ulcerated sore or occasionally a hard pimple. Ninety-five percent of the primary lesions are located on or near the genitals. The chancre may seem so insignificant that it is ignored and will disappear within four to six weeks, even without treatment.

2. The second stage of syphilis is characterized by the appearance of a copper-colored skin rash which resembles measles or smallpox. The rash may be limited or it may be quite severe and cover the entire body, and it may involve the mucous membranes. In addition to this rash, secondary syphilis may be accompanied by headaches, fever, loss of appetite, indigestion and loss of hair.

3. The third stage of this disease is known as latent syphilis. The signs and symptoms of secondary syphilis have spontaneously disappeared and the individual may be unaware of the disease. During this period, however, the spirochetes are vigorously attacking many internal organs. These attacks on the blood vessels, heart, spinal cord, bone marrow, or the brain

can go on for years unnoticed but will cause permanent degeneration if treatment is delayed.

4. It is during the fourth stage of syphilis that the previous bodily destruction becomes apparent. It may take ten, twenty, or more years after the initial infection for the final effects of syphilis to become apparent. Among the most common occurrences during this period are heart disease, blindness, loss of motor coordination, liver disorder and mental disturbances. All of these may be brought about by the destruction occurring during the latent period.

It is the effects of the infection on the brain and nervous system which are of special concern to the psychologist. When damage is done to the central nervous system the individual may begin to manifest serious disturbances of personality. The most common of these are general paresis, juvenile paresis and cerebral syphilis.

General Paresis

General paresis is the most common type of neuro-syphilis. This disorder accounts for approximately 1.8 per cent of admission to mental hospitals in the United States.

The physical symptoms of general paresis include motor disabilities such as a shuffled, unsteady walk, frequent tremors of the face, lips and tongue, and a loss of some reflexes. The pupils may also be of irregular size and there may be an absence of the pupillary reflex to light. Speech functions of the individual may also be disturbed. In attempting to pronounce "Methodist Episcopal" the individual may reply "Methdis Pispal," "Meodist Epispal," or "Mesdus Episfal."

Psychological symptoms become more apparent as the disease progresses. Initially, the individual may show occasional lapses of memory, impaired judgment and carelessness. As the disease continues, he may exhibit a loss of moral restraints and a deterioration of his personal habits. This intellectual deterioration is more evident as the person becomes unable to understand simple problems and to recall even recent events.

The variety of psychological symptoms manifested by those suffering from general paresis is determined by the extent of organic damage caused by the infection, the emotional makeup of the person before the onset of the disease, the stage of the disorder at which treatment is initiated and the life situation to which the individual must adjust. Three major categories are used to classify the various psychological symptoms of general paresis.

1. *The expansive type* is characterized by a sense of well-being and delusions of greatness. He talks readily of his vast projects involving millions of dollars and entirely unrealistic ideas. When asked how he is feeling he will answer that he is feeling great, that everything is going fine for him and that he has never felt better.

2. In contrast to the expansive type is the *depressed person*. This individual has serious feelings of depression and discouragement. He may have some insight into his condition but this understanding only serves to make him more worried and upset. The depressed patient may also experience hypochondriacal delusions. He may fear that entire organs of his body have either disappeared or stopped functioning. The severely depressed individual may also attempt to take his own life.

3. The demented or *simple type* does not show the marked degrees of either euphoria or depression exhibited by the above types. Instead, he may gradually withdraw from his environment and may experience delusions and hallucinations.

Juvenile Paresis
This is a mental disorder resulting from congential syphilis. It is a condition of general paresis which occurs in childhood and adolescence. The psychological disturbances are caused by deterioration of the brain tissue brought about by the spyhilitic infection. The major symptoms of juvenile paresis are progressive physical and mental deterioration.

The person suffering from juvenile paresis shows a lack of memory and progressively poorer judgment. Although the child was infected with the disease before birth, most of the symptoms do not begin to appear until he reaches the age of ten to twelve. In countries where adequate prevention and treatment is unavailable, syphilitic infections are often responsible for extremely high infant mortality rates and for many cases of blindness in children at birth.

Cerebral Syphilis

This is a mental disorder brought about by syphilitic damage to the blood vessels and meninges surrounding the brain tissue. The physical symptoms accompanying this disorder include persistent headaches, dizziness, disorders of pupillary reactions and insomnia.

Mental symptoms include impairment of memory, confusion and inability to concentrate. These symptoms generally emerge earlier than those of general paresis, often within two or three years after the original infection. Early in this disorder the symptoms are not as marked as general paresis, but if treatment is not begun this disease will soon progress to the more severe symptoms of untreated general paresis.

Treatment

Treatment for syphilitic conditions is primarily a medical specialty. The most commonly used treatment includes fever therapy and the administration of anti-syphilitic drugs. The syphilitic spirochete is highly vulnerable to high temperatures. Physicians are able to artificially induce above-normal bodily temperatures which will destroy the spirochetes.

Antibiotics such as penicillin are also used in large doses and have proven very beneficial when combined with some form of fever therapy. The success of medical therapy is dependent on the amount of cerebral damage which has accrued before treatment. This being true, it is of utmost importance that medical treatment be initiated early in the course of the disease.

After medical treatment is begun psychotherapy is often employed to enable the person to better adjust to his situation. Since syphilis results in many psychological problems, these must be dealt with individually. Therapeutic techniques for these various emotional disturbances are the same for similar problems with solely psychological causes. However, the person who has suffered from syphilis needs special help in understanding the specific effects of the disease upon his physical and mental functioning.

62. Thyroid Dysfunction

Description

The thyroid gland is a part of the endocrine system of the body.[1] It secretes a hormone, thyroxin, which plays a major role in regulating the metabolism of the body. Malfunction of this gland may produce exophthalmus (bluging eyes), goiter, fine tremor, weight loss, intolerance to heat, nervousness, irritability and emotional instability. Persons with an improperly functioning thyroid gland may manifest only a few of these symptoms and in some cases just the emotional ones.[2]

Physical and emotional disturbances may result from either oversecretion or undersecretion of this gland.

Hyperthyroidism. An oversecretion of the hormone, thyroxin, may result in both physical and psychological symptoms. Among the most frequent physical symptoms associated with hyperthyroidism are sleeplessness, restlessness and loss of weight. The person with an overactive thyroid gland may also become tense and emotionally excitable.

Hypothyroidism. An insufficient supply of thyroxin in the adult or older child leads to a disorder called *myxedema*. This slowing down of body metabolism results in an overall sluggishness, memory defect and obesity. In more severe cases, states of depression may accompany the fatigue and listlessness.

Thyroid hormone deficiency dating from birth is known as *cretinism.*[3] This early childhood condition is due to an insufficient supply of thyroxin and is characterized by both physical and mental abnormalities. Prominent physical characteristics of the cretin are dry, coarse skin; short, broad hands and feet; bulky and protruding abdomen; dry hair which falls out easily; short thick neck; poorly formed teeth which decay easily; and

[1]See the discussion of ENDOCRINE DYSFUNCTIONS in this volume.
[2]For a medical discussion of thyroid dysfunction, see: Harrison, T. R. and others (Eds.): *Principles of Internal Medicine*, McGraw-Hill Book Company, Inc., New York, Fourth Edition, 1962.
[3]See *Dorland's Illustrated Medical Dictionary*, W. B. Saunders Company, Philadelphia, 23rd Edition, 1957.

coarse sounding voice. The intelligence of the cretin is seriously deficient. Most cretins have I.Q.'s in the idiot or imbecile ranges. They are unable to profit from formal education, and have only limited ability to benefit from training.[4] The cretin shows little response emotionally.

Etiology

The primary factor in these disorders is the *abnormal functioning of the thyroid gland,* for which the causes are not well understood. The nature and extent of the malfunction greatly influence the severity of the symptoms.

In hyperthyroidism some feel there is a tie-in between *episodes of iodine and the ingestion of goitrogenic agents.* The use of iodized salt has greatly reduced the incidence of endemic goiter in iodine-deficient areas.

Hypothyroidism manifested as cretinism can result from *failure of the thyroid gland to develop,* from a *deficiency of maternal iodine,* or from *genetic factors.* When it is manifested later in life as juvenile and adult myxedema, it can be caused by *destruction of thyroid gland tissue from disease, atrophy or ablative procedures (thyroidectomy or radiation).*

The personality of the individual is also important in understanding these disorders. The emotional makeup of the person determines to a large extent the effect which this physical malady will have on his behavior.

Illustration

Identification; White female, age 37
Presenting Problem: The patient has been a nervous individual for several years. She becomes easily upset by trivialities and often has difficulty in sleeping. She has also lost over fifty pounds in the past few years.
Personal and Family History: The subject is the third of four children. She was a happy, well-adjusted child and did well in school. There is no history of mental or emotional disturbance in her family. The patient married at 24 and now has three

[4]See the discussion of MENTAL DEFICIENCY in this volume.

children. About five years ago, shortly after the birth of her last child, she began to lose weight and became nervous and irritable. She often complained of being quite warm when others were comfortable. She was advised by her family physical to see an endocrinologist.

Treatment

Therapy for hyperthyroidism can include (1) drugs such as iodine or certain antithyroid preparations, (2) surgery involving subtotal or total removal of the thyroid gland (thyroidectomy), and (3) radiation, the taking of radioactive iodine orally. These methods are best administered by a medical specialist when available.

The early diagnosis and treatment of cretinism is very important. It is primarily a medical concern and early, effective care in some cases has brought almost complete remission of symptoms. Patients with juvenile or adult myxedema (hypothyroidism) are given thyroid hormone substances. In some cases, iodine may be indicated.

Psychotherapy has proven helpful when used in connection with medical treatment. Therapy is aimed at giving the person a better understanding of the nature of his illness and the ways in which he can adjust to his new energy level. Since these disorders may bring serious physical and emotional symptoms, it is important that the person learn to accept his limitations. In developing a realistic approach to his handicaps, the person needs much spiritual growth and insight. As he begins to understand and accept the will of God for his life, he is better able to accept his current condition and to feel satisfied with his circumstances in life.

Perhaps the counselor's greatest contribution is made when he works with the parents of children who have the above disorders. Through several sessions, parents can come to understand and better accept their child's problem. As parents realize his limitations, they can make life more satisfying for him as well as for themselves.

63. Tics

Description
Psychological tics are persistent, intermittent muscle twitches or spasms usually limited to a localized muscle group. They may include facial grimaces, blinking of the eyes, twitching of the mouth, licking of the lips, clicking of the teeth, shrugging of the shoulders, twisting of the neck, clearing of the throat, blowing through the nostrils and many other motions. A person may be aware of the tic, but in some cases he may perform the act so involuntarily that he is not cognizant of it. A young woman, for example, was thinking of giving up her library position because she had been told that she had a noticeable and persistent clearing of the throat. She had previously been unaware of this and could not tell when it occurred.

Tics occur most frequently between the ages of 6 to 14, but are also common among adults. Some nervous reactions are found in all children and adults, but they are not sufficiently severe to warrant special attention. In other cases, however, they become persistent and sufficiently exaggerated to signal rather serious emotional disturbances.

Etiology
Tics may have an organic cause, but the great majority are psychological in origin. They usually represent some *inner tension and anxiety.*

Nervous mannerisms or tics are common *when a person feels embarrassed or self-conscious.* Public speakers and singers, for example, often clear their throats repeatedly before speaking or singing. The average person, however, does not carry this over to usual social situations. The individual with a tic is almost always under stress because of *feelings of self-consciousness and inadequacy,* or as a result of special tension. A man, for example, who is overworked may develop a nervous mannerism, but when he is able to relax more and assume a normal work load, the tic disappears.

Sometimes *repressed sexual desires or hostility* may lead to the accumulation of tension and to feelings of uneasiness, restlessness and irritability. These, in turn, may be reflected by a tic. Usually, the greater the tension, the more frequently the tic occurs.

Illustration
Identification: White female, age 14
Presenting Problem: The patient sought psychological assistance because of a persistent, irritating blinking of eyes.
Personal and Family History: The parents of the subject were hard-working people with an above-average income. Although they had received little education, they had become quite successful economically. Both the mother and father were extremely concerned that the girl make an outstanding academic record and become successful in personal and social relationships. At home they constantly supervised her study and saw that she had everything done "perfectly." She was also under pressure to take part in many social activities and to be the center of attention.

The subject's facial tic became apparent when she entered first grade in school. However, it did not become serious until the third grade when she was under much pressure both at home and at school. During the past two years it become sufficiently serious that her school counselor suggested she receive psychological help.

Treatment
Calling attention to a tic and encouraging a person to rid himself of the "nervous habit" does little good. This concern will only intensify the disturbance. Treatment of a person suffering from a tic is directed toward better personality and health adjustment with the aid of a more appropriate means of reducing tension. It is important that parents and teachers of children with this nervous condition learn to provide a more desirable environment with less strain. When children are provided with a stable and secure environment, they can be freed of the ten-

sion which produces the nervous mannerism. As a client finds an accepting counselor who understands the basis of the problem, the person is then free to bring his inner conflicts to the surface and resolve them.[1]

[1]For a discussion of related disturbances, see ANXIETY REACTION and INSECURITY in this volume.

64. Unfaithfulness in Marriage

Description

Unfaithfulness in marriage may be defined as breaking of the marriage vows. It involves intimate sexual relations with a married or single person who is not a marriage partner.

In much of western civilization there is an alarming upswing in unfaithfulness. In certain circles it seems almost the norm, yet this utter disregard of the sacredness of the marriage vows is undoubtedly a major factor in the rapidly increasing divorce rate. Children in such marriages are often the innocent victims, suffering in many ways and becoming predisposed toward adult maladjustments.

Etiology

Lack of spiritual dedication. This condition is probably responsible for more unfaithfulness than all other causes combined. The unsaved nature of man is corrupt and apart from God. The Bible aptly describes it in the following diagnosis: "The heart is deceitful above all things, and desperately wicked: who can know it?" (Jeremiah 17:9). It should be no surprise, then, that without godly restraint, men and women find extra-marital sexual relations difficult to resist.

Even the believer in Christ is not immune from falling into the sin of unfaithfulness if he is content to remain a babe, spiritually speaking, or to follow the Lord afar off. There is no standing still in the Christian life. If there is not growth and maturity, then there is retrogression, which leads to disobedience. Although the carnal nature does not need to dominate the life of the Christian, it is still within him and is capable of gross immorality. Marital unfaithfulness is but one pitfall of a believer who refuses God's daily leading and who gives in to his carnal appetites.

General immaturity. This is one of the most common causes of unfaithfulness on the part of either husband or wife. Couples who marry young are particularly susceptible to immature actions, although maturity and age do not necessarily go hand in hand. One who has been accustomed to having his or her own desires satisfied immediately is hardly equipped for the demands of constant sharing imposed by marriage. Extreme self-centeredness contributes strongly to marriage unhappiness which often leads to unfaithfulness.

Lack of vocational skills. Highly industrialized societies demand high levels of vocational skills. Unless one has a reasonably adequate education and specialized training he is unable to secure a satisfying job. This fact bears directly upon one's happiness and success in marriage. If an individual is not happy at work and if he is unable to furnish the home with necessary finances, many problems will ensue. Such dissatisfaction leads to bitter quarreling and outright deprivation. In these instances it is only natural for a marriage partner to turn to another for help and for comfort.

Unwillingness to accept family responsibilities. The coming of children into the home and the unwillingness of either partner to accept his or her parental responsibility can lead to an illicit relationship. The husband or wife who views children as something to tie one down and keep one from enjoying life is fair game for an outsider who capitalizes on such attitudes.

Overcritical partners. The husband or wife who demands perfection of the marriage partner, who seldom compliments or praises, and who nags constantly, is inviting unfaithfulness. Although this does not excuse unfaithfulness, it should, nevertheless, be recognized as a major factor in driving one's mate into the arms of another to seek solace for a wounded ego.

Sexual dissatisfaction in marriage. Oftentimes, husband and wife have come from different backgrounds where the wonder and mystery of sex was viewed from entirely different perspectives. Some husbands see sex as only the fulfillment of a biological urge, and some wives view sex as something vulgar to be endured or tolerated but certainly not to be enjoyed. A lack of sound sexual information, unwholesome ideas, inconsiderate or selfish attitudes, and impatience in adjustments in the marriage relationship can lead to seeking sexual satisfaction with someone else.

Hostility toward the parent of the opposite sex. Anger that was felt by a girl toward her father during childhood and that has persisted through adolescence and young adulthood may be projected later upon her husband. The faults of a father may take on greater proportions in the imperfections of a husband. Similarly, the smothering overprotectiveness of a mother may seem to be repeated in a wife who is somewhat domineering. Sometimes this hostility becomes generalized toward all those of the opposite sex, causing one to leave the marriage partner, seeking in vain for happiness from another.

In-law interference. Well-meaning parents can contribute to unfaithfulness on the part of a son-in-law or daughter-in-law by constant and unwarranted interference. The inability of in-laws to permit a newly married couple to make their own decisions and live their own lives has, at times, been responsible for a weakened resistance on the part of a husband or wife to an outsider who offered sympathy and physical response. In-laws who constantly take sides, who make unfavorable comparisons with former girl friends and suitors, and who fail to retire into the background at critical moments, may contribute to a broken marriage as much as does the third party in a triangle.

Lack of confidence in people. Some persons, because of early experiences, seem incapable of trusting another human being. Consequently, they are suspicious and distrustful of their mates. Other things being equal, trust begets trust in marriage. But some unfortunate persons, by their utter lack of confidence, drive a wedge between themselves and their marriage partners. This is often due to unhappy childhood experiences such as a broken home or the death or desertion of one or both parents. Sometimes it is caused by the traumatic betrayal of a trust by a close friend or a respected adult.

Lack of teaching regarding the sanctity and permanence of marriage. This is another principle causing unfaithfulness. An increasingly prevalent attitude says, "Let's go ahead and get married anyway; if it doesn't work out, we can always try it with somebody else." It is felt that marriage partners can be shed or exchanged in much the same way as a piece of merchandise. Certain segments of society smile patronizingly upon the person who has extra-marital affairs as long as he does not get caught. Moral and spiritual standards are largely ignored.

Illustration
Identification: White male, age 30
Presenting Problem: The couple came to a marriage counselor because of unfaithfulness on the part of the husband. During separate sessions the wife said she wanted to keep the marriage together but felt that she could not handle the problem emotionally if her husband continued in this way. The husband admitted his infidelity and stated that he saw nothing wrong with it. "She can take it or leave it," he said.
Personal and Family History: As a child, the husband was dominated by his mother. The father was a weak although expressively loving personality. The husband's mother was undemonstrative and very strict religiously, without any demonstration of spiritual maturity. As a child, the client was submissive for the sake of "peace." He claimed he had an unhappy, "stifling" childhood.

During counseling he revealed that his sexual relations with his wife were unsatisfactory. He claimed that she could not meet his needs. As a result, he became moody and uncommunicative. The wife was submissive and tried to please him. He felt that most of the time she was "doing him a favor" rather than enjoying the relationship herself.

In therapy it became evident that the husband felt inadequate as a man and was attempting to prove his masculinity by extra-marital affairs. He was also perceiving his wife as a mother-substitute.

On the other hand, he feared women and withdrew from desirable emotional relationships with them. He dared not love his wife deeply since he felt this would involve domination and consequent loss of personal adequacy. He feared that she would dominate him, yet he wanted his wife to be a strong personality. He attempted to control her, yet he was dependent and resentful of his dependency needs. His wife's submissiveness angered and frustrated him, causing him to lose respect for her.

However, when she attempted to show strength, he rebelled for fear she would rob him of his self-confidence.

Treatment

To approach the problem of marital unfaithfulness caused by general immaturity, it is of little value to lecture or rebuke the unfaithful partner. Much more is accomplished through the process of discussion and insight. The direction which therapy takes will often be determined by the results of psycho-diagnostic testing. Modern treatment of personality problems usually involves the use of psychological tests. They are helpful in identifying particular areas that the counselee may conceal, either deliberately or unconsciously. The general concept of maturity should be considered in relationship to a variety of situations in married life. The ingredients of healthy, wholesome emotional development should be examined. In this process the counselor should seek to help the client uncover past experiences that have hindered his development. Through insight and understanding, maturity will begin to emerge. Willingness to forego illicit sex relations can then be viewed as leading to greater permanent happiness, thus helping to resolve the outward problem of unfaithfulness.

Some couples are unprepared emotionally and psychologically to cope with the responsibilities of a family. In some cases, the unfaithfulness of a wife has resulted partially from the persistent, never-ending pressure of being responsible for young children with little if any help or recognition from the husband. Changing diapers, preparing meals, cleaning house, applying bandages, answering the phone, settling quarrels, giving baths, teaching discipline—these and other responsibilities, without any break, can drive a woman to utter discouragement, and sometimes to unfaithfulness. Husbands need to be encouraged to provide periodic release for their wives from household duties and the care of children, even if only for a few hours each week. The wife's physical condition, too, is vitally important.

When unfaithfulness has been the result of an overcritical mate, counseling is needed to uncover the causes of such attitudes. The person who critizes, nags and constantly complains, needs to understand what is causing his behavior. Frequently, a person who has this problem is attempting to compensate for feelings of inadequacy and inferiority. The counselor and counselee should examine acceptable, non-critical ways of gaining self-respect and the respect of one's mate. Most important, yieldedness to Christ as Lord of one's life will be seen as the ultimate answer to a critical spirit, either on the part of the sinning or sinned-against partner. The counselor may wish to apply the keen edge of such appropriate Scripture as Luke 6:38, "For with the same measure that ye mete withal it shall be measured to you again."

If a married couple is complaining of sexual dissatisfaction, the counselor should seek to convey an understanding and appreciation of the vastly different viewpoints regarding sex that a husband and wife may bring to their marriage. An adequate understanding of the basic differences between the sexes, biologically and psychologically, should never be taken for granted on the part of the counselor. The recommendation of a sound marriage manual may be especially helpful in the prevention or treatment of unfaithfulness.[1] The counselor's own attitude toward sex will, of course, be a crucial one in treating the problem of unfaithfulness. The wise counselor will neither overemphasize nor minimize the significance of sex. He attempts to interpret it in proper perspective—normal and God-given, to be satisfied and enjoyed within the limits of marriage as outlined in the Word of God.

In treating the problem of hostility toward the opposite sex, the counselor discusses with the subject the feelings of anger, hostility or resentment that may be traced to early childhood experiences. A sorting process is encouraged to help separate feelings toward a parent figure from those toward a husband or wife. When differences between the parent and the marriage partner are discussed, it is sometimes helpful in resolving hostility. An open confession and discussion of such feelings, to-

[1]The counselor who works with marriage problems should periodically examine various marriage manuals available at bookstores and add to his library those which meet various needs. One volume which has proved helpful to some couples is: Lewin, S. A. and Gilmore, John: *Sex Without Fear*, The Medical Research Press, New York, 1962.

gether with an unreserved forgiveness of real or imagined wrongs, will usually result in a new appreciation of one's mate, thus eliminating the temptation to seek happiness elsewhere.

In-law interference represents a delicate area, and treatment here involves both the intellect and the emotions. The needs and characteristics of parents emerging into the "golden years" can be discussed and explained by the counselor with considerable benefit to husband and wife. The "leave and cleave" principle of Scripture may profitably be examined from many angles; in other words, the new relationship of husband and wife takes precedence over the old tie to parents. "Therefore shall a man leave his father and his mother and shall cleave unto his wife: and they shall be one flesh" (Genesis 2:24). The former may still be cherished and respected, but it becomes secondary to the primary responsibility to husband or wife. The counselor's role here is largely an educative one in viewing in-law relationships in their proper perspective and at the same time encouraging emotional tolerance and consideration for relatives acquired by marriage. In addition, mutual agreement is sought in certain areas where in-law interference cannot be tolerated.

Experienced counselors know that unfaithfulness in marriage may stem from experiences one had as a child or youth. If the counselee reveals that his own parents were separated, divorced or unfaithful, or otherwise maladjusted, he should be led to discuss these factors. He may well discover that his lack of confidence in his parents has interfered with his feelings of confidence in his own spouse, and hence has led to infidelity in marriage. With adequate insight, he will be able to distinguish between his parents and his spouse, thereby causing him to love and trust his mate. This improved attitude of mutual respect and confidence will mitigate a tendency to unconsciously "punish" his parents via his wife.

Some marriage partners are deeply disturbed, requiring long-term therapy. As one wife told the psychologist during her first visit, "I don't think we need marriage counseling. Basically, we love each other, and that's not our problem. I think we've been this way all our lives, and it would be bad enough if just one of us was crazy, but we *both* are. Maybe that's why we got married in the first place!" Through psycho-diagnosis and initial interviews it became apparent that the woman was not far from accurate. Both were disturbed and confused and needed professional help over a long period of time. Counselors will do well to consider the nature and seriousness of the maladjustment presented by one or more of the marriage partners. Indeed, there are many who will respond only to professional diagnosis and long-term, Christ-centered therapy.[2]

Undoubtedly the most significant factor in overcoming unfaithfulness and other problems in marriage is spiritual conversion and dynamic Christian growth. When a client is led to a saving knowledge of Christ, he is the recipient of a new nature as well as new desires. He is also empowered by the Holy Spirit to control himself and to live an exemplary life. When he is yielded each day to Christ he is sustained and led into paths of righteousness which allow no place for ungodliness. The Christian counselor, therefore, helps the client to understand that he is a spiritual being in need of spiritual help. This should be followed by a definite commitment to Christ and a life that is pleasing to God. As a person is gradually led into a close walk with the Lord the counselor will need to help him resolve his feelings of guilt over his former unfaithfulness.[3] When one resolves his past feelings he is able to develop new and wholesome attitudes toward his total marital and sexual adjustment. A process of counseling, combining both the emotional and spiritual aspects of the problem of unfaithfulness, can help a person completely overcome this problem and reestablish his marriage on a new and secure foundation.

[2]See the discussion of SOCIOPATHIC PERSONALITY in this volume.
[3]See the discussion of GUILT in this volume.

65. Unwed Mothers

Description

The number of unwed mothers in most modern societies is increasing much out of proportion to the increase in population. The problem reaches into all levels of society, affecting girls of wealthy, prominent families as well as those of moderate and lower income. The problems associated with unwed mothers have come to the attention of many organizations. Churches, community social agencies, and governmental organizations are now giving considerable attention to girls who bear children outside of marriage. It is recognized that the experiences of an unwed mother often lead her to thoughtful reflection. During such a time she may be counseled and helped to achieve a better adjustment in life and to become a respected and worthwhile citizen.

The problem of births out of wedlock affects the mother, the father and the child itself. It is also a serious consideration for both families involved. Because of the far-reaching effects of the problem, the counselor should earnestly consider his responsibility for such cases.

Etiology

A study of girls who have had children out of wedlock points to a variety of causes for their behavior. Some of these causes are evident, whole others are more subtle. Many such girls are driven by reasons which they really do not understand.

Every person desires to love and to be loved. If a girl does not receive the recognition and acceptance from her parents, *she may seek affection through an illicit affair.*

In some homes young people have never been taught adequate moral codes and standards. As a result, they have little or no conviction about immorality. The parents may have even set standards of immorality which the children have adopted for themselves. In such cases, girls may become unwed mothers, feeling only deep hostility yet not understanding their own responsibility in the behavior.

In the Christian home it may be the *lack of genuine spirituality.* Power to control the sex drive is aided by a dedicated life in Christ. When a girl is not committed to Christ, the temptation of an illicit love affair may become overwhelming.

Social pressure and the desire to be accepted by peers may be so strong that a girl will have sexual relations *to gain the approval of others.* This need is so great that many times an adolescent will choose to follow the crowd rather than remain chaste.

The desire to explore and experiment may cause a girl to participate in premarital relations. This is often related to a *lack of sex education.* If the parents do not properly educate their children, they may experiment and, in so doing, bring much heartache and unhappiness to themselves as well as their families.

Some men have, of course, taken advantage of a girl's innocence and have brought about pregnancy with no thought of marrying the girl or caring for the child. Still other girls are *victims of rape and extreme cruelty.* In such cases, traumatic aftereffects are commonly evident.

Knowingly or not, *a single girl may seek to punish her parents* by doing something that she knows will hurt them. Her feelings or rejection may be so great that she feels justified in becoming pregnant.

A girl may have such a strong desire to get married that she will deliberately attempt to become pregnant. This is often used as a lever against her parents, who may be unwilling to allow her to marry; so, becoming pregnant forces them to do so.

Girls sometimes testify to the fact that by becoming pregnant they either are *attempting to hold a boyfriend or force him into marriage.* The following quotation expresses the feelings of many girls who believed they were in danger of losing their boy friends: "I loved him so much that I knew I could not live without him. But he was dating another girl, too. So I decided that the only way I could be sure of marrying him was to have relations with him and have a baby."

The lack of any definite aims or worthwhile life plans can cause a girl to become involved in sexual relations outside of marriage. In any area of life, motivation is an important element. Many girls would be less likely to become involved if their eyes were set on meaningful goals.

Treatment
The handling of unwed mothers is frequently done in a hastily and poorly-planned manner. The emphasis is too often concerned with secrecy and even deception rather than with thoughtfulness. Discretion and confidentiality are essential, but due consideration should be given to the girl's parents, to her future, and to her immediate problems.

Counseling With the Parents
The counselor can help parents of unwed mothers and fathers to understand their role as loving parents. Although a girl and boy may have disgraced themselves, they are still worthy of love and guidance. God's Word teaches, "Brethren, if a man be overtaken in a fault, ye which are spiritual, restore such an one in the spirit of meekness; considering thyself, lest thou also be tempted" (Galatians 6:1). Through counseling sessions, family members can be led to see that they can assume a positive, helpful attitude and not necessarily magnify the negative aspects of the situation. Parents can also be shown that illegitimate sex relations on the part of their children are usually symptomatic of basic personality problems with which parents can help.

A Christian counselor can point parents to prayer and to meditation in the Word of God which will bring infinite wisdom and comfort. "Blessed be God, even the Father of our Lord Jesus Christ, the Father of mercies, and the God of all comfort; who comforteth us in all our tribulation, that we may be able to comfort them which are in any trouble, the comfort wherewith we ourselves are comforted of God" (II Corinthians 1:3, 4).

Assessing the Girl's Abilities
It is essential to look beyond the pregnancy condition and to understand the person involved if genuine care and counsel are

to be given the unwed mother. The counselor will want to consider such questions as (1) "What is this girl's intelligence?" (2) "What are her abilities?" (3) "What are her interests?" (4) "What are her attitudes toward education?" (5) "How can she be helped to develop her potential?" and (6) "What type of work would be appropriate for her five, ten or twenty years from now?" Such questions must be carefully examined if the counselor is to help her adequately. Intelligence and vocational guidance tests are useful to evaluate her potentials. In many cases special educational arrangements are necessary. The girl's opportunities to experience normal fulfillment of life's goals are vital to her future happiness and well-being.

Considering the Girl's Personality Adjustment and Self-Understanding

Research studies of unwed mothers show that girls are less likely to have problems of this type if they have desirable home conditions and if they are well-adjusted themselves. In most cases, girls who become pregnant have serious maladjustments. Thus, in order to understand the needs of the young expectant mother, appropriate psychological tests should be given. These tests, combined with interviews, will reveal the extent and nature of emotional disturbances that may have contributed to the problem.

A counselor should arrange several counseling sessions to consider the causes of the unwed pregnancy, then help the girl to insulate herself against a recurrence, with the minimum of fear and guilt.

Some girls are unsure of their attractiveness and femininity. The close embrace of a lover and his fond admiration and sweet words help to reassure them of their feminine qualities. The effective counselor will be alert to this need for acceptance and will help the unwed mother to understand its part in causing her to have illicit sex relations.

Another area which counselors should explore with the unwed mother is her basic need for love and appreciation. Many young people are hungry for love which they never receive in their own home. In such cases illicit romance becomes an adventurous adolescent experiment. The heart tries in vain to fill the vaccum left by inadequate parental love. This deprivation can easily set the stage for petting and deep sexual involvement. Such boys and girls are like the starving who suddenly discover food. When a counselor helps the unwed mother to understand the relationship between this basic need and her promiscuity, she can consider other ways of fulfilling this need.

Experienced counselors know that many cases of illegitimacy are reflections of the attitude of young people toward their homes and schools. During therapy a counselor should help the unwed mother to consider her own hostile feelings. One girl, for example, said, "I don't care if I *am* pregnant. Mother will be moritified and I'll be glad of it. Now I hope she learns how I feel for being criticized all my life. She made life miserable for me and I hate her for it!"

These and other feelings often cause girls and boys to throw all responsibility aside and engage in sexual relations. A counselor should help unwed mothers and unwed fathers to understand the causes behind their behavior. As they do come to know the dynamics of their actions, they can discuss and resolve their strong feelings and live happier, more gratifying lives.

Helping the Girl to Handle Her Guilt Feelings

Most premarriage sexual experiences are soiled with remorse and shame. The unwed mother usually has severe guilt feelings. During counseling she should be encouraged to talk frankly about the feelings of guilt and shame. She needs to understand that God forgives and that adultery and fornication are not unpardonable sins. Through the Scriptures she can be taught that God forgives and restores because He loves her in spite of her sin. She should come to realize that God sent Jesus, His Son, to die for sin and that He stands ready to forgive (I John 1:9). A study of the woman taken in adultery (John 8:1-11) can be especially helpful in freeing an unwed mother from feelings of guilt and sinfulness. Professional counselors should help the unwed mothers to see that God wants to restore every penitent sinner. Unwed mothers often have so extremely contradicted and violated their ideal for themselves that they feel worthless and unacceptable. They have difficulty forgiving themselves and facing society. Scripture portions such as the following are especially helpful: "He hath not dealt with us after our sins; nor rewarded us according to our iniquities. For as the heaven is high above the earth, so great is his mercy toward them that fear him. As far as the east is from the west, so far hath he removed our transgressions from us. Like as a father pitieth his children, so the Lord pitieth them that fear him. For he knoweth our frame; he remembereth that we are dust" (Psalm 103:10-14). Unwed mothers should be shown that God wants them to accept His forgiveness and accept themselves as justified, cleansed and free. The counselor can show her that others have committed sins like this, yet God in His mercy has forgiven them completely and has raised them up to serve Him. Isaiah 1:18 says, "Come now, and let us reason together, saith the Lord: though your sins be as scarlet, they shall be as white as snow; though they be red like crimson, they shall be as wool." When an unwed mother accepts God's forgiveness and regains her faith in herself and her self-esteem, she is prepared to face the future with confidence.

Assisting the Girl to Plan and Care for Her Child

Some unwed mothers want to keep their child. If the father is available and if conditions are favorable, it may be best for them to marry and bear the responsibility for their own son or daughter. However, in many cases, either the father is not available or willing, or it would be undesirable to consider marriage. Then it is necessary to plan for the care of the child either by adoption or in a foster home. Sometimes a foster home is arranged until the mother is married and receives her own child. In some instances it is best to make the child available to Christian parents through an adoption agency. A few retain the care of the child in the home of the girl's parents or in a nursery until the girl can establish a home of her own. Whatever the decision, it should be made early in the pregnancy period, with careful consideration for the baby's best advantage and the mother's optimum adjustment.

Considering the Possibility of Marriage
If the unwed mother-to-be is to marry the father of her child, effective counseling is usually needed. Several session of pre-marriage counseling are especially helpful. Discussions should center in the following areas: (1) Personality adjustments, (2) finances, (3) attitudes toward children, (4) in-law considerations, (5) ethics in marriage, (6) sexual compatibility, and (7) spiritual development.

Uppermost in the minds of many unwed mothers is the question of whether they should ever marry. A girl may feel that she will never want to have sexual relations again, or that she is unworthy—that no decent man would want to live with her. She may also have deep resentments toward all men. The counselor should be sensitive to the girl's desire to discuss these matters. She may hide such desires from all else, yet want to clarify her feelings with a counselor who is not a member of her family. Such discussions will help her to develop wholesome attitudes about herself and, more specifically, about sex and future marriage.

66. Withdrawal

Description

The withdrawn person evades social contacts in order to avoid anxiety. He sees threats in social situations, but security and safety in seclusion. He retreats from situations which he has found to be discouraging or threatening—where he feels he may be a failure. Such a withdrawn person may long to participate but he usually recoils from activities in which he feels he will experience frustration and defeat.

In childhood the severely withdrawn youngster may refuse to attend school and, if forced to do so, will refrain from entering into group activities. Classroom teachers ordinarily single out the noisy and rebellious children as those who they believe are maladjusted. But, in reality, the withdrawn individual may have a much more severe disturbance. The person who is shy and withdrawn is often overlooked. Since he does not interrupt activities or cause dissension, he may not be recognized as having serious emotional problems.

Etiology

Research indicates that *parents of withdrawn individuals are themselves often shy and seclusive.* In their reluctance to engage in a variety of social contacts, they may unconsciously inflict on their children this means of adaptation.

Some *overprotective parents* will not allow their child to participate in experiences which they fear he is unable to handle. They take pains to see that their child is never in a threatening situation and that there is little opportunity for the child to be engaged in argument or conflict. The person who is raised in this environment usually does not develop adequate means of reacting to normal situations of stress and frustration.

Children who experience *no love or security in their own home* find it difficult to enter into social experiences with others outside the immediate family. They are unsure about their own worth and they wonder if they will be accepted by others.

Some adults have developed withdrawn behavior largely because of the *lack of opportunity for social contacts in their childhood*. For example, the child from a rural setting may have no playmates his own age and may not develop normal pre-school social skills.

Therapists often find that clients who are withdrawn come from homes where their *parents were overcritical*. In fact, a variety of conditions could cause a growing child to develop a damaging self-image and a serious fear of associating with others.

Illustration

Identification: White female, age 12

Presenting Problem: The subject was brought by her mother to a psychologist. The mother reported that the girl did not like school. Headaches and stomach discomfort were reported, especially beginning on Sunday evening. Generally, two days of school were missed weekly and the days of attendance were prefaced by crying. There has been virtually no classroom participation verbally. As the weeks passed, she became more alone, withdrawing from playground activities and remaining by herself.

Personal and Family History: The subject is a nice-appearing girl with average intelligence. She has a brother and a sister, both younger than she. As a young child she had several severe illnesses but she is in reasonably good health now.

The subject's mother is an overanxious woman who is deeply concerned that her daughter do well in school. The father is rather quiet in the home and has little to do with the children. He is intensely interested in church work and often spends several nights a week in some type of church activity.

The family has moved four times since the subject was seven years of age. She found each adjustment to the new situation progressively difficult. At age nine she suffered a traumatic experience when her cousin, age eight, with whom she was riding in an automobile, was killed in an accident. She began to withdraw noticeably at that time.

At school, the subject is seriously withdrawn. She has no special friends and makes little or no effort to contact other children.

Treatment

Children
The child who has developed withdrawn behavior as a result of lack of adequate playmates and social contacts may be aided by a gradual introduction into social situations. Parents of pre-school children should see that there are occasional opportunities to play with others their age, even if it requires extra time and effort for the parents.

If the child has developed his attitudes of withdrawal from his parent's seclusiveness, it is necessary to work closely with them. It is vital to show them the importance of encouraging the child to develop proper social contacts.

Rejecting and unloving parents must learn to exhibit affection more freely if their child is to develop the feelings of security and adequacy which are necessary for confident social interaction.

Group therapy has proven effective in treating some withdrawn children. A skilled group therapist can work with several shy children in a non-threatening situation and assist each to gradually develop confidence and poise. In working with withdrawn children in a group, it is important not to include those who are overaggressive. One such child in a group of withdrawn children may talk continually and completely dominate the situation. The withdrawn children, then, would be discouraged from developing social skills.

Adults
Seriously withdrawn adults often respond well to individual counseling therapy. In such an environment they feel free to express themselves and to explore the causes of their extreme shyness. As the counselor begins to accept them, they in turn learn to accept themselves and to express their fears. Group therapy is also beneficial provided the group is not too large and the members are congenial and supportive to quiet members.

Both children and adults who are seriously withdrawn may find unusual help through spiritual means. As they trust in Christ and grow in the faith, they develop a self-concept which is supportive and helpful. Probably nothing means more to one's confidence than to realize that he is a child of God and the object of His love. Too, as a person studies the Scriptures he realizes that God is always with him and anxious to meet his needs. The counselor, then, can make an unusual contribution to the withdrawn person by leading him into paths of spiritual maturity.[1]

[1]For a closely related problem, see the discussion of INSECURITY in this volume.

References

This list includes the publications to which the reader is referred throughout this volume and from which the author has drawn material.

Abt, I., Adler, H. M., and Bartelme, Phyllis: "The Relationship Between the Onset of Speech and Intelligence," *Journal of the American Medical Association*, vol. 93, pp. 1351-1356, 1929.

Alexander, Franz: *Psychosomatic Medicine*, W. W. Norton and Company, Inc., New York, 1950.

Anderson, F. N.: "Psychiatric Aspects of Enuresis," *American Journal of Diseases of Children*, vol. 40, pp. 591, 818, 1930.

Areti, S. (Ed.): *American Handbook of Psychiatry*, Basic Books, Inc., New York, Vol. II, 1959.

Bakwin, H. and Bakwin, R.: *Clinical Management of Behavior Disorders in Children*, W. P. Saunders Company, Philadelphia and London, 1953.

Barbara, Dominick A. (Ed.): *Psychological and Psychiatric Aspects of Speech and Hearing*, Charles C. Thomas, Springfield, 1960.

Bellak, Leopold, M. D., and Benedict, Paul K., M. D. (Eds.): *Schizoprenia: A Review of the Syndrome*, Harper, New York, 1961.

Benda, Clemens E., M. D.: *Mongolism and Cretinism*, Grune and Stratton, New York, 1949.

Benda, Clemens E., M. D.: *The Child With Mongolism (Congential Acromicria)*, Grune and Stratton, New York, 1960.

Bieber, Irving, and others, (Society of Medical Psychoanalysts): *Homosexuality, A Psychoanalytic Study*, Basic Books, Inc., New York, 1962.

Birch, H. G.: *Brain Damage in Children*, Williams and Wilkins Company, 1964.

Bleyer, Adrien: "The Role of Advanced Maternal Age in Causing Mongolism," *American Journal of Diseases of Children*, vol. 105, pp. 79-92, 1938.

Bolt, W. H.: "Postnatal Trauma as an Etiological Factor in Mental Deficiency," *American Journal of Mental Deficiency*, vol. 103, pp. 247-267, 1948.

Carlson, Earl R.: *Born That Way*, John Day Company, New York, 1942.

Coleman, James: *Abnormal Psychology and Modern Life*, Scott, Foresman and Company, Chicago, Fair Lawn, 1964.

Committee on Nomenclature and Statistics: *Diagnostic and Statis-*

tical Manual, Mental Disorders, American Psychiatric Association, Washington, D.C., 15th Edition, 1962.

Cruickshank, William M., and Raus, G. M. (Eds.): *Cerebral Palsy,* Syracuse University Press, 1955.

Cruickshank, William M. and Johnson, G. Orville (Eds.): *Education of Exceptional Children and Youth,* Prentice-Hall, Englewood Cliffs, New Jersey, 1958.

De Haan, Robert F., and Havighurst, Robert J.: *Educating Gifted Children,* University of Chicago Press, Chicago, 1957.

Dorland's Illustrated Medical Dictionary, W. B. Saunders Company, Philadelphia, 23rd Edition, 1957.

"Drug Addiction," *Collier's Encyclopedia,* vol. 8, p. 394.

Finch, Stuart M.: *Fundamentals of Child Psychiatry,* W. W. Norton and Company, Inc., New York, 1960.

Fletcher, John Madison: *The Problem of Stuttering,* Longmans, Green Company, 1928.

Glueck, Sheldon, and Glueck, Eleanor: *Unraveling Juvenile Deliquency,* Harvard, New York, 1950.

Gregory, Ian: *Psychiatry: Biological and Social,* W. B. Saunders Company, Philadelphia and London, 1961.

Harrison, T. R. and others (Eds.): *Principles of Internal Medicine,* McGraw-Hill Book Company, Inc., New York, Fourth Edition, 1962.

Henninger, James M.: "Exhibitionism," *Journal of Criminal Psychopathology,* vol. 2, pp. 357-366, 1941.

Kanner, Leo: *Child Psychiatry,* Charles C. Thomas, Springfield, Illinois, Third Printing, 1960.

Kirk, Samuel A.: *Educating Exceptional Children,* Houghton Mifflin Company, Boston, 1962.

Kisker, George W.: *The Disorganized Personality,* McGraw-Hill, New York, London, 1964.

Lennox, W. G.: "Sixty-six Twin Pairs Affected by Seizures," *A. Res. Nerv. and Ment. Dis., Proc.,* vol. 26, p. 11, 1947.

Levin, Nathaniel M.: *Voice and Speech Disorders; Medical Aspects,* Charles C. Thomas, Springfield, 1962.

Levinson, Abraham: *The Mentally Retarded Child,* John Day Company, New York, 1952.

Lewin, S. A., and Gilmore, John: *Sex Without Fear,* The Medical Research Press, New York, 1962.

Lewis, Richard S.: *The Other Child: The Brain-Injured Child,* Grune and Stratton, Inc., New York, 1951.

Longerich, M. C., and Bordeaux, J.: *Aphasia Therapeutics*, The Macmillan Company, New York, 1954.

Money, John (ed.): *Reading Disability: Progress and Research Needs in Dyslexia*, The Johns Hopkins Press, Baltimore, 1962.

Morley, D. E.: "A Ten-Year Survey of Speech Disorders Among University Students," *Journal of Speech and Hearing Disorders*, vol. 17, pp. 25-30, 1952.

Myerson, A., and Neustadt, R.: "The Bisexuality of Man," *Journal of the Mount Sinai Hospital*, New York, vol. 9, pp. 668-678, 1942.

Narramore, Clyde M.: (The author's books referred to in this volume are published by Zondervan Publishing House, Grand Rapids, Michigan.)

Noyes, A. P., and Kolb, L. C.: *Modern Clinical Psychiatry*, W. B. Saunders Company, Philadelphia and London, 1963.

"Patterns of Disease," *Parke, Davis and Company*, May, 1963.

Putnam, Tracy J.: *Epilepsy*, J. B. Lippincott Company, New York and Philadelphia, 1958.

Schilder, P.: "The Psychogenesis of Alcoholism," *Quarterly Journal of Studies on Alcohol*, vol. 2, pp. 244-292, 1941.

Seliger, Robert V., M.D., and Cranford, Victoria, edited by Goodwin, Harold S.: *Alcoholics Are Sick People*, Alcoholism Publications, Baltimore, 1945. .

Selye, Hans: *The Stress of Life*, McGraw-Hill Book Company, New York, 1956.

Shepherds, Inc., P.O. Box 1261, Milwaukee, Wisconsin, Sunday school materials for slow learners.

Shneidman, E. S., et al: "Some Facts About Suicide," *Public Health Service*, Printing Office, 1961.

Silverman, Daniel: "The Electroencephalograph and Therapy of Criminal Psychopaths," *Journal of Criminal Psychopathology*, chapter 5, pp. 439-466, 1944.

"Statistical Abstract of the United States," *U. S. Bureau of Census*, 1964 (85th edition), Washington, D.C., p. 309, 1964.

Terman, Lewis M., and others: *Genetic Studies of Genius*, Stanford University Press, Stanford, 5 vol. 1925-1959.

Thorpe, L., Katz, B., and Lewis, R.: *The Psychology of Abnormal Behavior*, Ronald Press Company, New York, 1961.

Van Riper, Charles: *Speech Correction*, Prentice-Hall, Inc., Englewood Cliffs, 1963.

Wolk, Robert L., Psychologist, and Diskind, Meyer H., Parole Officer: *Special Narcotic Project*, New York.

Glossary
A

ABERRATION: A deviation from the normal.

ABREACTION: The release of pent-up emotion associated with a painful experience.

ACROMEGALY: A disease caused by hyperfunction of the pituitary gland. It is characterized by progressive enlargement of the face, hands and feet.

ACROPHOBIA: Morbid fear of high places.

ACTING-OUT: Expression of unconscious emotional conflicts through overt behavior rather than internalizing these conflicts.

ADDICTION: Habitual emotional and physiological dependence upon alcohol or drugs.

ADDISON'S DISEASE: A disease of the adrenal glands characterized by anemia, emaciation and weakness, digestive disturbances and a brownish coloration of the skin.

ADJUSTMENT: The individual's attempts to harmonize his needs with the demands of his environment.

ADOLESCENCE: The period when a child is becoming an adult. It begins at puberty (approximately 10-14) and ends when the person comes of age (approximately 17-19).

ADRENAL ANDROGENS: Hormones secreted by the adrenal cortex which control the development of secondary sex characteristics.

ADRENAL CORTEX: The outer portion of the adrenal glands which is responsible for secretion of androgens and other hormones.

ADRENAL GLANDS: Two endocrine glands at the upper end of the kidneys. The outer layer, the cortex, influnces secondary sex characteristics. The inner layer, the medulla, secretes hormones which help supply the body with extra energy for emergencies.

ADRENALINE: The hormone secreted by the adrenal medulla. This secretion helps the body mobilize for stress situations.

AFFECT: A person's experience of feeling or emotion.

364 Encyclopedia of Psychological Problems

AGGRESSION: Attack upon an object, individual or idea that stands in a person's way.

AGITATION: A condition marked by exaggerated restlessness.

AGNOSIA: Inability to recognize and interpret sensory stimuli.

AGORAPHOBIA: Morbid fear of open places.

AGRAPHIA: Inability to express thoughts in writing due to a cerebral disorder.

ALCOHOLISM: A diseased condition caused by the habitual use of alcohol.

ALEXIA: Inability to understand written language due to a cerebral disorder.

ALZHEIMER'S DISEASE: An unusually early onset of senility associated with deterioration of the brain.

AMBIVALENCE: The existence of opposing desires or feelings toward an object.

AMENTIA: Inadequate intellectual ability. Mental deficiency.

AMNESIA: Partial or total inability to recall past experiences.

ANALGESIA: Loss of the sense of pain resulting from either physical or psychological causes.

ANDROGEN: Hormone which stimulates the development of male sex characteristics.

ANESTHESIA: Total or partial loss of sensitivity.

ANOREXIA: Severe and prolonged loss of appetite.

ANOXIA: Deprivation of sufficient oxygen supply.

ANTIDEPRESSANT DRUGS: Drugs which are used to relieve anxiety and depression.

ANTISOCIAL PERSONALITY: A person who chronically exhibits antisocial behavior.

ANXIETY: A state of being uneasy, apprehensive or worried.

ANXIETY REACTION: A psychoneurotic disorder characterized by morbid dread and anxiety.

APATHY: A condition marked by the absence of feeling and emotion.

APHONIA: Loss or impairment of ability to utter vocal sounds.

APTITUDE: An inborn, potential ability to learn a specific kind of activity.

ARTERIOSCLEROSIS: The thickening and hardening of the walls of the arteries, occurring usually in old age.

ASTHENIC REACTION: A psychoneurotic disorder characterized by fatigue, listlessness and general lack of vitality.

ASTRAPHOBIA: Morbid fear of thunder and lightning.

ATAXIA: Disturbance in the coordination of voluntary muscular movements.

ATHETOSIS: Uncontrollable, jerky, twisting movements of the extremities.

ATONICITY: Loss of normal muscle tone which results in inability to maintain good posture.

ATROPHY: Reduction in size or wasting away of a bodily organ.

ATTITUDE: A mental set to respond in a certain manner to an object or experience.

AURA: A premonitory subjective sensory phenomenon. Such sensations usually precede an epileptic seizure.

AUTISTIC THINKING: An attempt to gratify unfulfilled desires in fantasy rather than in reality.

AUTOEROTICISM: Masturbation. Gratification of sexual desire without another person.

AUTONOMIC NERVOUS SYSTEM: The portion of the nervous system which controls internal organs.

AUTONOMY: The ability to control one's own actions and conduct. Self-reliance.

B

BEDWETTING (ENURESIS): Involuntary urination while asleep, continued past the usual age (4-5).

BEHAVIOR: The way in which an organism reacts to a stimulus.

BESTIALITY: Sexual intercourse with animals.

BIRTH TRAUMA: Physical injury received at birth.

BLOCKING: The inability to recall an idea or experience to consciousness due to emotional conflict.

BRAIN PATHOLOGY: Disease and malfunctioning of the brain.

BULIMIA: An abnormally large appetite for food.

C

CATALEPSY: A condition in which the muscles are rigid, and limbs remain in position where placed.

CATATONIA: A type of schizophrenia characterized by muscular rigidity and inflexibility. There may be alternating periods of excitement and hyperactivity.

CATHARSIS: The discharge of emotional tension associated with painful and upsetting ideas by "talking it out" with an understanding listener.

CATHEXIS: Attachment of special significance or emotional feeling to an idea, object or person.

CEREBRAL: Pertaining to the brain or the cerebrum.

CEREBRAL ARTERIOSCLEROSIS: (See Arteriosclerosis).

CEREBRAL PALSY: A motor disability caused by a brain dysfunction.

CHARACTER DISORDERS: Personality disorders characterized by developmental defects and lack of anxiety.

CHEMOTHERAPY: The use of drugs in treating mental illness.

CHOREA: A nervous disorder characterized by involuntary twitchings and jerking movements. Also called St. Vitus' Dance.

CHROMOSOMES: Small bodies found in the nucleus of cells. They contain the genes and determine hereditary characteristics.

CHRONIC: Persistent or continuing for a long time.

CLAUSTROPHOBIA: Morbid fear of being in small, enclosed spaces.

CLIENT-CENTERED PSYCHOTHERAPY: An approach to counseling developed chiefly by Carl Rogers. It emphasizes the importance of the client seeking his own solutions rather than being actively directed by the counselor.

CLIMACTERIC: The period of somatic changes occurring at the termination of the reproductive period in the female. The period of menopause. The male also experiences a decline in sexual activity during this period.

COITUS: Sexual intercourse.

COMA: A state of unconsciousness.

COMBAT REACTION: A personality disturbance which results from the stress of a war experience.

COMPENSATION: A defense mechanism by which an individual covers up an undesirable trait by exaggerating a desirable one.

COMPULSION: An irresistible urge to perform some act even though the individual realizes it is irrational.

CONCUSSION: An injury to the head or spine which causes rupturing of small blood vessels in the brain. This may cause circulatory disturbances, tissue damage, shock and unconsciousness.

CONFABULATION: Falsification of material to fill memory lapses.

CONFLICT: Stress characterized by incompatible desires, needs or environmental demands.

CONGENITAL: A condition existing from birth but not necessarily hereditary.

CONSCIENCE (SUPEREGO): The attitude of an individual toward the moral or social implications of his behavior. It is responsible for feelings of guilt.

CONSCIOUSNESS: A state of awareness.

CONVERSION REACTION: A condition in which inner emotional conflicts are converted into physiological symptoms.

CONVULSION: An uncontrolled contraction of a group of muscles caused by malfunctioning of the central nervous system.

COUNSELING: The process of one person helping another to solve a conflict or improve his life adjustment.

CRETINISM: Severe throid deficiency at an early age, accompanied by arrested physical and mental development.

CUNNILINGUS: A form of sexual perversion in which the tongue or mouth is use in erotic play with female genitals.

D

DAYDREAMING: Wishful or purposeless thinking during waking hours. A form of fantasy.

DECOMPENSATION: Personality disorganization under excessive stress.

DEFENSE MECHANISMS: Ways of dealing with ego-involving conflicts. They are attempts to protect and enhance the person's self-concept.

DELINQUENCY: Illegal or antisocial behavior engaged in by a minor.

DELIRIUM: A state of mental disturbance which may include confusion, disorientation, excitability, illusions, delusions or hallucinations.

DELIRIUM TREMENS: A condition characterized by anxiety, tremors and hallucinations. It is due to prolonged use of alcohol.

DELUSION: A belief which is out of keeping with reality and the individual's level of maturity.

DEMENTIA: A condition involving deterioration of mental ability.

DEMENTIA PRAECOX: An old term for the condition known as schizophrenia.

DENIAL: A defense mechanism by which a person avoids unpleasant emotional conflicts by denying or refusing to perceive some aspect of reality.

DEPERSONALIZATION: Feelings of unreality about oneself, one's body or the environment.

DEPRESSION: Undue sadness, dejection or melancholy. Feelings of worthlessness and guilt and, often, of apprehension.

DEREISTIC THINKING: 1. Autistic thinking or fantasy. 2. Thought processes in which the individual ignores reality.

DESENSITIZATION: The process of reducing the tension and fear associated with unpleasant experiences by repeatedly exposing the individual to them.

DETERIORATION: The degeneration of intellectual or emotional functioning.

DEVIANT BEHAVIOR: Behavior which is a variation from the average. It is usually used in a pathological sense.

DIAGNOSIS: Identification of the nature and extent of a disorder by an analysis of the symptoms.

DIPSOMANIA: Uncontrollable craving for alcohol.

DISINTEGRATION: The process by which organized material gradually loses its organization and integration.

DISORIENTATION: Loss of awareness of one's position with respect to time, place or person.

DISPLACEMENT: A defense mechanism in which an emotional attitude is transferred from its original object to a more acceptable object.

DISSOCIATIVE REACTION: A psychoneurotic reaction characterized by a separation of mental processes in such a way that they become split off from the main personality.

DIZYGOTIC: Twins from two ova. Fraternal twins, as contrasted with identical twins.

DRUG ADDICTION: Habitual emotional and physiological dependence upon drugs.

DUALPERSONALITY: A dissociative reaction in which a person exhibits different personality structures.

DYNAMICS: The determination of the causes and effects of an emotional or behavioral pattern.

DYSARTHRIA: Impaired speech, usually due to organic disorders of the nervous system.

DYSFUNCTION: Impaired functioning of an organ.

DYSGRAPHIA: A cerebral disorder resulting in impaired ability to write.

DYSSOCIAL REACTION: Antisocial behavior resulting from living in an abnormal moral environment.

E

EGO: The conscious part of personality which mediates between the individual's impulses and the demands of reality; the self.

EGOCENTRIC: Preoccupied with one's own concerns; self-centered.

EGO-SYNTONIC: In harmony with or acceptable to the aims of the ego.

ELATION: A condition marked by feelings of well-being and pleasure.

ELECTROENCEPHALOGRAPH (EEG): An apparatus for recording the electrical activity of the brain.

ELECTROSHOCK THERAPY: The administration of a carefully regulated electrical current to the brain in the treatment of severe mental disorders.

EMOTION: A mental state characterized by strong feelings such as fear, anger, love or hate.

EMOTIONAL IMMATURITY: Inadequate development of adult emotional control in areas such as independence and self-reliance. The use of childish behavior to meet stresses which most people can handle satisfactorily.

EMOTIONAL INSULATION: A defense mechanism in which the individual reduces anxiety by withdrawal and refusal to become emotionally involved with others.

EMOTIONAL TENSION: An aroused emotional state (anger, fear, etc.) in which the body's preparation for action has not been consummated in action.

EMOTIONALIZED ATTITUDES: Attitudes which are based upon emotions and feelings rather than objectives and rational causes.

EMPATHY: An insightful awareness and understanding of the feelings, emotions and behavior of another person.

ENCEPHALITIS: Inflammation of the brain.

ENCEPHALITIS LETHARGICA: Sleeping sickness. Inflammation of the brain which results in weakness, fatigue and somnolence.

ENDOCRINE GLANDS: The glands of internal secretion. They secrete hormones which regulate body functions and growth.

ENDOCRINOLOGIST: A medical doctor who specializes in the treatment of the endocrine glands and the internal secretions of the body.

ENDOGENOUS: Produced from or due to internal causes.

ENURESIS: Involuntary urination while asleep, continued past the usual age (4-5).

ENVIRONMENT: The world a person lives in, such as home, school, office, family, church and other social contacts.

EPIDEMIC ENCEPHALITIS: A disease of the brain resulting in apathy, drowsiness and muscular weakness. Also called sleeping sickness and lethargic encephalitis.

EPILEPSY: A chronic disease of the nervous system, characterized by convulsions and often unconsciousness.

EROGENOUS ZONE: An area of the body which, when stimulated, causes sexual excitement.

EROTIC: Pertaining to sexual stimulation.

ESTROGEN: Female hormone produced by the ovaries.

ETIOLOGY: The investigation of the causes of a disorder.

EUNUCH: A male who has been castrated or whose testes have never developed.

EUPHORIA: An exaggerated feeling of well-being and comfort.

EXHIBITIONISM: Public exposure of the sex organs.

EXOGENOUS: Produced from or due to external causes.

EXTRAPUNITIVE: The tendency to direct hostility outward, toward one's environment.

EXTROVERSION: Interest in environment and in other people more than in one's self.

EXTROVERT: A person whose interests are directed toward his environment rather than toward inner experiences and himself.

F

FABRICATION: Telling of imaginary events or stores as if they were true; confabulation.

FAMILIAL: Relating to characteristics which run in families.

FANTASY: A defense mechanism by which an individual escapes from the world of reality and seeks gratification through imaginary activities; daydreaming.

FEAR: An emotion to recognized sources of danger which is characterized by a feeling-tone of unpleasantness and accompanied by activity of the sympathethic nervous system.

FEEBLEMINDEDNESS: Mental deficiency; mental capacity considerably below average.

FELLATIO: Sexual stimulation by insertion of the penis in the mouth.

FETISHISM: A sexual deviation in which the individual receives sexual gratification by means of an object such as a handkerchief, glove, hair or panties.

FETUS: The unborn young of an animal. In man, from the end of the fifth week after conception until birth.

FORNICATION: Sexual relations outside of marriage.

FRATERNAL TWINS: Twins from two separate ova, as contrasted to identical twins coming from one divided ova.

FREE ASSOCIATION: The uninhibited verbalization by a client of every idea that comes to mind during a therapy session.

FREE-FLOATING ANXIETY: Anxiety which is not attached to any specific object. It occurs in all situations.

FRIGIDITY: Lack of or deceased sexual desire in a woman.

FRUSTRATION: Thwarting of a person's efforts to satisfy basic needs and drives.

FUGUE: A form of dissociation. An episode of non-remembered activity of considerable duration which usually involves an actual physical change of environment.

FUNCTIONAL: An illness which has no organic or structural basis; psychogenic.

FUROR: An acute outburst of excitement, anger and violence.

G

GENE: An element of the germ plasm concerned with determination of hereditary characteristics.

GENERAL PARESIS: Mental illness associated with degeneration of the brain due to syphilitic infection.

GENETICS: The branch of science dealing with heredity.

GENITALIA: The reproductive organs.

GERIATRICS: The science which studies and treats the aged.

GERONTOLOGY: The study of the phenomena of old age.

GIGANTISM: A condition of abnormal size due to oversecretion of the pituitary gland.

GOAL: The object toward which an individual strives; an objective.

GONADS: Testes or ovaries, sexual glands.

GRAND MAL: Gross convulsive seizures with loss of consciousness.

GROUP THERAPY: Counseling or psychotherapy with a group of patients.

GUILT: Feelings of apprehension and sinfulness. A distinction must be made between real guilt which is induced by the Holy Spirit for transgression of God's law, and pseudo guilt which arises from an overly-critical environment.

GYNEPHOBIA: Morbid fear of women.

H

HALLUCINATION: Sense perception which does not have an external stimulus.

HALLUCINOGENS: Drugs or chemicals which produce hallucinations.

HEBEPHRENIC REACTION: The schizophrenic reaction characterized by silly mannerisms and inappropriate affect and behavior.

HEMIPLEGIA: Paralysis which affects one side of the body.

HEREDITY: Genetic transmission of characteristics from parents to their offspring.

HETEROSEXUALITY: Attraction, interest and physical relationships between individuals of the opposite sex.

HOMOSEXUALITY: Inverted sexual orientation. Sexual attraction or relationships between members of the same sex.

HOSTILITY: An emotion or feeling of enmity, ill-will, unfriendliness or antagonism.

HUNTINGTON'S CHOREA: Disease of the nervous system characterized by jerky, involuntary movements and mental deterioration.

HYDROCEPHALUS: An abnormal accumulation of fluid within the cranium which results in abnormal enlargement of the head. This frequently causes mental deficiency.

HYPNOSIS: An artificially induced state resembling sleep, in which the person is more fully influenced by suggestion.

HYPNOTHERAPY: Use of hypnosis in treating mental illness.

HYPOCHONDRIASIS: Psychoneurotic reaction characterized by exaggerated concern about one's physical health.

HYPOMANIA: A slight degree of manic excitement in a manic-depressive reaction. Common symptoms include elation and over-activity.

HYSTERIA: A psychoneurotic disorder which is characterized by organic symptoms even though there is no actual organic pathology.

I

ID: A term used to denote a person's unconscious, instinctual urges.

IDENTICAL TWINS: Twins which developed from one fertilized ovum. They are always of the same sex and look very much alike.

IDIOT: A severely mentally-retarded person. Usually denotes an I.Q. score below 25.

IMBECILE: A mentally-retarded individual with an I.Q. score between 25 and 49.

IMPOTENCE: Inability (usually in a male), to achieve orgasm.

IMPULSE: An urge to action which has little forethought or anticipation.

IMPULSIVENESS: A tendency to act without thinking. A lack of self-mastery.

IMPUNITIVE: A reaction to frustrations in which the person minimizes the situation or exhibits a conciliatory attitude instead of blaming either himself or others.

INADEQUATE PERSONALITY: An individual who does not respond adequately to intellectual, social, emotional and economic situations in spite of the fact that he is not seriously handicapped either physically or mentally.

INCEST: Sexual intercourse between two closely related individuals such as brother and sister or father and daughter.

INCOMPETENT: A lack of the mental qualifications needed to manage one's own affairs. This may be due to either mental illness or mental deficiency.

INCORRIGIBLE: A minor who is hostile, defiant and unmanageable.

INFANTILISM: The presence of immature and childish behavior in an adult.

INFERIORITY COMPLEX: A person's feeling that he is inadequate and doesn't measure up to desired standards.

INSANITY: A legal term for mental disorders which make an individual incompetent to act in accordance with conventional standards and to be responsible for his own actions.

INSIGHT: The sudden recognition of the cause or solution to a problem. The discernment of relationships between data or experiences.

INSTINCT: The innate tendency to react to a stimulus in a particular manner.

INTELLECTUALIZATION: A defense mechanism in which the individual avoids emotional hurt by substituting an intellectual for an emotional interpretation of a threatening situation.

INTROJECTION: The process of incorporating the values of the environment or a person into one's own personality structure.

INTROPUNITIVE: Responding to frustration by blaming oneself.

INTROVERT: A person is quiet and reflective rather than interested in his external environment.

INVOLUTIONAL MELANCHOLIA (INVOLUTIONAL PSYCHOTIC REACTION): A psychotic depressive reaction associated with the involutional period (usually occurring between 40 and 60 years of age).

ISOLATION: A defense mechanism in which the disturbing emotional content of an experience is kept from awareness, preventing upsetting emotional reactions.

J

JACKSONIAN EPILEPSY: Muscle spasms in a small group of muslces or a limb.

JUVENILE DELINQUENCY: Antisocial and illegal behavior by minors.

JUVENILE PARESIS: General paresis in a child or adolescent, usually due to congential infection.

K

KLEPTOMANIA: An irresistible compulsion to steal. The individual frequently has no need for the stolen object.

KORSAKOFF'S PSYCHOSIS: Psychotic disorder due to chronic alcoholism. It is characterized by memory defects, confabulation, loss of orientation and other deteriorative symptoms.

L

LATENT: Inactive or dormant.

LESBIAN: A female homosexual.

LIBIDO: In a broad psychanalytic sense, the unconscious energy or instinctive drives of the id. In a limited sense it may be used to denote sexual drives.

LIFE STYLE: The patterns of thought and action which characterize a person's behavior.

LITERATE: Having the ability to read and write.

LOBOTOMY: Brain operation in which some nerve fibers between lobes are severed in order to alleviate severe symptoms of mental illness.

M

MACROCEPHALY: A pathological condition characterized by an abnormally large head.

MALADJUSTMENT: The inability to adapt to problems and tasks of everyday life.

MALARIA THERAPY: Inducing fever through malaria germs in order to treat paresis.

MALINGER: To consciously feign illness in order to gain personal benefit.

MANIA: A state of extreme excitement and overactivity.

MANIC-DEPRESSIVE REACTION: A psychotic disorder characterized by extreme mood disturbances. Manic states evidence excitability and overactivity while depressive states are characterized by dejection and underactivity.

MARASMUS: Progressive emaciation which may result from inadequate mothering in infancy or from malnutrition.

MARIJUANA: Leaves from the plant canabis sativa which are smoked as a cigarette. It gives a sense of elation and freedom from inhibitions.

MASOCHISM: A sexual perversion in which a person receives sexual gratification by having pain inflicted upon him.

MASTURBATION: Sexual gratification through self-stimulation of the genitals.

MELANCHOLIA: A mental condition characterized by extreme depression.

MENINGES: The membranes which cover the brain and spinal cord. This consists of the pia mater, arachnoid and dura mater.

MENINGITIS: Inflammation of the meninges.

MENTAL AGE (MA): A measure of an individual's intellectual development. A mental age of eight, for example, means that the person has the intellectual ability of an average eight-year-old child.

MENTAL DEFICIENCY: Generally used as synonymous with

mental retardation. Low intelligence, which makes a person unable to operate effectively in his environment.

MENTAL RETARDATION: Inability to function effectively in one's environment because of low intelligence.

MICROCEPHALY: A pathological condition characterized by an abnormally small head and mental deficiency.

MIGRAINE: A severe headache, often on only one side. Common symptoms include neusea, dullness and visual disturbances.

MILIEU: A person's physical and social environment.

MONGOLISM: A form of mental deficiency which is characterized by facial features resembling the Mongolian race.

MONOMANIA: A psychotic condition in which the disturbance appears to center upon one basic idea or experience.

MONOZYGOTIC: Identical twins, coming from the same ovum.

MORES: The social customs and moral values of society.

MORON: An individual with a mild degree of mental retardation (I.Q. score between 50 and 70).

MOTIVATION: Incentive or drive which results in action.

MULTIPLE PERSONALITY: A dissociative reaction in which a person exhibits two or more distinct personality structures.

MUTISM: State of refusing or being unable to speak.

MYXEDEMA: A disease caused by decreased functioning of the thyroid gland, which results in dry and thickened skin, thinness of hair, fatigue and mental dullness.

N

NARCISSISM: Love for self.

NARCOLEPSY: An abnormal desire for sleep, usually temporary in nature.

NARCOTHERAPY (NARCOANALYSIS): The use of drugs such as sodium pentathol to help a person more freely ventilate his feelings in therapy.

NECROPHILIA: Sexual attraction toward dead bodies.

NEGATIVISM: An attitude of hostility or resistance to suggestions. The person may refuse to obey commands or do just the opposite of what is suggested.

NEOLOGISM: A meaningless word coined by a person. This is sometimes found among psychotic patients who are unable to distinguish reality from fantasy.

NERVOUS BREAKDOWN: A popular term referring to a vareity of emotional disturbances which interfere with a person's ability to deal adequately with daily activities.

NERVOUSNESS: A condition characterized by tension, apprehension and restlessness.

NEURASTHENIA (ASTHENIC REACTION): Psychoneurotic disorder characterized by listlessness and fatigue.

NEUROLOGIST: Medical doctor who specializes in the diagnosis and treatment of diseases of the brain and nervous system.

NEUROPSYCHIATRY: The branch of medicine which deals with both neurology and psychiatry in treating disorders.

NEUROSIS (PSYCHONEUROSIS): A broad category of emotional disturbances which have the basic common element of anxiety.

NEUROSYPHILIS: Syphilitic infection of the central nervous system.

NEUROTIC-DEPRESSIVE REACTION: Psychoneurotic disorder characterized by worry, discouragement and pessimism.

NONDIRECTIVE THERAPY: An approach to counseling developed by Carl Rogers. It emphasizes the importance of the client seeking his own solutions rather than being actively directed by the therapist.

NYCTOPHOBIA: Morbid fear of darkness or the night.

NYMPHOMANIA: An insatiable sexual desire in females.

O

OBSESSION: Persistent, irresistible idea or thought which an individual cannot remove from consciousness.

OBESSIVE-COMPULSIVE REACTION: Psychoneurotic reaction characterized by persistent thoughts and uncontrollable impulses to perform a certain act.

OCHLOPHOBIA: Morbid fear of crowds or crowded places.

OLFACTION: The sense of smell.

OLIGOPHRENIA: Mental deficiency.

OPIUM: A drug which leads to physiological and psychological dependence. It is prepared from a type of poppy. Major derivatives of opium are morphine, heroin, paregoric and codeine.

ORGANIC PSYCHOSIS: Psychotic disorder resulting from organic brain pathology.

OUT-PATIENT CLINIC: Clinic where individuals are treated on a non-hospitalized basis.

OVARIES: The reproductive glands of the female. They function in the producing of ova and certain internal secretions.

OVERCOMPENSATION: The attempt to compensate for feelings of inferiority by excessive striving for power and achievement.

OVERPROTECTION: Sheltering a child from all possible dangers to such a degree that he is unable to stand on his own.

P

PALPITATION: An extremely rapid pulsation.

PARALYSIS AGITANS (PARKINSON'S DISEASE): A disease of the central nervous system characterized by tremors, contraction of the muscles and mask-like facial expression.

PARANOIA: A psychotic mental disorder characterized by well-systematized delusions of persecution or grandeur.

PARANOID STATE: A psychotic disorder characterized by poorly systematized delusions of persecution or grandeur.

PARASYMPATHETIC DIVISION: The cranial and sacral parts of the autonomic nervous system which control many vital bodily functions such as digestion.

PARESIS: Disorder caused by syphilitic infections of the brain. Common symptoms include speech disorders and memory and judgment defects.

PARKINSON'S DISEASE (PARALYSIS AGITANS): A disease of the central nervous system characterized by tremors, contraction of the muscles and mask-like facial expression.

PASSIVE-AGGRESSIVE REACTION: Aggressiveness which is expressed in a quiet manner such as pouting, stubborness or inefficiency.

PATHOLOGY: Diseased or disordered physical and mental condition.

PEDERASTY: Sexual intercourse between males through the anus. Sexual intercourse with youths through the anus.

PEDOPHILIA: Sexual deviation in which an adult has an erotic attachment for children.

PEER: An equal in age and status.

PERFECTIONISM: Excessive attention to detail. This behavior often serves as a defense against feelings of insecurity and guilt.

PERIPHERAL NERVOUS SYSTEM: Nerve fibers connecting the central nervous system with the receptor and effector organs.

PERSEVERATION: Persistent continuation of a word or action after it has been initiated.

PERSONALITY: The sum total of a person's attitudes, drives, aspirations, strengths, weaknesses, interests, and abilities.

PERVERSION: Deviation from normal. Often used in a limited fashion to denote sexual abnormality.

PERVERT: A sexual deviate.

PETIT MAL: Mild form of epilepsy characterized by a partial loss of consciousness.

PHALLIC: Related to the male sex organ.

PHOBIA: Irrational fear or dread of an object or situation.

PHOBIC REACTION: Psychoneurotic disorder characterized by irrational fear.

PHOTOPHOBIA: Morbid fear of strong light.

PINEAL GLAND: Small oval gland at the base of the brain. The function of this gland is currently unknown.

PITUITARY GLAND: An endocrine gland which controls body growth.

PLACEBO: A neutral substance administered in place of a drug. Some people report "cures" of ailments after therapy with this inactive substance.

PLAY THERAPY: Use of play activities in therapy with children. In enables a child to act out his feelings in an accepting environment.

POST-HYPNOTIC SUGGESTION: A suggestion given to an individual during hypnosis to perform some act after he is brought out of the hypnotic state.

PRECIPITATING CAUSE: The specific experience or stress which serves as the final factor causing a disorder.

PREDISPOSITION: A condition which makes it likely that an individual will develop certain symptoms under stressful situations.

PREGNANCY: The stage between conception and childbirth.

PRENATAL: Before birth.

PRIMARY CAUSE: The major etiological factor in a disorder.

PROGNOSIS: A judgment concerning the duration, course and outcome of a pathological condition.

PROJECTIONS: Defense mechanism in which an individual places blame for his difficulties upon others or ascribes his own unacceptable impulses to others.

PROJECTIVE TECHNIQUE: Psychological technique for diagnosing personality adjustment by using unstructured stimuli. This causes the person to bring his own feelings and attitudes into the unstructured situation.

PROMISCUITY: Sexual relations outside of marriage.

PROSTITUTION: Engaging in sexual intercourse for financial remuneration.

PSYCHASTHENIC REACTION: Psychoneurotic disorder characterized by phobias, anxiety, obsessions and compulsions.

PSYCHIATRIC NURSING: Nursing specialty concerned with mental disorders.

PSYCHIATRIC SOCIAL WORK: Social work primarily concerned with the mentally ill.

PSYCHIATRIST: Medical doctor who deals with mental and emotional disorders.

PSYCHIATRY: A specialized field of medicine which deals with mental disorders.

PSYCHOANALYSIS: The method of approach to human behavior originally outlined by Sigmund Freud. This approach places emphasis on unconscious processes. It comprises a theory of personality development and functioning and repressed experiences in the formation of psychotherapeutic techniques, and research techniques for the mental disorders.

PSYCHODRAMA: Therapeutic technique in which the client acts out a number of significant experiences in order to gain insight into his personality adjustment.

PSYCHOGENIC: A disorder arising from psychological factors.

PSYCHOLOGICAL TEST: Standardized examinations designed to yield information on an individual's mental and emotional adjustment.

PSYCHOLOGIST: Person holding an M.A. or Ph.D. degree in psychology. Among the areas of specialization in this field are clinical, experimental, industrial and school psychologists.

PSYCHOLOGY: The branch of science which deals with human behavior and adjustment.

PSYCHOMOTOR EPILEPSY: Type of epilepsy in which the individual experiences an impairment of consciousness, confusion or psychic disturbance rather than convulsions.

PSYCHONEUROSIS: A broad category of emotional disturbances which have the basic common element of anxiety.

PSYCHOPATHIC PERSONALITY (ANTISOCIAL PERSONALITY): An individual who exhibits marked immaturity and whose behavior is chronically antisocial.

PSYCHOPATHOLOGY: Science dealing with the causes and solutions of behavioral deviations.

PSYCHOPHYSIOLOGIC DISORDER (PSYCHOSOMATIC DISORDER): Maladjustment characterized by bodily symptoms which result from continued emotional stress.

PSYCHOSIS: Severe form of mental illness characterized by loss of contact with reality. Delusions and hallucinations may also be present.

PSYCHOSOCIAL DEVELOPMENT: An individual's development of social relationships.

PSYCHOSOMATIC DISORDER (PSYCHOPHYSIOLOGIC DISORDER): Maladjustment characterized by bodily symptoms which result from continued emotional stress.

PSYCHOSURGERY: Use of brain surgery in treating severe mental disorders.

PSYCHOTHERAPY: The use of psychological techniques in treating emotional disturbances.

PSYCHOTIC: Pertaining to or caused by psychosis.

PUBERTY: The beginning of adolescence. The time when the reproductive functions mature.

PUBERTY PRAECOX: Oversecretion of adrenal hormones in

childhood which results in premature or unusually early appearance of puberty.

PYROMANIA: Morbid compulsion to set fires.

PYROPHOBIA: Morbid fear of fire.

R

RAPE: Forcible sexual intercourse against the will of the partner, usually the female.

RAPPORT: Empathic relationship between two individuals characterized by mutual cooperation and confidence. Used in psychology to denote a desirable patient-therapist relationship.

RATIONALIZATION: Defense mechanism in which the individual attempts to justify his actions or beliefs.

REACTION FORMATION: Defense mechanism in which a person exhibits (and consciously believes he possesses) the opposite feelings or impulses of those he actually has on an unconscious level.

REACTIVE DEPRESSION: Psychoneurotic disorder characterized by worry, discouragement and pessimism.

RECIDIVISM: Repetition of delinquent or criminal acts in spite of punishment or treatment.

REFERRAL: Sending a person to another specialist for diagnosis or treatment.

REGRESSION: Defense mechanism in which the individual reverts to earlier and more immature patterns of behavior in the face of stress and frustration.

REALITY: The world as it actually is. The ability to correctly perceive reality is impaired in some forms of mental illness.

REMISSION: Improvement or removal of symptoms in the course of a disease.

REPRESSION: Defense mechanism by which a person forces threatening ideas or impulses into the unconscious mind.

RESISTANCE: Opposition to uncovering repressed thoughts or to making progress in therapy.

RIGIDITY: Inflexibility and resistance to change.

ROLE PLAYING: Technique of psychotherapy in which the individual acts out a conflict situation in order to gain insight into his behavior.

S

SADISM: Sexual perversion in which pleasure or sexual gratification is obtained by inflicting pain upon others.

SATYRIASIS: Insatiable sexual desire in males.

SCHIZOID PERSONALITY: Personality type characterized by seclusiveness, inability to relate to others, serious-mindedness and tendency to excessive daydreaming.

SCHIZOPHRENIA: Psychotic disorder characterized by loss of contact with reality, confused thought processes and withdrawal.

SCOTOPHILIA: (Voyeurism): Sexual deviation characterized by receiving sexual gratification from observing others in a state of nudity.

SECONDARY CAUSE: Etiological factor which contributes to a maladjustment, but which is not the major or primary cause.

SECURITY: A sense of safety and ability to meet the needs of life.

SELF-ACTUALIZATION: Full development of one's potential.

SELF-CONCEPT: A person's attitudes toward his personal worth.

SELF-DEVALUATION: Self-criticism associated with feelings of unworthiness.

SELF-LOVE: Nacissism.

SENILITY: Mental and psychological deterioration with old age.

SEXUAL DEVIATION: Any perversion of sexual behavior.

SHOCK THERAPY: Use of convulsive drugs such as insulin or metrazol, or electro-shock in treating mental disorders.

SOCIALIZATION: The process of developing interpersonal skills and learning to function adequately in society.

SOCIOECONOMIC STATUS: A person's level of social and economic functioning.

SOCIOPATHIC PERSONALITY: An individual who exhibits chronically irresponsible and antisocial behavior.

SODOMY: Sexual intercourse by the anus.

SOMATIC: Pertaining to the body.

SOMNAMBULISM: Sleepwalking.

SPASM: Involuntary contraction of muscles.

SPASTIC: A person who lacks normal coordination because of dysfunctions of the brain.

SPERM: Male reproductive cell.

SPONTANEOUS REMISSION: Alleviation of a disease symptom without treatment.

STRESS: A condition which is threatening to an individual's adjustment.

STRESS TOLERANCE: The amount of stress which a person can handle without developing serious personality disturbances.

STUPOR: A state of partial unconsciousness with unresponsiveness and lethargy.

STUTTERING: Speech disorder characterized by a disturbance in the rhythm of speech. This may include either blocking (inability to articulate certain sounds) or repetition of a sound.

SUBCONSCIOUS: Mental activities which are outside an individual's awareness or consciousness.

SUBLIMATION: Defense mechanism in which an unacceptable drive is chaneled into socially acceptable activities.

SUBSTITUTION: The process by which an unacceptable or unattainable goal is replaced by one which is acceptable or attainable.

SUPEREGO: (Conscience): The attitude of an individual toward the moral or social implications of his behavior. It is responsible for feelings of guilt.

SUPPRESSION: Conscious attempt to force threatening desires or thoughts from awareness.

SURROGATE: A substitute person, often for a parent.

SYMBOL: An object, expression, or activity which is used to represent something else.

SYMPATHETIC DIVISION: Division of the autonomic nervous system which is important in reacting to emergency situations such as extreme cold or threat.

T

TENSION: A condition characterized by anxiety, suspense or strain.

TESTOSTERONE: Male sex hormone.

THERAPEUTIC: Related to treatment or healing of maladjustments.

THERAPY: Procedure designed to treat maladjustments.

THREAT: A situation which poses danger to an individual.

THYROID GLAND: Endocrine gland which plays an important role in regulating body metabolism.

THYROXIN: Hormone secreted by the thyroid gland.

TIC: Persistent, intermittent muscle twitch or spasm.

TOXIC: Poisonous.

TRAIT: A distinctive physical or emotional characteristic of an individual.

TRANQUILIZER: Drug which has a quieting or calming effect on an individual.

TRANSFERENCE: Unconscious attachment of attitude to a person who represents a signficant figure in the person's past.

TRANSIENT SITUATIONAL PERSONALITY DISORDERS: Personality maladjustments which are temporary in nature.

TRANSVESTISM: Sexual deviation in which a person dresses in clothing of the opposite sex.

TRAUMA: Psychological or physical injury.

U

UNCONSCIOUS: That portion of the mind of which a person in unaware.

UNCONSCIOUS MOTIVATION: Incentive or drive of which a person is unaware.

UNDOING: Defense mechanism in which an individual repeatedly performs some act in an attempt to atone for a past misdeed.

V

VACILLATE: To waver or fluctuate.

VISCERA: The internal organs of the body.

VOYEURISM: A condition in which an individual gains sexual stimulation from watching members of the opposite sex undress or in a state of nudity.

W

WASSERMANN TEST: A serological test used in the diagnosis of syphilis.

WITHDRAWAL SYMPTOMS: Physical and emotional symptoms usually because of feelings of insecurity.

WITHDRAWAL SYMPTOMS: Physical and emotional symptoms resulting from the removal of a drug from an addicted individual.

WORRY: Excessive concern over real or anticipated danger.

Z

ZOOPHILIA: Sexual deviation characterized by abnormal affection for animals.

ZOOPHOBIA: Morbid fear of animals.

ZYGOTE: Cell formed by the union of two gametes.

Index

THERAPY (discussed in each problem area)

THYROID DYSFUNCTION (see Endocrine Dysfunction)

TICS   336

TRANSIENT SITUATIONAL PERSONALITY DISORDERS (see Anorexia Nervosa, Enuresis, Pica, Speech Disturbances and Tics)

TRANSVESTISM (see Sexual Deviation)

TRUTHFULNESS (see Lying)

ULCERS (see Peptic Ulcer)

UNFAITHFULNESS IN MARRIAGE   339

UNWED MOTHERS   347

VISIONS (see Psychotic Disorders and Schizophrenic Reactions)

VOYERISM (see Sexual Deviation)

WAKEFULNESS (see Sleep Disturbances)

WITHDRAWAL (see Depression, Inferiority, and Insecurity)

WORD DEAFNESS (see Aphasia)